ALSO BY CHRIS BALLARD

The Butterfly Hunter

Hoops Nation

Sports Illustrated

THE ART OF A
BEAUTIFUL
GAME

THE THINKING FAN'S TOUR OF THE NBA

CHRIS BALLARD

Simon & Schuster

NEW YORK LONDON TORONTO SYDNEY

Simon & Schuster
1230 Avenue of the Americas
New York, NY 10020

First Simon & Schuster hardcover edition November 2009

SPORTS ILLUSTRATED is a registered trademark of Time Inc.
Used with permission.

SIMON & SCHUSTER and colophon are registered trademarks
of Simon & Schuster, Inc.

For information about special discounts for bulk purchases,
please contact Simon & Schuster Special Sales at 1-866-506-1949
or business@simonandschuster.com.

The Simon & Schuster Speakers Bureau can bring authors to your
live event. For more information or to book an event contact
the Simon & Schuster Speakers Bureau at 1-866-248-3049
or visit our website at www.simonspeakers.com.

Text designed by Paul Dippolito

Manufactured in the United States of America

3   5   7   9   10   8   6   4   2

Library of Congress Cataloging-in-Publication Data
Ballard, Chris.
The art of a beautiful game: the thinking fan's tour of the NBA / Chris Ballard.
p. cm.
1. National Basketball Association—Anecdotes. 2. Basketball players—Anecdotes. I. Title.
GV885.515.N37B345 2009
796.323'64—dc22   2009024308

ISBN 978-1-4391-1021-8
ISBN 978-1-4391-4117-5 (ebook)

To Callie and Eliza

Contents

THE ART OF A
BEAUTIFUL
GAME

Introduction

Some years ago I had the unenviable task of guarding Mark Aguirre in a pickup game. I'd like to say I held my ground as he posted me up, absorbing each of the bargelike blows he delivered with his hips and prodigious backside, holding strong against the Nor'easter of Ass he unleashed upon me. But I did not. Like so many opponents during Aguirre's NBA days, I slid and stumbled and shuffled backward until he was essentially standing under the basket and I out-of-bounds. At which point he could merely reach up and lay the ball into the basket.

How I came to be guarding Aguirre was a matter of circumstance. I was in Indianapolis writing a story for *Sports Illustrated* and had wandered over to a local health club looking for a run. Aguirre, then an assistant coach for the Indiana Pacers, arrived a half hour later. My teammates, kind souls that they were, agreed that I should be the one to guard Aguirre.

This was what an NBA coach might refer to as "a matchup problem." Aguirre was a 6' 6", 230-pound NBA legend who averaged 20 points during his 13-year career with the Mavericks and the Pistons, and even at 43 years old, he was still in remarkably good shape. I, on the other hand, was a 6' 1", 175-pound former small-college player who had a difficult enough time defending the guys in my local rec league.

For the most part Aguirre took it easy on me in the post, backing me down only a handful of times. Not that it mattered; he turned out to be just as adept on the perimeter. At one point I was guarding him on the wing and he fooled me so completely, using a ball fake together with a subtle push on my leg and hip, that I actually turned around to try to beat him to the baseline. In mid-sprint I heard Aguirre chuckle behind me. He was standing in the same spot, having not moved an inch, and calmly fired up and swished a three-pointer. (He was a much better outside shooter than I recalled.) "What in the world," I asked him, "did you just do?"

He only smiled. Mark Aguirre did not get where he was by giving away his secrets to random dudes he meets at the gym.

That night I saw him at Conseco Fieldhouse, before the Pacers game, and his face lit up with recognition—and amusement. "Hey, still waiting for that baseline drive?" he asked.

I laughed, then asked if I might pick his brain at some point, this time in the name of journalism. "Check back with me after the game," he said.

I did, and he was true to his word. That night, after a Pacers win, Aguirre spent nearly 45 minutes in a back corridor of Conseco showing me the secrets of his post moves: how to leverage a defender, which arm to use to swim past an opponent, how to "lock in" an opposing big man on a lob pass and, best of all, how to "push the refrigerator" (that is, use your outside leg to drive into a defender, as if he were a Frigidaire).

As Aguirre talked, I realized that in all those years of watching him play, I'd never fully appreciated what he was doing. I just figured . . . well, I don't know what I figured. That he just used his butt to move guys out of the way? That he'd been born a little quicker and trickier around the basket than the rest of us?

Unmistakably, though, there was an art to what he was doing, one honed over years, one only certain players have mastered, one only certain players *can* master, for it requires a rare combination of dedication, talent and intuition. To appreciate it, you need only watch one of those young, springy big men who enter the league each year. You know the type—long-limbed, imposing, throwing down monster dunks. These players may be freakishly athletic, but their post moves are so rudimentary as to be nonexistent. Pump fake? Never. Freeze fake? What's that? Moving the refrigerator? They're not even good at moving their feet.

Still, it is the resplendent jams of these high-flyers that we see on the highlights, and that 10-year-old boys mimic on Nerf hoops. And there's nothing wrong with that—I admire the dunk as much as anyone—but it is a shame that few fans are privy to a true craftsman like Aguirre breaking down his art.

Instead, we often hear about how the pro game is flawed, full of remarkable athletes who boast unremarkable skills. As a writer who covers the NBA, I run into this mind-set on occasion: "No one plays defense, no one passes and it's all about getting paid," some people say. "How can you enjoy watching *that*?"

In response I'll usually mumble something about Chris Paul and drop steps and bank shots, but that's not much of a comeback. What I should say is, Sure, there's a lot about the pro game that's messed up, like guys who can hit their head on the rim but can't dribble with their left hand, and, yes, there are some lackadaisical millionaires; but it's still a beautiful, complicated game, the best ever invented in my opinion, and there are plenty of guys who treat it as such.

Then I could explain why that's true. I could describe the way Ray Allen squares up on his jump shot so perfectly that, were he on sand, he would spring up and, upon returning to earth, land precisely in his own footprints. I could talk about underhand scoop shots that rise like helium balloons. I could describe nine seconds left, the floor spread and the arena roaring like a 747 as Kobe Bryant holds the ball at the top of the key, about to break thousands of hearts.

I could talk about reverse layups with so much spin they hit the backboard and then shoot sideways as if yanked on a leash. I could evoke the *ka-smack* of the one-handed rebound and the *ka-thunk* of a three-pointer from the top of the key that sinks off the back of the rim as it drops in.

I could mention The *Noooooo!-then-Yesssss!* Shot and the way bench guys in the NBA hold each other back, as if saving one another from oncoming traffic, because that last play was just too damn exciting. I could relate how, after 40 years of pulling out a little pump fake to the right before shooting a jump hook, my 70-year-old father still employs it every time he plays, not because it works (though occasionally it does) but because it's like catching up with an old friend.

I could describe shots so pure the net snaps up and has to be untangled from the rim, and the way an NBA three-pointer arcs so high it looks as if it was shot from the moon, and seeing a play on Sunday afternoon on NBC, then seeing it again a few hours later down at the playground, reenacted a hundred different ways. I could talk about back picks you can practically hear through the TV, especially when they result in alley-oop dunks, and how the only thing better is when a help-side defender comes flying over to block that alley-oop.

I could confess that I can spend an hour talking to someone at a dinner party and never make the kind of real, true connection that comes from running one seamless give-and-go with a stranger during a pickup game. I could talk about the most compelling moment in sports—one second on the clock, down two, first of two free throws—and how it has made men's careers as well as ruined them.

I could explain how the pick-and-roll can be the oldest play in the book, or even the only play in the book, and people *still* can't stop it. And I could pull out tape of an old Princeton game to illustrate what is perhaps the most beautiful play in sports, a perfectly executed back-door cut.

But I don't say any of that, of course. Instead, what I've done is write this book. And while it's not necessarily about all the aforementioned things, it is a celebration of the game and those who play it at the highest level, the players for whom it truly is both an art and a science.

Because while the majority of what we read and hear about the NBA may be the day-to-day drama—who wins, who loses, who might get traded, who threw whom under which bus—this doesn't mean that NBA stars don't adore the game in all its myriad intricacies.

All you have to do is ask one. Not in vague generalities, but speaking his language. Ask LeBron James for the umpteenth time about his impending free agency, or his friendly rivalry with Dwyane Wade, and he will likely say one of the same things he's said the umpteen other times he's been asked. But sit down with James and watch film and ask him to dissect a pick-and-roll, or how he draws a weakside defender's attention, and it's amazing what happens. He leans forward, he gets excited, he talks quickly. He becomes a teacher, eager to explain. Gone are the marketing catchphrases and one-game-at-a-time clichés, replaced by staccato observations. He becomes like anyone else talking about something he loves: passionate.

This book is about passionate players. It is not about one season or the inner workings of a team or the "genius" of a coach, but rather about the beauty of basketball, because even the "ugly" aspects—like, say, defense and rebounding—become beautiful in the hands of the masters.

The material herein comes from research conducted over the course of nearly three years, some of it while working on stories for *SI*. I gathered much in league arenas and locker rooms, but just as often my work was done over beers (as with Rockets forward Shane Battier, who graciously broke down his approach to perimeter defense while sipping pale ales at a bar in Portland), or in a coffee shop in Washington, D.C. (as with Idan Ravin, the NBA trainer known as "the hoops whisperer"), or in the case of Steve Kerr, while shooting jumpers together at AmericaWest Arena.

But no matter what my method, for a week or two after researching each chapter, almost without fail, I became obsessed with whichever aspect of the game I'd just explored. And because of that, I'd like to publicly thank the noon hoops crew at the Berkeley YMCA for putting up with these obsessions. For no sooner had I returned from reporting on, say, rebounding, than I was suddenly trying to grab every weakside board at the Y by jumping laterally, the way Ben Wallace does. Three weeks later I'd be trying out Kobe's jab-step-fake-and-go, even though a simple rocker step would have worked fine. And, of course, I preached to all who would listen. I became the Deepak Chopra of the drop step, a Mormon missionary of the motion offense.

It is my hope that, in writing this book, I might inspire some of you to feel similarly: to see the game from a different perspective (or a dozen different ones), to gain a renewed appreciation for the at-times misunderstood giants who roam our nation's arenas and, above all, to revel in the art of what is truly a beautiful game.

Killer Instinct: Why Kobe Bryant Wants to Beat You at Everything

Consider the following hypothetical situation. Let's say you are playing for your high school basketball team and have persuaded one of the team's bench warmers to stay afterward to play one-on-one. Let's also stipulate that you are much, much better than this bench warmer, who, for our purposes, we shall call Rob.

Now let's say the two of you are playing a game to 100 points, with each basket worth one point, winner's outs after a made shot, and you are having your way with poor Rob, backing him down and driving by him and pulling up for jumpers. Pretty soon you've built an almost embarrassing lead—say, 40 baskets to none. Now, in this situation, do you:

a) begin to feel bad for Rob, who is, after all, doing you a favor by staying late, and perhaps ease up a bit so he can at least score a few baskets?

b) continue playing hard but maybe start taking only outside jumpers, so that Rob might have a fighting chance, thus making it more competitive?

c) never let up for a second, hounding Rob on defense and punishing him on offense, because the only way to win is to do so *absolutely and completely,* and only the weak relent, even for a moment?

If you answered "c," congratulations. You share a mind-set with Kobe Bryant, the most competitive life-form on the planet.

Bryant, in fact, lived the above scenario while at Lower Merion High in Pennsylvania—and did so more than once. Only Bryant didn't just get up 40–0. Sometimes he would take an 80–0 lead on Rob Schwartz, a good-natured, if undersized, junior guard. Think about that: 80 baskets to none. Can you imagine the focus, the ruthlessness, required to score 80 times on someone before they score once? Kobe can. To Kobe, this is just *what you do*. It is *how you play*.

"You'd think he'd have a tendency to ease back, but he doesn't have that in him," remembers Schwartz, who now works as a strength-and-conditioning coach near Philadelphia. "I think the best I ever did was to lose 100–12." Naturally, Bryant doesn't want to concede that Schwartz had even that much success. "I think he's lying about that," Bryant says when I tell him of Schwartz's recollection. "I told Rob that too. We were talking about it, and I said, 'You never got 12. I never let you get double digits. Most you got was five.'" Bryant is smiling when he says this, but it's a forced grin. He really does want to set the record straight. Because God forbid any of us think for a moment that this Schwartz kid got double digits on Kobe Bryant.

Call it what you will: killer instinct, competitive fire, hatred of losing or, as Sam Cassell once said, "that Jordan thing." No one in the NBA embodies it like Bryant. It is at once one of the most valuable skills and the hardest to teach. Sports psychologist Jim McGee, quoted in Michael Clarkson's book *Competitive Fire,* describes elite athletes such as Bryant as "neurological freaks," positing that they have a different hormonal and neurological makeup than the rest of us.

It manifests itself in various ways. Some, like Magic Johnson, competed with an ever-present grin. Others, like Larry Bird, would rather cut off a finger than be congenial to an opponent. When Bird first met Michael Jordan, the two men were warming up for an exhibition game—NBA stars versus collegiate Olympians—on opposite ends of the court. When Jordan's ball rolled to where Bird was shooting, Bird picked it up, looked at Jordan and proceeded to punt the ball over Jordan's head. Welcome to the show, kid.

Jordan, of course, was himself famous for berating teammates in practice and for befriending opponents only to crush them later (once prompting coach Jeff Van Gundy to call him a "con man," whereupon, the next night, Jordan scored 51 points against Van Gundy's Knicks). Jordan so loathed losing that when he once dropped three consecutive games of pool to then-assistant Roy Williams while at North Carolina, Jordan refused to talk to him the next day. Asked to provide a one-word summation of Jordan, former Bulls center Luc Longley chose "predator." Yet, during his pro career, Jordan somehow managed to come off as lovable—just your friendly neighborhood athletic super-hero who stars in underwear commercials and cartoons.

Because Kobe is Kobe, however, he cannot conceal his mentality the way Jordan did, behind a who-would-have-thunk-it smirk or an endorsa-riffic smile. With Bryant, his competitive fire manifests itself during practice, during games, during summer workouts, during conversation. When he dreams, Bryant is probably kicking someone's ass at something, perhaps swatting Bill Russell's hook into the third row. "He can't turn it off, even if he tried," says veteran swingman Devean George, one of a handful of NBA players who are relatively close to Bryant. And for that Kobe has often been pilloried—by fans, by the media, even by fellow players. But is that really fair? "Kobe wants it so badly that he rubs an awful lot of people the wrong way," says Lakers basketball consultant Tex Winter, guru of the triangle offense, who has known Bryant since 1999. "But they're not willing to understand what's inside the guy."

O.K. then, let's try. First, though, it's necessary to put aside any preconceived notions about Bryant. Maybe you love him, which is fine. But you may look at Kobe and think of Shaq. Or Phil Jackson. Or Nike. Or Colorado. Or his, um, considerable self-regard. While most players understand that it is their role to play well and the role of others—media, teammates, coaches—to point out that they've played well, Bryant prefers to multitask on this front. After scoring 25 points in the second half against the Spurs in Game 1 of the 2008 Western Conference finals, Bryant explained his performance to the media by saying, "I can get off"—that is, score at will—"at any time. In the second half I did that."

Granted, Bryant was merely being honest, but even so, tact dictates that he let *us* say such things about him. As you've probably noticed, however, Bryant has never been big on tact. Time and again over the years he has announced to us the particulars of his awesomeness. As teammate Luke Walton puts it, in succinct understatement, "Kobe does not lack for confidence."

Even as this bravado has irked some—O.K., many—over the last decade or so, it's also what makes it so mesmerizing to watch Bryant when he does go off. Because, like the man himself, it's never subtle. Spurs defensive specialist Bruce Bowen, Bryant's foil these many years, claims there's no indicator of an impending detonation, joking that you can't tell what's coming "by the way he chews his gum or something," but that's not true at all. Rather it's almost comically evident. George, the former teammate, describes it as "that Kobe face where he starts looking around all pissed off." His high school coach Gregg Downer says he can recognize it even watching on TV. In these moments Bryant reverts to his younger persona, the one that used to flummox Del Harris when he was Lakers coach during Bryant's first two years in the league, in 1996–97. "Kobe would put it on the floor and start going between his legs, back and forth, back and forth," says Harris, "and only then would he decide what to do."

So there was Kobe in that '08 conference finals game against the Spurs, with the Lakers down 20 in the third quarter, whipping the ball between his legs and shaking his noggin at Bowen like some enormous, ticked-off bobblehead. What followed seemed, in retrospect, inevitable: the jump shots, the twisting drives, the scowls and, finally, a cold-blooded Bryant jumper in the lane with 20-odd seconds left to seal a comeback win.

Watching Bryant in such moments can be electrifying, but it doesn't make it any easier to understand him. After all, how does one get inside the mind of a man that single-minded, a player who, in a one-on-one contest, feels compelled to go up 80–0?

Perhaps the answer is to start at the beginning, examining Bryant's life moment by basketball moment.

———————————

It's 1985, and Bryant is seven years old, living in Italy, where his father, Joe Bryant, is playing professional basketball. During Joe's afternoon practice, Kobe stands in the corner shooting baskets. During halftime at games, Kobe runs on the court and starts hoisting 15-footers, much to the delight of the Italian spectators. On weekends Joe and Kobe sit and watch videos of NBA games that Kobe's grandparents dutifully mail over from the States. Young Kobe studies the tapes over and over and over, the way most children do a Disney movie, until he knows what each player will do next, when Magic Johnson will fake and when he will pass. "As far back as I can remember," Bryant says, "I had this desire to understand the game."

Now it's 1989, and Kobe is 11 years old, no longer content to be the kid shooting in the corner at his father's practices. He keeps bugging Brian Shaw, then a star player in Europe, to play him one-on-one. Eventually Shaw relents, and the two play H-O-R-S-E. "To this day, Kobe claims he beat me," says Shaw. "I'm like, right, an 11-year-old kid, but he's serious." Even back then, Shaw saw something different. "His dad was a good player, but he was the opposite of Kobe, real laid-back," says Shaw. "Kobe was out there challenging grown men to play one-on-one, and he really thought he could win."

Now Kobe is 13 years old and an eighth-grader in the suburbs of Philadelphia, skinny as a paper clip. He is scrimmaging against varsity players at Lower Merion High in an informal practice. They are taken aback. "Here's this kid, and he has no fear of us at all," says Doug Young, then a sophomore on the team. "He's throwing elbows, setting hard screens." Bryant was not the best player on the floor that day—not yet—but he was close.

Now it's 1995. Kobe is the senior leader on the Lower Merion team, and he is obsessed with winning a state championship. He comes to the gym at 5 a.m. to work out before school, stays until 7 p.m. afterward. It's all part of the plan; when Lower Merion lost in the playoffs the previous spring, Kobe stood up in the locker room, interrupting the seniors as they hugged each other in an attempt at closure, and guaranteed a state title, adding, "The work starts *now*." (To this day, Bryant remains so amped about his old high school league that when he taped a video message for the Lower Merion team a few years ago, it contained none of the usual platitudes; instead it was Bryant reeling off a string of expletives and exhorting the boys to "take care of fucking business!")

During the Kobe Era at Lower Merion no moment was inconsequential, no drill unworthy of ultimate concentration. During one practice, "just a random Tuesday," as Coach Downer recalls, Bryant was engaged in a three-on-three drill in a game to 10. One of his teammates was Schwartz, then a 5' 7" junior bench warmer. With the game tied 9–9, Schwartz had an opening and drove to the basket but missed, allowing the other team to grab the rebound, after which they scored to win the game. "Now, most kids go to the water fountain and move on," says Downer. Not Kobe. "What do you think you're doing taking the last shot?" he demanded of Schwartz. The younger player looked at Bryant, amazed. "Dude," Schwartz said, "It's a three-on-three drill. It doesn't matter that much."

It was, Schwartz should have known, the wrong thing to say. He headed into the hallway to get a drink of water, but Kobe raced after him and berated him, and they nearly came to blows. It didn't stop with a reprimand either. "Ever get the feeling someone is staring at you—you don't have to look at them, but you know it?" says Schwartz. "I felt his eyes on me for the next 20 minutes. It was like by losing that drill, I'd lost us the state championship."

Now it's 1996 and the Lakers call in Bryant, fresh off his senior prom—he took the singer Brandy as you may recall—for a predraft workout. He flies in to Los Angeles and heads to the Inglewood High gym. In attendance are Lakers G.M. Jerry West and two members of the L.A. media-relations team, John Black and Raymond Ridder. Bryant, now 17, is to play one-on-one against Michael Cooper, the former Lakers guard and one of the premier defenders in NBA history. Cooper is 40 years old but still in great shape, wiry and long and much stronger than the teenage Bryant. The game is not even close. "It was like Cooper was mesmerized by him," says Ridder, now the Warriors' director of media relations. After 10 minutes, West stands up. "That's it, I've seen enough," he says. "He's better than anyone we've got on the team right now. Let's go."

It would be a pattern: Bryant bearing down on players he'd once idolized. There was the time down in Orlando at Magic Johnson's summer benefit game in 1998 that Bryant went after Penny Hardaway so hard—*in a charity game*—that Hardaway spent the fall telling people he couldn't wait to play the Lakers so he could go back at Bryant. And, more famously, there was his attempt to go one-on-one against Michael Jordan during the 1998 All-Star Game, waving off a screen from Karl Malone. *Take your pick-and-rolling ass out of here. I've got Jordan iso-ed.* That one didn't go over so well either.

In Bryant's mind no one was unbeatable. As a rookie with the Lakers, despite missing all of training camp with a broken hand and being only a few months removed from high school, he approached Harris, the head coach. According to Harris, "He said, 'Coach, if you just give me the ball and clear out, I can beat anybody in this league.'" When that didn't fly, Bryant went to Harris again. "He'd say, 'Coach, I can post up anybody who's guarding me. If you just get me in there and clear it out, I can post up anybody.'" Harris chuckles. "I said, 'Kobe, I know you can, but right now you can't do it at a high enough rate for the team we have, and I'm not going to tell Shaquille O'Neal to get out of the way so you can do this.' Kobe didn't like it. He understood it, but in his heart he didn't accept it."

Now it's 1999, and Bryant is coming off a season in which he averaged 19.9 points. At this juncture, already accomplished, most 21-year-olds might see fit to spend part of their summer screwing around. Bryant, however, spends his downtime fine-tuning his game. He watches boxes of videotape, pores over *Dean Smith's Basketball: Multiple Offense and Defense* and practices relentlessly. By himself. In a gym with chairs set up to simulate defenders. He is driven by the doubters, like the reporter who wonders if he'll burn out and fade away like another Harold Miner. "People didn't know that I was getting up at six and going to the gym and working for eight hours," Bryant says. "They didn't realize that I wasn't planning on going anywhere. I'd worked too hard." Shaw, who played for the Lakers from 1999 to 2003 and is now an assistant coach, tries to explain the mind-set. "It was like he was put on earth to be a great basketball player, and everything that he does is dedicated to becoming that," he says. "The only other guy I've been around with that kind of work ethic is Larry Bird."

Now it's 2000, and Bryant is an All-Star and a franchise player. Still, when guard Isaiah Rider is signed as a free agent by the Lakers, Bryant forces Rider to repeatedly play one-on-one after practice to housebreak this newest potential alpha male. (Bryant wins, of course.) When Mitch Richmond arrives the next year, it's the same. "He was the man, and he wanted us to know it," says Richmond. "He was never mean or personal about it; it's just how he was."

Not that Bryant always wins these one-on-one games—he says he's "lost games before but never a series"—but beat him at your own risk. Decline a rematch and, well, you can't. "If you scored on him in practice or did something to embarrass him, he would just keep on challenging you and challenging you until you stayed after and played him so he could put his will on you and dominate you," says Shaw. This included not allowing players to leave the court. Literally. "He'd stand in our way and say, 'Nah, nah, we gonna play, we gonna play. I want you to do that move again,'" says Shaw. "And you might be tired and say, 'Nah, I did it in practice.' But he was just relentless and persistent until finally you'd go play, and he'd go at you."

And, just as he once did with Rob Schwartz, Bryant now kept NBA teammates after practice as guinea pigs. "He was notorious for asking me to stay late to work on a move," says George, who played for L.A. from 1999 to 2006. "He'd say, 'Stand there for a minute. I want to try something.'" And then Bryant would unveil a spin move, or a cross-over, or something else he'd picked up watching tape, and do it over and over and over. "The crazy thing about it is, he has the ability to put new elements in his game overnight," says George. "Like, for example, he might say, 'Stay after and guard this move. Let me try it on you,' and he'll do it the *next day* in the game." George pauses to let this sink in. "Most of us, we'll try it alone, then we'll try it in practice, then in a scrimmage, and only then will we bring it out for a seven o'clock game. He'd do it the next day—and it would work."

This is how Bryant sees it—the game as laboratory. I first witnessed it in 2002, while I was interviewing him for a *Sports Illustrated* story. We were in an empty room at the Lakers practice facility and, when the conversation turned to dribble-drive moves, Bryant started getting worked up. He described to me a variation on a traditional move: a jab step-and-pause, where you sink deep, hesitate to let the defender relax and, instead of bringing the jab foot back, push off it. Soon enough, Bryant was out of his chair and positioning me as a "defender" on the carpeted floor.

"O.K., when I go here," he said, lunging forward, "now I just hesi-tate for a second and then"—and here Bryant pretended to exhale deeply—"Bam! I'm by you."

He stepped aside and, not content with the lesson, motioned for me to catch the imaginary ball he was holding. "You try it."

I jabbed, hesitantly.

Kobe shook his head. "Sell it man, really sell it!"

And so I did. And as we jabbed and relaxed and jabbed, it occurred to me that, deep down, Kobe Bryant is a total nerd. It's just that, while some people are *Star Wars* nerds, Bryant is a basketball nerd. "I think Kobe's actually a little bit embarrassed by his love of basketball," says Downer, the high school coach. "People called him a loner, but it's just that basketball is all he wants to focus on. I think he's part of a dying breed that loves the game that way."

If you doubt this, just listen to how he personalizes the game when talking about it. This is what he said when I asked whether he misses life before the NBA. "Sometimes I think back to going to school in

Lower Merion, waking up in the morning, having all the snow on the ground, and going to school at five o'clock in the morning to work out before school even started. I remember how nobody knew who I was, how pure the game was, and the dreams that I had of playing at this level and the hunger that I had. I miss that. Sometimes you miss the baby steps. You hear parents say all the time, 'My daughter is 15 now; I wish I could just shrink her back down to when she was only one.' I feel that way sometimes. Because you miss those early steps. Because it was so much fun, and it was so much mystery, and you didn't know what was going to happen."

It is this affection for the game that gets Bryant so excited about meeting kindred souls. Asked about Spurs coach Gregg Popovich during the 2008 playoffs, Kobe's face lit up as he recalled his chance to play for him in an All-Star Game. "I was really hoping he'd run us through one of those rigorous practices he does," said Bryant. When he got his wish, he deemed it "fun."

Now it's the summer of 2008, and Bryant is an Olympian on a team that will go on to win the gold medal. When around U.S. teammates, he refers to himself as "the old dog," as in, when Magic center Dwight Howard is being called to the bus as the team departs from a practice, "Don't worry, those motherfuckers aren't going anywhere without me. Stick with the old dog, and you'll be fine." (Howard does, and he is). It's a role Kobe's been waiting to play his whole career. Now, finally, he can be the alpha dog—all the time.

It is not easy to coach an alpha dog, of course. Especially one like Bryant, who not only knows the game chapter and verse but also understands both his own limitations and those of his teammates. As such, he is at times given to making, shall we say, executive decisions. "He's sure got a grasp of the game," says Tex Winter, the Lakers' assistant. "He understands the game. But—and don't misinterpret this—he understands it a lot better than he plays it."

O.K., Tex, so as not to misinterpret: Are you saying that he knows the right thing to do but sometimes chooses not to do it?

"Yup, that's it," says Tex.

Now it's the fall of 2008 and Bryant is finally where he wants to be. He's an MVP playing on *his* team, without any behemoth Hall of Famers to get in the way of post-ups. His team made the Finals in June of 2008 and is in good position to do so again. He is also by most accounts, the best player of his era. "Only two guys should be mentioned in the same breath, and those are Oscar Robertson and Michael Jordan," says one Western Conference scout. "I know people—like our coach—who think he's better than Jordan."

Better?

"Mike couldn't handle the ball like Kobe and had nowhere near his range," says the scout, aware he's trafficking in basketball blasphemy. "Defensively, he's just as good. Not as strong as Michael, but he has faster feet."

The scout has other things to say about Bryant. For example, on his weaknesses: "Um, let me think. . . . [Long pause.] No, I don't think he has any." On his athleticism: "There are probably 10 better in the league"—he names Andre Iguodala, LeBron James, Josh Smith, Dwight Howard and J.R. Smith as examples—"but no one uses it as well as Kobe. Just watch his footwork sometime." And on his focus: "There's a difference between loving basketball and liking basketball. There are only about 30 guys in the league who *love* it, who play year-round. Iverson loves to play when the lights come on. Kobe loves doing the shit *before* the lights come on."

This thing, this freakish compulsion, is the element of the game most difficult to quantify. There are no plus-minus stats or fancy equations to measure a player's ruthlessness, that desire to beat you so badly you need therapy and a six-pack to recover. One thing's for sure: You can't teach it. If so, Eddy Curry would be a six-time MVP, and Derrick Coleman would be getting ready for his Hall of Fame induction. But people know it when they see it. Ask around the league—G.M.'s, scouts and coaches—and only a few names get mentioned alongside Bryant's: Tim Duncan, Kevin Garnett, Deron Williams, Steve Nash, Chris Paul and Manu Ginobili. ("I *love* Manu," says Bryant. "He plays exactly the way I play, balls to the wall.") None are considered in the same league as Bryant, though. In a *Sports Illustrated* poll in 2008, for example, Bryant was a runaway winner when NBA players were asked which player they feared most. Kobe got 35% of the vote—no one else was close.

What players like Paul, Bryant and Ginobili have in common is that they see pressure not as most of us do—*Oh, crap, I better perform*—but as an opportunity. Says Ginobili, "It's the most fun part of the game when you have all that adrenaline, all that responsibility."

Even some of the great ones lacked the fire. Kareem Abdul-Jabbar says that when he was young, rather than challenging everyone who crossed his path, as Kobe does, he "just wanted peace." Says Abdul-Jabbar, "I think it's a quirk of personality. Some of us are like Napoleon, and some are Walter Mitty." Bill Russell, the dominant Celtics center, saw it as a necessity of the game. "You got to have the killer instinct," Russell told *SI* in 1965. "If you do not have it, forget about basketball and go into social psychology or something. If you sometimes wonder if you've got it, you ain't got it. No pussycats, please."

Idan Ravin is a basketball trainer who works with Paul, Elton Brand, Gilbert Arenas and Carmelo Anthony and is known by some in the league as "the hoops whisperer" for his effect on players (Chapter 9). Ravin has gone so far as to break killer instinct down into components. (He's a former lawyer, so this is the kind of stuff he does.) They are: love of the game, ambition, obsessive/compulsive behavior, arrogance/confidence, selfishness and nonculpability. He sees them all in Bryant.

"If he's a ruthless s.o.b., I kind of respect that," says Ravin. "He has, what, maybe 15 or 16 years in the league? Why should he be passing up opportunities now? Why pass the ball to a guy who doesn't work as hard, who doesn't want it like you do?"

The story about Schwartz, and 80–0, may be the most instructive as to how Kobe's brain works. How many of us can imagine thinking that way? How do you maintain focus when you're beating someone 79–0? How do you say, O.K., this point matters every bit as much as the previous 79 even when it clearly doesn't? I ask Bryant this question, and he shrugs. "I don't know, man," he says. "I just do it, to be honest. It's nothing for me. *It's just what I do.* I just keep going."

But, Kobe, what's the benefit? How does that make you better?

Bryant grins his Nike grin, the one that's designed to mask his intensity but usually fails. "I'd try to control him," he says. "So when I played Rob, I always worked on something different. I challenged myself to say, O.K., can I manipulate him defensively to do this, so maybe I can work on going left, so I can do that."

I can't help but ask: "Didn't you at any point feel like an asshole?"

"Nope, not at all," Bryant says. "To me, I enjoy doing it. I enjoy beating guys and beating them and beating them. If you're going to beat somebody, you have to beat them to a pulp. To see what happens, to see what they're made of."

That's why, even now, as an MVP, every little challenge matters to him. Here's a telling snapshot of Bryant from the 2008 playoffs. At the end of practice on the day before the Lakers learned who their Western Conference finals opponent was going to be, each member of the team had to shoot one free throw with the caveat that the team had to make a certain cumulative number or they'd all run sprints. As it turned out, everybody hit their free throw except Bryant, who rimmed one out. The only shooter left was Derek Fisher, he of the 81.4% lifetime percentage. The team had already met its mark, so even if Fisher missed it, there would be no sprints. But Bryant didn't care about the running; he cared about keeping score. So he stood to the side of the basket, fidgeting. As Fisher's shot arced toward the rim, Bryant suddenly took two quick steps and leaped up to goaltend the shot, smacking it away. "Of course," Lakers forward Lamar Odom explained later, "he couldn't be the only one to miss."

It is Bryant's blessing and his curse: There is no off switch on his drive. In the Lakers' locker room there is a popular joke that Kobe, father of two preteen girls, will be the worst soccer dad ever, the guy going crazy on the sideline. But I doubt this is true. I think Bryant understands that his will to win is not a transitive property. It's what makes the game both so easy for him (when he has the ball) and so frustrating (when he doesn't). It's also what it makes it so rewarding when he achieves his goals.

———————

Now it is June of 2009 and the Lakers are playing the Orlando Magic in the NBA Finals. It is Bryant's second opportunity to win his inaugural title UBS (Unsullied By Shaq) and he is on a mission, trying to balance team leadership with his desire to destroy everything in his path. At the moment, late in the first half of Game 1 at Staples Center, it is safe to say he is focusing on the latter. He sticks one jumper, then another, then drops in an implausible fadeaway after stopping his dribble and pivoting, spinning and pivoting again, a move that causes the normally sedate LA crowd to roar and Bryant to bare his teeth like a feral animal. At times like these, Bryant says, he can sense the fear in his opponent, in this case 6'6" swingman Mickael Pietrus. "They get kind of nervous and are scared to touch you," Bryant explains. "It's no fun playing against players like that." He prefers a confident opponent. "It becomes more fun for you," he says, "because it becomes a challenge."

This desire for challenges—and only Kobe would crave additional obstacles during the NBA Finals—is what Bryant has spent the past few seasons trying to harness. In recent years, at Jackson's suggestion, he has turned to meditation. Bryant says he's also coming to terms with the idea that it isn't that his teammates don't want to win as much he does (though this is true), but that they don't have the *capacity* to want to win as much as he does. Says Downer, the high school coach, "As difficult as Kobe can be, as demanding as he is, I think [he and his teammates] all found some middle ground, a center."

Part of that is Bryant allowing his teammates to succeed, something that is an ongoing struggle for him. Though he is the Lakers' leading playmaker during the 2009 playoffs, often flirting with triple-doubles (something that is not easy to do), he still remains reluctant at times to make the right swing pass (something that is). "He likes to make the pass for the assist of the score," explains Shaw. "We would like him to make the pass that would lead to the pass."

Even so, it's hard for the coaches to get too upset. "There's a trust that we have because we know that he's trying to win the game," Shaw says. "There are a lot of times when Phil will call a play, but [Kobe] will have a feel for what's going on out on the floor and say, 'No, no, no. I already got something going.' Phil trusts that."

Now it is 2 a.m. on Thursday during the second week of the Finals and Kobe cannot sleep. The Lakers lead the Magic 2–1 but are recovering from a painful loss in which Bryant missed late-game free throws. So he sits in a high-backed leather chair in the lobby of the Ritz-Carlton in Orlando, surrounded by chandeliers and white orchids and gleaming white floors, in the company of friends—a group including his security guy, team employees and trainers—but alone. He says little, the hood of his sweatshirt pulled over his scalp, his eyes staring into the inky night, past the windows and the palm trees. He holds a Corona but rarely brings it to his lips. He looks like a man so tired he cannot sleep, a man nearing the end of a long journey. It is one that began well before November, when this season started, or even last June, when the Lakers fell to the Celtics in the Finals. As he will later explain in a quiet moment, he divides his career into two bodies of work: "the Shaquille era and the post-Shaquille era." Since the post-Shaq era began in 2004, when the Lakers traded O'Neal to Miami, many have doubted, again and again, that Bryant would ever earn a ring on his own. And while he has dismissed those who classify his legacy as Shaq-dependent, calling them "idiotic," he also knows how close he is to banishing that perception.

Minutes pass. Bryant stares and says nothing. He has waited this long. He can wait a little longer.

Now it is 5:30 in the morning after Game 4, and Bryant is headed to the gym. Only hours earlier the Lakers pulled out a dramatic 99–91 win to take a 3–1 series lead, and with three more chances to finish the series, the players could finally relax. There are two nights off before Game 5, and it was time to celebrate a bit, and Kobe did. For all of four hours. Now, before he goes to sleep, it is time to get in some work.

At the urging of his trainer, Tim Grover, Bryant heads to the fitness center at the Ritz-Carlton, where a couple of early-bird businessmen are shocked to share their treadmill time with an 11-time All-Star. For an hour and a half Grover takes Bryant through a series of exercises: weights, stretching, muscle-activation routines. Grover's logic is that if Bryant gets his work in now, he can have a block of uninterrupted sleep and not disturb his rest pattern.

Bryant's work ethic is renowned, but this season he has become even more obsessive. Unhappy with his physical stamina during the Finals a year ago, he asked Grover, with whom he'd worked during the off-season, to become, in essence, his personal trainer: travel with him, monitor his workouts. For Grover, who runs his business out of Chicago, and whose clients include Dwyane Wade (and, for many years, Michael Jordan), it was asking a lot. "There are only about three guys in the league I would have even considered doing this for," says Grover. "With Kobe, I knew he'd take it very seriously."

Grover's modifications were small but important. Bryant had never been an advocate of cold tubs; Grover had him taking ice baths frequently for muscle recovery. He focused on strengthening Bryant's ankles, wrists, hips—"areas that don't make you look better in your jersey but can become nagging injuries," Grover says. The result is that, despite having played for nearly three years straight due to his Olympic commitments, Bryant came into these Finals free of ankle braces, shoulder wraps and sleeves—although his right ring finger, dislocated earlier in the season, remained taped. He even wore low-top shoes. (Bryant believes they give him a greater range of motion, and Grover concurs.) When Bryant missed those free throws in Game 3, finishing 5 of 10 from the line, Grover had him show up early the next day and spend 40 minutes just shooting foul shots. "The superstars aren't superstars just by accident," says Grover. "Michael was Michael because of what he did on and off the court; it didn't just happen. Same with Kobe. It's because of the time and effort and the knowledge that he gains and his willingness to listen to people." It is an interesting notion, that a man long criticized for not listening to people is succeeding now because he does.

Now it is half an hour before Game 5, and it seems as if every camera in Amway Arena is trained on Bryant. His eyes are hooded, his jaw is set. This is what he came for. When center Andrew Bynum says of Bryant, "Only he knows what motivates him," well, that's not really true at all. Don't we all know what motivates Bryant? As Fisher says, "He wants to be the best player to have ever played this game. That's what he works at every day." Thus while it is often easy to question Bryant's sincerity, it is hard to do so when the subject is his drive. "I push and push and push—that's the only way I know," Bryant says. A day earlier I had asked him about the future, when he's in his mid-30s, and whether he could ever see himself being a third option on a team. "Third option?" he said, and then he paused. He frowned slightly, rolling the idea around in his head, entertaining an existence where he orbits others, not the other way around. He wrinkled his nose at the thought, then finally answered. "I don't know; that's tough to see," he said. "One thing I've always been great at is scoring the ball. Even when I'm 35, I think I'll be a bad motherfucker." And with this, Bryant laughed. It must have felt good to tell the truth.

Now there is 1:12 left in Game 5, and the Lakers have both the ball and a 95–84 lead. Finally, the moment—his moment—is here. During the final Lakers timeout, Bryant heads back to the bench. He tries to lean back in his chair but cannot sit still. He attempts to control his breathing, which is quick and shallow. He bites his nails, shifts his eyes; he looks nervous, like a teenager about to ask a girl out on a first date. Then, finally, almost sweetly, he smiles. It is a genuine smile, oddly naked. It is a Bryant we rarely see.

Soon he will accept the MVP trophy and bring his daughters Natalia, 6, and Gianna, 3, onstage. Then he will run back to the locker room, slithering through the hallway crowd, shouting, "Oh! My! God!" and he will make sure to drench Jackson in champagne, and then he will sit before the media at a podium and grin goofily and talk about getting "a big old monkey off my back" and rest his cheeks in between his hands and say how it feels as if he's dreaming and how he "can't believe this moment is here." And then he will head to the Ritz to celebrate, still wearing his champagne-soaked T-shirt and shorts, a cigar protruding from his mouth, punch-drunk and pleased to take photos with all comers, no longer the child prodigy, no longer the petulant sidekick, no longer the selfish ball hog, no longer the Michael Jordan wannabe, but just Kobe Bryant, champion. And he will revel in this for hours, if not days, before waking up one morning and deciding there's been enough celebrating. Because, of course, there remains so much left to do.

So, add it all up and who is Kobe Bryant? He's a guy who can break down in detail any Western Conference team's plays and any star's strengths and weaknesses. (For example, Bryant believes Tracy McGrady isn't good at coming back to the ball once he's given it up, making it easy to deny him.) He's a guy who, according to former teammate Coby Karl, considers himself "an expert at fouling without getting called for it." (Watch how Bryant uses the back of his hand, not the front, to push off on defenders, and a closed-fist forearm to exert leverage.) A guy who makes up to 500 jumpers a day during the off-season, usually shooting 80 to 90%.

A guy who, even at the height of his success, believes he can never let his guard down. (Example: When Dwight Howard allowed 5'9" Nate Robinson to leapfrog him in the dunk contest in February '09, effectively ceding the dunk crown to Robinson and emasculating himself in one three-second span, Howard said it was all in fun, as did many others. Not Kobe. When I asked him whether he'd ever let someone dunk over him in a similar situation, he grimaced. "Fuck no!" he said. "Especially not to lose no goddam dunk contest!")

He's a guy who, according to Nike spokesperson Kejuan Wilkins, had the company shave a couple millimeters off the bottom of his shoe because "in his mind that gave him a hundredth of a second better reaction time." A guy so intense he talks to himself during games. ("You'll see him literally giving himself a pep talk," says Downer.)

A guy who lit into teammate Andrew Bynum during a timeout when the 21-year-old center came out lackluster in Game 3 of the 2009 Finals, yelling, "Get your head in the fucking game!" loud enough that a sideline reporter could overhear. A guy who, at 30, has four championship rings (or one more than Michael Jordan at the same age), two scoring titles, an MVP award and now a Finals MVP award; who has won for six coaches and as part of starting lineups that included Travis

Knight and Smush Parker, suffering but one losing season (and when it comes to Bryant, suffering really is the right term).

A guy who, lest we forget, played the better part of a year with a finger on his shooting hand in need of surgery. A guy who says of being guarded by Bruce Bowen, the Spurs' exasperating pest/forward, "It's fun," and actually *means* it. A guy who, no matter what he does, will never get the chance to play the one game he'd die for: Bryant vs. Jordan, each in their prime.

When I ask Tex Winter about that hypothetical game, he says, "There'd be blood on the floor by the end," then pauses. "But I wouldn't bet against Michael."

When I relay this to Bryant, he becomes serious. "I wouldn't bet against *me*, either," he says. But there is not the same edge as with his other boasts. Clearly, with Michael it is different. Would playing him have been, in some ways, the ultimate test? "Yeah," Bryant says, "because he's the only guy I know that's as serious about it as I am."

How serious? Ask Bryant to explain his competitive fire, and he talks about effort, about playing "balls to the wall" (one of his favorite laudatory phrases) and says things like, "A lot of players just want to look cool; they don't want to get their hands dirty." Then he tells a story about when he returned to the U.S. as a 12-year-old. Because of his father, he was invited to play in the esteemed Sonny Hill summer league in Philadelphia. As Bryant tells it, he was competing against collegians, players like Rasheed Wallace and Alvin Williams. "I didn't score one point the whole summer," he says, spitting the words out. "Not even a technical free throw." To most people, this would be considered part of a learning process. After all, he was *12 years old*. To Bryant, it was a wake-up call. "From that point on, I've always had a mentality of it's like I'm trying out for a ball team. Look at the movie *Rudy*"—and surely this is the first time anyone has ever compared Kobe Bryant to Rudy, the runty walk-on football player at Notre Dame. "This guy could do that with no talent whatsoever, but if I have the talent and I play that hard all the time, what are the results going to be?" He pauses, nods. "I'm curious to see. I want to find out."

You mean, like an experiment?

"Yeah, my own personal thing. And now I want to see how far I can push this thing. I keep pushing it and now"—he pauses for a moment and then chuckles, a man in awe of himself—"now I'm on autopilot and I don't know how to turn this shit off. It just goes."

Pure Shooter: A Double-Barrel Duel with Steve Kerr

During his playing days, former Bulls guard Steve Kerr occasionally used to write a reminder to himself on the tops of his shoes. If he fell into a shooting slump or began to lose confidence—the worst thing that can happen to a shooter, tantamount to a surgeon suddenly getting the shakes—Kerr needed only to look down, where, written in black ink on the toes of his hightops, were the letters FI.

Fuck it.

At the start of a game, as he took the floor, Kerr would repeat this mantra to himself, under his breath, over and over. *Fuck it. Fuck it. Fuck it. Fuck it.*

When he got the ball for the first time on offense in the half-court, no matter where he was or who was guarding him, he shot it. If his man was crowding him, he pump-faked, then took a dribble and launched a jumper. If he was unguarded but three feet behind the line, he shot it anyway. *Fuck it.*

If doubt began to creep back in, he buckled down even further, following the advice of an old high school friend to go "double barrel." This meant walking to center court, raising his arms to the crowd—and thus to his own wavering confidence—and extending both middle fingers. *Fuuuuuck iiiiit!* Only, of course, he didn't actually do this; he just imagined doing it. That was usually enough, though. "I needed a reminder to myself to stop thinking and just shoot," explains Kerr, now the G.M. of the Phoenix Suns. "You have to find ways to lose your self-consciousness. If you're self-conscious as a shooter, you're doomed."

Rather, the pure shooter aims not to think, to be, as they say, "unconscious." Perhaps the most impressive instance of Kerr's achieving this state came in the spring of 2003, during the gloaming of his career, when he put on one of the more remarkable shooting demonstrations in NBA history. It was Game 6 of the Western Conference finals, and the San Antonio Spurs were in danger of getting blown out by the Dallas Mavericks, which meant the series would head back to San Antonio for a do-or-die seventh game. With starting point guard Tony Parker felled by food poisoning from a bad crème brûlée and Tim Duncan facing constant double teams, the Spurs had struggled all night. So, with San Antonio down 15 points near the end of the third quarter and nowhere else to turn, coach Gregg Popovich looked down his bench and motioned to Kerr.

It was, by any measure, a desperation ploy—"totally unplanned," as Popovich later admitted. At age 37 Kerr was in the final season of his 15-year career and had played only three minutes so far in the series and only 13 minutes in the entire postseason. For the year he'd averaged but four points in 12.7 minutes a game. He was, in most people's mind, finished.

Still, he was Steve Kerr, the same man who would retire with the highest three-point percentage in NBA history (45.4%) and who had hit all those jumpers alongside Michael Jordan with the Bulls. Maybe, Popovich hoped, putting Kerr in would at least change the tenor of the game.

Immediately, Kerr's presence spread the floor for the Spurs. Two minutes after entering the game he drained a three-pointer from the left baseline. Remarkably, it was the first game shot he'd hit in a month and a half. Kerr recalls thinking that perhaps this could be his night, and he felt the first surge of confidence.

Six minutes later he got open again, this time at the top of the key. Again he swished a three, and now the game was tied. Then, on the very next possession, Dallas again left Kerr in order to double Duncan in the paint. And again he calmly sank a three-pointer from the top of the key. It was the Spurs' first lead since the first quarter, and even the announcers were feeling it. "YESSSS!" roared play-by-play man Marv Albert, with even more gusto than usual, while on the San Antonio bench reserves Danny Ferry and David Robinson hopped around like a couple of giddy four-year-olds on Christmas morning, lifting their knees in the air, pumping their fists and grinning maniacally. (Really, it is worth finding this clip on YouTube just to watch their reaction.)

Finally, with five minutes left in the game and the Spurs up five, Mavs guard Steve Nash doubled down on Duncan one final time. On the right wing Kerr caught the kick-out, and the entire arena seemed to groan. To no one's surprise, and with utter calm, Kerr sank another three, his fourth in four tries, all of them perfect swishes. And with that, the Mavs were done. The Spurs never relinquished the lead, pulling away to win 90–78. Two weeks later they defeated New Jersey for the NBA title. Shortly after, Kerr retired. To this day he says people approach him at least once a month to talk about that night. "I think a lot of people lived through me," he says. "It was just one of those moments."

For some players, such a moment might be considered a stroke of luck, a hot streak or a night "in the zone." Kerr is different, though. Not only did he expect to make those shots, but most everyone else in the arena expected it too. Kerr is what's known in basketball parlance as a "pure shooter," a rare breed that includes the likes of Ray Allen, Reggie Miller, Larry Bird, Chris Mullin and Dell Curry, among others. Some, like Curry, seem to shoot only with their arms, while others, like Allen, spring high into the air before releasing spinning jumpers. Mullin didn't even need to square up his body, only his wrists. All of them were deadly if left unguarded.

There is a common coaching adage that to make a shot half the time in the game you need to be able to knock it down 70% of the time in practice. Well, for these men 70% is an abomination. Without a defender, a pure shooter is upset if he *ever* misses. As a result, unbelievable tales circulate around the league. Like the time Brent Barry reportedly drained 97 out of 100 threes during practice, or the afternoon when Mullin is said to have sunk 194 consecutive jumpers during a workout. So pure is the stroke of such shooters that it is oblivious to all attempts at sabotage, both external or internal. A journalist buddy of mine has a friend who used to work at a beach club on Long Island. He recalls once coming upon Mullin at the club, a few years after Mullin left St. John's and before he quit drinking. It was late one summer night, almost dark, and the friend heard sounds coming from a nearby basketball court. Checking it out, he discovered Mullin, standing there by himself, taking swigs of beer with his right hand and launching one-handed three-pointers with his left, a partially completed six-pack at his side. Shot after shot sank through the net. Swig. Swish. Swig. Swish. Swig. Swish.

Much of the allure of the Pure Shooters Club is that it is so exclusive. You can become a better shooter, it is said, but you cannot become a pure shooter; that is a birthright. If you're needing genetic evidence, look at Dell Curry's son, Stephen Curry, who was drafted by the Warriors in the summer of 2009 after a remarkable career at Davidson, where he set the NCAA single-season record with 162 three-pointers as a sophomore. Then there are the shooting broods: Rick Barry sired a lineup of sweet-shooting sons, including Brent, Drew and Jon, while Chuck Person was departing the league just as his little brother, Wesley, came in, armed with the same moon-ball arc.

For those not blessed with it, a perfect stroke can seem an almost magical attribute. Most every NBA player can dunk and run and jump, but only a select few are true pure shooters; all others, it seems, aspire to their ranks. Some, like the well-traveled forward Antoine Walker, seem to hope that merely by shooting enough they will gain entrance; in 2005 Walker launched 645 three-pointers, over 100 more than anyone else in the league, but hit only 34.4% of them. (During the 2003–04 season, he shot a deplorable 26.9%, but he didn't let that deter him from launching 305, or almost four a game.) Walker did not fool anyone (though he did utter one of my favorite hoops quotes of all time; once asked why he shot so many threes, Walker responded, "Because there are no fours"). Others have trained themselves to shoot only from certain spots, like Damon Jones, formerly of the Heat and Bucks, who is a deadeye three-point shooter (lifetime 39.0%) but has relative trouble when faced with an unguarded 15-footer (72.4% on free throws). This is akin to being a tennis player who has a huge serve but often flubs easy ground strokes.

Still others, like four-time Defensive Player of the Year Ben Wallace, spend their afternoons daydreaming wistfully. While with the Pistons, Wallace regularly spent an extra half hour after each practice launching three-pointers, even though he never shot them in games. Who can blame him? There is great glory in being a shooter. Even the lingo is heroic, evoking characters from the Old West: marksman, gunslinger, deadeye.

Pure shooters are held in such esteem, they change a game without even taking shots. Put a player like Miller, or three-point specialist Jason Kapono, on the floor, and the opposition must be aware of him at all times. His defender can't sag off or gamble for steals; if Kapono stands 25 feet from the basket, that's where his defender stands. Even in transition, defenders race to the wing to make sure there are no open threes, lest their coach go bonkers because *That's the one guy you can't leave open!* Remarkably, this works even if Kapono misses his shots, because everyone expects him to make his next one.

More than any other part of the game, shooting is a matter of confidence. To be a truly great shooter, you must *believe* that you are one, even when the results say otherwise. That's easy in theory and quite difficult in practice. And that's also what separates those who are automatic shooters from those who are merely streaky, the Reggie Millers of the world from the Antoine Walkers.

How does one become the former? That is up for debate. Some argue that you can become a great shooter through practice. In his book *Sport Science,* the physicist Peter Brancazio took it a step further, claiming to have discovered a way to create a pure shooter by following the laws of physics. After much study and "fairly extensive mathematical calculations," he decided that launching shots at the trajectory that requires the least amount of force would lead to a greatly increased level of accuracy. So for someone of average height shooting a 15-footer, for example, that ideal trajectory would be 49 degrees. (For a sense of what this looks like, a 49-degree shot should peak just below the height of the top of the backboard.) To detail the reasoning here would require a page full of equations, but Brancazio's general point is that shooting the ball with a higher arc than the ideal trajectory requires more effort, thus making the shot less replicable, whereas shooting it with less arc means it has to be more precise to go in.

While Brancazio should be commended for his enthusiasm—his proof for his theory was that he tried it himself and became a better shooter—the more accepted pure shooter theory is the born-not-made version. These players, it is believed, come out of the womb with perfect form and go to the grave demonstrating perfect follow-through. They are able to maintain the skill even when they rarely play and long after their careers have ended. So innate is the ability, it is said, that a man like Larry Bird will still be able to kick your ass at Pop-a-Shot when he's in a nursing home. (And who is to doubt that claim?)

Kapono, who won two All-Star three-point shootouts and currently trails Kerr by a whisker (.002%) for best career three-point percentage (45.4%), compares it to golf. "You can teach anyone how to hit a flop shot, but unless you have that feel, that understanding and that feeling in your hands and your body to pull that shot off like Tiger Woods or Phil Mickelson, it won't be the same," he told me. "You have to be able to have that sense, when things are going short or long. It's not that much of a technical thing, it's more of a feel thing."

In the interest of adding to the body of knowledge about pure shooters, and armed with the excuse of researching this book, I devised an experiment of sorts. I wondered: Could someone like Steve Kerr, five years removed from his NBA playing days, still stroll out on the court and drain threes? Or, like most mortals, would he succumb to the time away, the lack of practice and the effects of aging? It would by no means be a conclusive study—and until the NIH expands its funding guidelines considerably, there probably won't be one—but perhaps it would shed some light.

So I called the Suns and made my pitch to Kerr: a shooting competition, journalist versus G.M. My role would be minor, of course. I would (hopefully) provide some competition—the better to get Kerr's juices going and simulate a practice or game situation. A fringe benefit, I suggested to Kerr, is that he would get to do something many G.M.'s might relish: crush a sportswriter.

Why choose Kerr? First, because of his track record as one of the greatest spot-up shooters ever: Not only did he retire atop the career three-point percentage list, but he won an NBA three-point shootout, hit clutch jumpers to win Finals games and shot 86.4% from the free throw line for his career. Second, because he is just close enough to his playing days to be in decent shape but just far enough removed to have had a chance to become rusty. And finally, because perhaps no player in the last 20 years has seemed so much like the rest of us. To look at Kerr as a player was to think, Hey, *I* could take that guy. He was not only short (at least in NBA terms), white and skinny but, unlike fellow SWGs (Short White Guys) such as Steve Nash and John Stockton, he also lacked the speed and athleticism to compensate for his physical shortcomings. Kerr *was* his jump shot. It was the only reason he made the league and the only reason he hung around. Thus he became the standard by which every rec leaguer and high school hero judged himself. Secretly, we all thought we could compete against a guy like Kerr. Now I was hoping to get the chance.

Being a good-natured sort, Kerr agreed, and we set a date for October 2008, during the Suns' preseason.

The designated morning arrived, and I drove from the Phoenix airport to AmericaWest Arena, arriving at 10:30 a.m., near the end of a Suns shootaround. Behind one bench Kerr was chatting with a couple of staffers, watching his players amble through various offensive sets (which are ostensibly the reason for game-day shootarounds, though the real purpose seems to be ensuring that players are awake and functioning by 10 a.m.). He looked almost the same as he did in his playing days: the short blond hair, the thin frame, the freckly Dennis the Menace countenance that made him appear forever 15, somebody's gym-rat kid mistakenly let loose among NBA players. He was also, I noted, wearing slacks and a dress shirt. Taking a look at me, outfitted in hightops, shorts and T-shirt, he looked concerned: "Am I going to need my gear for this?"

I suggested that it would help, seeing as I was hoping we could do a fair amount of shooting—25 collegiate three-pointers followed by 25 NBA three-pointers and then 10 free throws.

Kerr nodded. He was in—he just needed to get his gear from his office, he told me. Though, as became apparent, he preferred to wait until all the Suns players left the court.

Half an hour later, Kerr emerged wearing a Suns T-shirt, ratty shorts that looked as if they'd been wadded up in a closet for months and tennis shoes. Fortunately for him, all but one of the Suns players had left by this point. Unfortunately for him, that one player happened to be Shaquille O'Neal, who was still chatting with a reporter courtside, his giant arms draped over two adjacent chairs. Shaq took one look at Kerr and me warming up and let Kerr have it: "Hey, look at the old guys!" Shaq bellowed. "When did we sign them?"

Kerr laughed it off. In reality, he was more worried about how his body was going to respond. It had been more than a year since he'd played, he told me, and he rarely even shot around anymore. His back had become creakier than an old barn door, and at 43 his legs stiffened up quickly. "Tennis is my game now," he said as we heaved up jumpers. "My body doesn't respond like it used to when I try to play basketball."

For my purposes, this was ideal. Here was a once-great shooter being pulled off the top shelf of a musty closet and dusted off. Would all the parts still work? I asked him for predictions.

He stopped shooting and grimaced. "On the college threes, I think I can make 18 out of 25. From pro I'm going to say"—he paused to do some mental calculations—"13, about half of them. When I was playing and practicing a lot, I could usually make about 20 out of 25. Now it's the distance that gets me. I shoot that NBA three with my legs, and you really have to push to get it up there."

And free throws?

Kerr fixed me with a grave look. "I'll be very disappointed if I miss one."

By now Shaq had (mercifully) left, so it was just Kerr, myself and an *SI* photographer on the AmericaWest floor. It was the first time I'd shot on an actual NBA court, and the immensity of the arena was disconcerting. There was the hoop, the sideline and then, stretching out and up and up, row upon row of seats, darkened for now. There was no shooting background and, on the floor, no college three-point line to orient by. Above, the lights bore down, isolating us. It really did feel like being onstage—and this is in an *empty* arena. I could only imagine the sensation of entering a game cold with 18,000 people roaring. It's not, I imagined, something one can practice.

Though, as it turns out, Kerr used to do just that. Midway through his career, he approached Chip Engelland, an old friend who now works as the Spurs shooting coach, with a problem. Increasingly, Kerr found himself in difficult shooting situations. He'd play 20 minutes one night, then six the next, depending on matchups. Some nights he'd get up four shots, other nights it would be two. Sometimes he'd sit two games, then be expected to come in cold—as he later did in that Mavs series—and hit a big shot. How could one prepare for such erratic opportunities?

Engelland had a solution. He told Kerr to meet him on the bench at the practice gym. Once there, the two men sat and talked for five minutes. Then, suddenly, Engelland leaped up, ball in hand.

"Start running the wing," he ordered Kerr. "Now!"

Startled, Kerr jumped up and followed. Engelland dribbled madly, leading a fast break. When he got to the top of the key, he fed Kerr on the wing for a three-pointer. Then the two promptly returned to the bench, where they sat and talked for five more minutes. Then they did it again, and again. "In 30 minutes, I'd only shoot six shots," Kerr says. "Psychologically it was awesome, because then the next game I was like, 'Hey, I just did this.'" ("I remember we did it three days in a row, says Engelland. "The first day he hit 3 of 9, the second day it was 5 of 9 and by the third day it was 7 of 9. He really got it quick.")

Our shooting contest was different though. In this case Kerr had effectively been sitting on the bench for more than a year. On the other hand there was nowhere near the pressure that comes with an arena roaring and an NBA defender chasing you. Or was there? When I mentioned this, Kerr countered that this wasn't entirely true. "I mean, I'm out here shooting threes cold, and you're going to write up the results and I'll be judged by this," he pointed out. "That's actually *a lot* of pressure."

And so we began, shooting five balls each from five spots—both baselines, both wings and the top of the key, moving around the arc from baseline to baseline, with the second guy rebounding and passing the ball back. We started with college threes—though without an arc we had to guesstimate the 20 feet. Here, Kerr looked entirely comfortable. He knocked down four of his first five from the baseline spot, then continued at this pace, eventually dropping in 20 out of 25, or two more than he predicted. His form looked the same as it did during his Bulls and Spurs days. As with many great shooters, Kerr's form is entirely replicable; only the distance changes. Whether he's shooting from 12 feet or 27, Kerr squares his body, bends his knees as if performing a squat, then pushes up and out, using his legs to drive the ball, his right arm firing up and his wrist snapping almost violently up and out—as if reaching up and into a jar placed on top of a high shelf. Watching him shoot was almost mesmerizing; catch, bend, shoot, snap.

My form was not quite so pure, and I struggled without the familiarity of a college arc, missing the comfort of the line itself. In essence, I am a trained three-point shooter. In high school, college and for years afterward in rec leagues, I spent much of my time floating along the three-point line, waiting for spot-up opportunities. Without the anchor of the arc, however, I felt lost. Kerr merely repeated his motion, no matter the distance, but I am accustomed to exactly 19 feet, nine inches. Six inches in, and I am liable to shoot it long; a few inches back, and it'll probably come up short. Out of 25 shots, I hit only 13, probably five or six fewer than I normally would. I felt a surge of disappointment. Not because I expected to beat Kerr, but because I had hoped to at least make it competitive.

I fared better on the next round of shots. After starting slow, I heated up and hit seven of my last 11 from the NBA arc to finish at 12 of 25.

I even managed to forget for a moment that it was Steve Kerr feeding me the ball. In a vacuum, with practice, I would have expected to do better, but considering the circumstances and my poor showing in the previous round, I was satisfied. "Pretty good," was Kerr's assessment.

At this point, with Kerr heading to the corner, it occurred to me that 12 made shots is only one fewer than Kerr predicted he would hit. Which in turn allowed me to entertain, if only fleetingly, the notion that I could conceivably walk away with one of the greatest bar boasts ever: *I beat Steve Kerr in a three-point shooting contest.* Hey, crazier things have happened.

He headed to the left baseline, set his feet and drained his first shot, then missed the next one. He made two more, then missed two, putting him at three out of his first six. So far, as predicted, Kerr was shooting 50%. Which, for perspective, is still pretty darn good from that range. In the NBA three-point shootout, held during All-Star weekend each year, players must take 25 shots in a minute from the same five spots Kerr and I were shooting from, with the fifth ball at each rack, the so-called "money ball," worth an extra point. Most years, a score of 14 or so is enough to advance out of the first round (and in 2009 Rashard Lewis put up a score of only seven in the final round). Some players, however, struggle to hit even 10; when Michael Jordan competed in 1990, he hit only 5 of 25 shots—the worst score in contest history. In 2008 Steve Nash finished with nine points. Naturally, when Kerr competed, he did quite well. In 1997 he won the event, scoring 15 points in the first round, 21 in the second and 22 points in the final.

Eleven years later and staring down a 3 for 6 start, those totals looked unlikely for Kerr. Perhaps the pure shooter had lost some of his touch after all. I would find out soon enough.

For now, let us leave Kerr where he is, in mid-release on the left wing, and consider for a moment the mechanics of the jump shot.

Depending on who's doing it, shooting a basketball can appear to be either the most natural motion in the world or, as when Shaq launches a "jumper," like watching a man trying to dislocate his own shoulder. The first player to shoot a true jump shot, feet leaving the ground, was—well, that's a matter of some contention. According to John Christgau's entertaining and authoritative tome, *Origins of the Jump Shot: Eight Men Who Shook the World of Basketball,* a number of players experimented with the shot during the 1920s and '30s before it was popularized by Stanford guard Hank Luisetti in a game versus Long Island University at Madison Square Garden in 1936. Many of these men came to it out of necessity. Kenny Sailors, for example, grew up outside Hillsdale, Wyoming, playing games of one-on-one against his 6'5" older brother, Bud, using a makeshift basket on the family farm. A foot and a half shorter than Bud, Kenny found the only way he could get a shot off—let alone score—was to leap and then shoot. His high school coach thought the shot "queer," but it sure worked; Sailors went on to play for the University of Wyoming and then in the NBA.

Men like Sailors tended to push their jumpers—enough so that sportswriters at the time referred to these strange, leaping efforts as "shot puts"—but over time the prototypical jumper evolved into an above-the-head, high-flick release, shot not off the palm but the finger-tips. There is perhaps no better example of the form than that of Ray Allen of the Celtics. He always squares up, always leaps perfectly verti-cally, and his shot never varies. It's not that he can't shoot a set shot (he told me he'd shoot "at least 80 percent" if he shot 100 with feet planted on the floor in practice), but that he believes it's foolhardy to vary one's form. "It's only going to get you in trouble," he explained, "because if you shoot a set shot one time, then the next time you're shooting from a different release angle. If you can shoot the same shot every time, that's the ultimate reward. Then you don't have to do any-thing different."

Though players like Allen and Kerr boast what's generally thought of as "textbook" form—an elbow-in thrust followed by wrist-snapping follow-through—many of the games' great shooters boast unconven-tional, if not downright peculiar, releases. Larry Bird launched his jumper from the right of his head, beginning his motion as if carry-ing a jug of water on his shoulder (a form he adopted as a boy having to shoot against older, stronger men while playing against local black hotel employees in French Lick, Ind.). Reggie Miller's left wrist snapped against his right on a follow-through so crooked it always seemed a mir-acle the ball went straight. Dallas forward Dirk Nowitzki releases every jumper only after a herky-jerky prelude in which, on three-pointers, he pigeon-toes his right foot to the line and leaves his left staggered behind him, like a man learning to surf, before raising the ball from below his hip, releasing it and then kicking his legs out in opposite directions. Michael Redd, the Milwaukee three-point specialist, also splays his legs when he shoots (generally considered a bad idea) and tends to slingshot the ball from behind his ear. He's also something of a self-taught gunner; in college Redd had neither the confidence nor accuracy to shoot long jumpers and spent much of his time driving to the basket. Only after leaving Ohio State did he focus on shooting, spending two summers hoisting hundreds of jumpers a day at a gym in Ohio, near where he grew up. In the NBA, Redd launches so often that former Milwaukee teammate Damon Jones once dubbed him Bombs over Baghdad because, as Jones explained to me with little concern for political correctness, "Sometimes he kills the enemy and sometimes he kills the civilians. And we"—he gestured around the Bucks' locker room—"are the civilians." (Shawn Marion, though not considered one of the great shooters, may take the prize when it comes to "the craziest form that still works." He shoots the ball from somewhere near his lower thigh and flips it at the basket as if shooing away a fly.)

And then there is Kevin Martin, the Sacramento guard whose form could make a CYO coach cry. He begins with the ball in his right hand by his side, as if restraining an unruly dog near his hip. Then his right leg turns inward, as if he's been hit in the shin by a blunt object, and he swings the ball up and across his body, only to release it with a pronounced heave from in front of his face. If you didn't know better, you might think he's physically disabled, so spasmodic is the motion. Despite this, last year Martin shot 40.2 % on three-pointers and 86.9% on free throws. It's unclear which is more remarkable, that he is so accurate or that there was never someone, somewhere to force Martin to change his form. David Thorpe, who runs the Pro Training Center and works with a number of NBA clients, says he was tempted to fiddle when he first began working with Martin in 2002. "I would never teach anyone to shoot like Kevin, but I wouldn't change it because it works for him," says Thorpe. "As coaches we have to remember we don't want to mess it up when something works. And Kevin is a natural shooter."

Unconvinced, I ask Martin about this after a Kings game. He told me he developed his shot when he was growing up because he usually played against guys four or five years older. "And if you've seen my body frame, you know I wasn't in there banging with them," he said. "So I was out at the three-point line, just shooting it. And to get it up there, I had to fling the ball up." He became so adept at the motion that, by the time Martin got to high school, his coach didn't dare mess with success. "That's what coaches always told me," Martin said with a shrug. "As long as it goes in, it can look as ugly as it wants." Thorpe believes that Martin would probably rank with the best shooters regardless of what form he'd developed. "I would argue that Kevin could throw a wadded piece of paper in a trash can better than most people. He just has that talent. There are all sorts of basketball abilities that can be refined, but with shooting there's a natural ceiling."

In certain respects, shooting is comparable to learning a foreign language. Some people can spend years and years struggling to become comfortable with it, taking classes and practicing diligently, while others just take to it naturally (and are despised for doing so by those who struggle).

Reggie Miller grew up shooting a one-handed push shot that began down by his thigh; it wasn't until high school that he developed the high-release jumper for which he was known—and that came only after much practice. As Miller told my colleague Jack McCallum in 1994, "When I was growing up [in Riverside, Calif.], my father had a little area of concrete for our backyard basket," Miller recalled. "My first goal was to master every shot in that area. After I did that, I said, 'Dad, we need more concrete.' Eventually we had an area that went back maybe 22 feet from the basket. Any more than that was in my mother's rose garden, and I shot from there, too. I apologize, but it paid off."

In Kerr's case, he says he was never explicitly taught how to shoot—he could just always do it. "Even as a six-year-old I could hit baskets," he says. "I had to heave the ball from my hip, but I could make them all day. It was just a feel thing." (In fact, Kerr says there's never been a time in his life where he felt frustrated shooting a basketball.)

Allen is the rare shooter who's also an exceptional leaper. (Often such players are seduced by their own athleticism at a young age and become drivers first, shooters second.) On most shots he rises 25 inches or more off the floor, and he carefully monitors this "lift," which he believes is the key to his success. When ankle injuries robbed him of some jumping ability during the 2007–08 season, he told me he felt "uneven" on some jumpers. The following season, healthy again, he flirted with what he calls "the promised land of shooting": 50% from the field, 90% from the free throw line and 40% from behind the arc. (Allen finished at 48.0%/95.2%/40.9%.) Very few players can maintain those percentages for a full season. In the last decade only Steve Nash (who pulled it off three times and came within one tenth of one percent another season) and Jose Calderon have done it, and they were both point guards, who have more high-percentage layup opportunities than a spot-up shooter like Allen.

(In researching this, I went deep into the NBA record book and compiled two lists. On the first list were those who, since 1980, had pulled off the 50/90/40 feat: Chronologically it is Bird, Bird, Mark Price, Reggie Miller, Kerr, Nash, Nowitzki, Nash and Calderon, Nash. The second list shows those in that same time span who came close. Combined with the names above, it's essentially a collection of the great shooters of the last three decades—but with a few surprises. Again in chronological order, here are those who came closest: Kyle Macy, Brad Davis, Byron Scott, Kiki Vandeweghe, Jeff Hornacek, Ricky Pierce, Drazen Petrovic, Kenny Smith, Bill Laimbeer, Dana Barros, Mario Elie, Chris Mullin, Danny Ferry, Ray Allen, Jon Barry, Peja Stojakovic, Wally Szczerbiak, Jason Kapono, Brian Cardinal [!] and Brent Barry. What's more, only one player in NBA history has ever pulled off a 50/90/50 season: Steve Kerr, in 1995–6.)

Allen's success is due to a shot that is almost obsessively calibrated. First, to ensure optimum lift and stamina, he attempts to maintain a body fat level of 4%, and varies his exercise depending on how his legs feel. Some summers he focuses on biking 30 miles a day, while during the season he may spend more time jogging, all the time monitoring his calorie intake. "Sometimes my body craves food, and I have to eat carbs," he explains. "There are times I get too slim, and my trainer will tell me, Go eat a cheeseburger." (Surely we can all relate to such a problem.)

Allen also follows an unvarying routine to hone his stroke. Before each game his regimen begins with hook shots and runners in the lane ("to get familiar with the ball"), then 10 free throws, then 25 mid-range jumpers around the key and then, depending on the opponent, either post ups or pick-and-rolls. To finish, he must make at least 100 of the shots, total. "If I'm not shooting the ball well, it might take 150 shots, max," he says. And on each release he repeats that same motion. As he explains: "Why give yourself any margin for error?" (How accurate is Allen? When in Seattle, Allen mentored Rashard Lewis, who would later lead the league in three-point attempts while with Orlando. Lewis followed Allen's routine religiously. Still, according to Lewis, when the two would have shooting contests, he would beat Allen "maybe once in 100 times." I asked if this was hyperbole. "No, I'm saying *maybe* once," Lewis said. "He's that good.")

Occasionally, however, a player changes his form while in the NBA and becomes a measurably better shooter. Spurs point guard Tony Parker, though frighteningly quick when he entered the league, was such an erratic jump shooter that teams could just lay off him—sometimes as much as five feet—and dare him to shoot. In NBA circles this is known as a "self-check," as in there is no need to defend (or "check") the player because he's doing the job himself merely by being more than 15 feet from the basket. (Kendall Gill, the old Nets guard, was a notorious self-check.) In his first three years in the league Parker shot 41.9%, 46.4% and 44.7% from the field, remarkably low percentages for a player who gets so many layups.

In the summer of 2005, after years of watching opponents back off Parker in the playoffs, the Spurs brought in Steve Kerr's friend Chip Engelland to tinker with his form. Engelland is something of an unlikely guru. A soft-spoken Duke grad (he was co-captain of the 1983 team), he went to law school before starting his own basketball camps, and he lacks the rah-rah intensity common to personal trainers and self-help coaches. His aphorisms are the practical kind—"You want to control the ball, not let the ball control you" and, referring to beginning shooting drills close to the basket, "You learn the game like golf—from the cup back."

In Parker's case, the first thing Engelland noticed was that while his form was exemplary on his one-handed runners and teardrops, Parker held the ball differently on his jump shot. Rather than keeping his right hand under the ball, Parker had it slightly higher up. So, beginning with training camp in the fall of 2005, Engelland reconstructed Parker's shot, moving his right hand down, his right thumb out to widen his grip, slowing down his motion and even changing his release point.

Eventually Parker's J began to improve; he was applying more backspin, and his line drives were turning into baby parabolas. Parker ended the 2005–06 season shooting 54.8%. Of course, that leap of improvement could be due to a host of reasons—maybe Parker shot more layups or became more proficient at them, or perhaps his teammates put him in better shooting situations. Examining shot chart breakdowns, however, we see that not only did Parker become better in the paint, but his jumpers indeed fell more often; in 2004–05 Parker shot 34.5% on shots outside the paint, whereas in 2005–06, post-Engelland, that rose to 39.7%. Looking even more specifically at mid-range shots, those outside the lane but inside the three-point line, we see that Parker's shooting increased from 39.3% to 41.6% the following season, and by 2008–09, it was up to a very respectable 45.5%, above the league average.

Parker turned himself into a proficient mid-range shooter, but he didn't develop true three-point range. Other players skip the mid-range and move straight beyond the arc, perhaps no one so dramatically as Dan Majerle, the Suns shooting guard from the mid-90s. "Dan was one of those rare guys who was better from 25 feet than from 17," says Kerr, who refers to his former teammate as "an either/or guy," as in either he launched the three or went all the way to the basket.

Sometimes a player becomes a better shooter simply because he's *allowed* to shoot. Take the case of Eduardo Najera. When Najera played for the Denver Nuggets in 2008, coach George Karl was running what could be loosely defined as a see-basket-shoot offense. While Karl preferred his players to (in this order) get to the rim, shoot free throws or take open threes, the only shot he considered a bad one was a contested two-pointer in the first 10 seconds.

So what did this have to do with Najera? After all, he is a 6'8", 235-pound reserve forward best remembered for his years as a defensive specialist on teams devoid of them, first with the Mavs and then with the Warriors and Denver. A classic banger, Najera spent the first seven years of his career setting retaining-wall screens and taking more elbows to the face than jump shots. But Karl saw in him a competent shooter, and one who could stretch the defense and open up driving lanes for his stars. After watching Najera hit 20-footers in shooting drills, Karl told him to take a step back and start launching threes in games. Assuming his coach was "just playing around," Najera did no such thing. ("I'm not dumb," says Najera, "I know what's kept me in the league the last eight years.") To Najera's surprise, however, Karl approached him a few exhibition games later. "Hey," Karl said, "I'm still waiting for you to shoot those threes."

Thus Denver fans were treated to the unlikely site of Najera not only occasionally pushing the ball on the fast break, which is a bit like seeing a tractor leading the Indy 500, but also spotting up behind the arc. Strategically, it even made sense; since Iverson and Anthony

often clogged the lane, Najera couldn't do his work inside, so instead
he spaced the floor. At first, ex-teammates were surprised, to put it
charitably. "What the hell are *you* doing shooting threes?" joked Mavs
forward Dirk Nowitzki. Mavs owner Mark Cuban thought the scenario
was hilarious. Until, that is, Najera nailed a big third-quarter three in
a December win over Dallas. Then Cuban wasn't so amused. For the
season Najera averaged nearly two three-point attempts a game and
hit a respectable 36.1%, despite averaging only eight attempts per *season* before that in his career. To Karl, it was just common sense. "It's
not that complicated. If you can make the three, I'm going to let you
take it."

————————

Let's return now to Phoenix and Kerr and our contest. When last we
left him, Kerr had started slowly from behind the NBA arc, and I, naturally, had felt a small flicker of competitive hope. Well . . . Kerr began
to heat up. He hit his next two from the wing, then two more, making him 7 of 10. "Sign him up," I yelled, only half-joking. "Give that
man a contract!"

Working his way to the top of the key, he hit a groove. The old
knees loosened up, the back flexed perfectly. Soon he was 8 of 11, then
10 of 14. I even tried throwing one of my passes a bit off to his right,
to try to break his rhythm, but to no avail. "Oh, trying to throw me
off!" Kerr chortled as he sank another one. He improved to 14 of 18,
the ball practically singing through the net, then 15 of 19, then 16 of
20, then over to the corner to get to 17 of 21, then 18 of 22. Two more
balls whistled through, and then he was loading up his final three and
sinking it to finish 21 of 25. It was a remarkable display, one worthy
of celebration. I began whooping while Kerr shouted and pumped his
fist and did a little jig. We were both jazzed, high-fiving like a couple
of high school kids. Counting it up, I realized that he'd hit his final 11
NBA three-pointers in a row.

"I know," he said, "and I'm shocked. I didn't think there was any
way I'd do that."

"That would have won the NBA three-point shootout," I pointed
out.

"Wow," he said to me. "Remember what you said about putting
me in a competitive shooting environment to make me shoot better?
I started to feel it. The juices just started to flow. When you get in a

game, your range increases because of the energy and competition. Well, I thought I'd struggle at the wings. I knew I could make the corners, because it's 22 feet. But the adrenaline carried me through the top 15."

I asked how his legs felt.

"Fine," he said, then continued analyzing his performance. "I find the further the shot is away from the hoop, it's really got to flow." He paused, mimicking the motion. "So I was thinking about releasing it a little earlier than I normally would, adjusting my release point to keep my range."

Rather conclusively, I suggested, we'd determined that he still had it. That someone can come out of retirement and, on his first try, knock down 21 out of 25 NBA threes certainly supports the idea that a pure shooter never loses his touch.

To reinforce this, Kerr proceeded to hit all 10 of his free throw attempts and then shut me out in a game of H-O-R-S-E in which I didn't even shoot that poorly. I began the game by hitting an NBA three from the left wing (he matched), then a shot with my feet on the NBA three-point line, in the hopes that this might throw him off ("You been practicing for this?" he asked before swishing that one too), and a number of other tough shots. Still the only shot Kerr missed the entire H-O-R-S-E game was when he shot over the backboard from out-of-bounds along the baseline. He hit runners, a "four-pointer" from the sideline out-of-bounds that was probably 26 feet, then finished me off with what he called "the Dan Majerle three," from about 30 feet deep, straight on.

Afterward, Kerr was practically bouncing. "I'm all fired up right now," he said, grinning. "I want to go play." (Later, it should be noted, the reality of age set in. Within hours, he told me, his elbow began to hurt from all the shooting. "No more pickup ball for me," he said with a touch of regret.)

He predicted he'd be thinking about the shootout for days (and he wasn't kidding; I later heard reports of his reliving the tale around the Suns offices, and that afternoon, when I asked about his favorite non-NBA shooting memory, he said with a laugh, "besides making 21 of 25 just now, you mean?"). This wasn't much of a surprise, really. After all, when he was playing, Kerr would sometimes wake up in the middle of the night and lurch suddenly to attention, hands at the ready to catch an imaginary pass so he could launch a jumper. "My wife thought I was crazy," he said, "but I guess my subconscious was thinking about jumpers."

This suggests that shooters have both an intimate, and at times mystical, connection with their shots. Perhaps my favorite philosophy comes from Szczerbiak, the Cavs forward. "You have to always respect the jump shot," Szczerbiak told me, dead serious. "Because on any given day that ball can start being one inch off and going in and out. You think you got it figured out and you really don't."

Which is where superstition comes in. Kerr would grow a good-luck goatee if he was in a slump, but that's nothing compared to other rituals. The most notorious of these belongs to Rip Hamilton, who has perhaps the best mid-range jumper in the game today (which, it might be noted, is by far the least-sexy shot in basketball; as Utah coach Jerry Sloan once put it, "There's not anything exciting about a 15-foot jump shot. How many times you ever see them show on television, or people write in the newspaper, anything about a guy making a 15-foot jump shot?"). In 2004, Hamilton suffered a facial injury and had to wear a plastic mask. Once recovered, he took it off only to find—or at least *believe*—he'd lost his shooting mojo. So, to this day, he still wears the mask, which he calls "my Superman cape." Ray Allen becomes upset if someone takes his pregame parking spot—it has to be the same one before every Boston home game—and once got mad at Paul Pierce when the Celtics forward attempted (and missed) a 360 dunk during warmups. Why in the world, the furious Allen asked, would Pierce do that? The team had been winning with its usual routine, and now Pierce had gone and messed it up. After Boston won the game, Allen then tried and failed to enforce a new decree that Pierce attempt (and miss) a 360 before every game, because now it was a winning superstition.

No one topped Reggie Miller though. To watch him warm up for a game, a pleasure I enjoyed on multiple occasions, was to see not only a master at work but also a man suffering from what appeared to be low-grade OCD. He would arrive at Conseco Fieldhouse three hours before tip-off. Save for a few techies laying down TV cables and the odd usher, the cavernous arena would be empty when Miller took the floor and began shooting: first free throws, then a precise routine of layups, jumpers and three-pointers, assisted by a ball boy who moved in tandem, knowing where to pass, when to do it. The only sound would come from the squeak of shoes, the *schwick* of the dancing net and the click of Miller's wrists snapping together. So consistent was his warmup—he'd typically make on the order of 35 of 36 free throws and 35 or 36 of 42 three-pointers—that it was disconcerting when he didn't connect, like seeing someone, midway through a meal, lift a forkful of salad and miss his mouth entirely.

That was just the beginning of his routine, though, which then–Pacers coach Rick Carlisle described to me as resulting from "a military mind-set." Among other superstitions, before every home game Miller always a) wore the same type of shirts (long sleeve with the cuffs cut off); b) watched film at the same time with the remote in the same hand; c) used only certain doors and hallways; and d) at the appointed moment, wielded a portable massager tool against hard surfaces in the locker room, creating a jackhammerlike din that he claimed served as "a dinner bell" to inspire his teammates. (When I asked Pacers forward Dale Davis if this was true, he just grinned and said, "That's Reggie. He's been doing that stuff forever, and for whatever reason, superstition or not, it works.")

Once on the court, Miller always dribbled down the final 30 seconds before the game began while facing the opponent's shot clock, then shot a three-pointer. (Naturally, he had a customized routine for each away-game arena, too.) The most unusual rite, however, came approximately eight minutes before the game would begin, when Miller would walk over to Pacers media relations director David Benner, who would be bearing a soda for Miller. (Benner always brought Pepsi, *unless* the team had lost the previous game, in which case he might switch it up and bring Sprite.) After taking a sip, Miller would listen as Benner berated him briefly with good-natured jibes, then respond by getting in Benner's face, wagging his finger and going nose-to-nose with him while cracking jokes about everything from Benner's hair to his clothes to his choice of music. The only topics off-limits were Benner's beloved wife and dog. "The fans sometimes think we're actually fighting," Benner told me. "They can't understand why he'd be bitching me out."

Then, and only then, was Miller ready to take the court, whereupon he'd unveil the full Reggie repertoire: the Baseline Fadeaway, the One-Knee-Up Runner, the Catch-and-Snap Three, the Free Throw Bait 'n' Flail and, throughout, the Reggie Run, that slithery, shirt-grabbing, shoulder-dipping dash around screen after screen—often 70 or more in a game—that made him look like a skier navigating slalom flags. Whether his pregame routine made him a better shooter is anyone's guess, but so long as Miller *believed* it made him a better shooter, well, that's all that really mattered, isn't it?

If we were to create a guide to the care and handling of the pure shooter, it would have these tenets. First, while only certain men are born blessed with the requisite hand-eye coordination to be great shooters, a pure shooter must be carefully maintained. His confidence must be nourished regularly, a process that may take the form of inspirational hightop slogans, or visualization, or elaborate superstitions— whatever makes a shooter believe he's invincible. Additionally, a pure shooter must himself provide proper polishing of his form, ensuring that it is both replicable and consistent.

Finally, he must be rock-solid in the one core conviction of the trade: that every shot is a made shot. When I asked Ray Allen how often, upon releasing a shot, he expected it to go in, he was surprised by the question. "How often?" he repeated. "I think I'm going to make every one I shoot."

In sum, sometimes myth can meet reality. Remember the implausible-sounding tale about Brent Barry hitting 97 out of 100 NBA threes in practice? Last winter I tracked down Barry in the Rockets' locker room before a game and asked him about it, telling him I'd heard a rumor of what he'd done.

"No, that was an exaggeration," he said, looking grim. "It was only 94."

Of course, *only* 94 out of 100 NBA threes. This number became even more impressive once he explained the situation. It happened while he was with San Antonio, during a drill the Spurs run that the players refer to as "shooting the hundred." Here's how it works: Using a rebounder-feeder, you start by shooting 10 spot-up three-pointers from six spots (baseline and two wing spots on each side) for a total of 60, then move on to five each from the same locations, though this time on the move (running down to the baseline to catch and shoot, then over to the wing, and so on) for another 30 and, finally, two spot-up shots each from the traditional five NBA shootout positions for a total of 100. Barry said he averaged "in the low 80s, like my golf game." Think about that for a moment—Barry shoots NBA three-pointers better than many players shoot free throws. Hell, he shoots NBA three-pointers better than many pickup players shoot *layups*.

Barry did not shoot in a vacuum. His competition most days consisted of the other Spurs wing players, and they turned it into a shooting Olympics. "Manu [Ginobili] would represent Argentina, Tony Parker represented France, Beno Udrih was Slovenia and I was the U.S.," Barry told me. "We'd have gold, silver and bronze medals for the day." And he fared pretty well, right? Barry smiled. "Yeah, I felt like Michael Phelps up there." He paused. "Though any other competition, like speed, and the U.S. would have been in big trouble."

By the way, when Barry hit 94, he broke the long-standing record of another former Spur, a mark that had stood for a while.

"The record was like 88 or 89," Barry said. And who had it? "This won't surprise you," he said. "It was Steve Kerr."

No, I told him, it did not surprise me at all.

The Rebound: Dwight Howard and the Science of Extra Possessions

If you were to try to engineer the perfect rebounding specimen, you could do a lot worse than Orlando Magic center Dwight Howard. At just under 7 feet tall, Howard carries a muscular 265 pounds on his frame, can bench 225 pounds more than 25 times and is so broad across the top that, with a T-shirt on, he looks as if he's wearing shoulder pads. His reach extends upward 113.5 inches (or just about 9½ feet); with a running start his vertical leap is 37 inches, and he says that on two occasions he has reached up and touched the top edge of the backboard. (He can also literally kiss the rim on a dunk.) What's more, his hands are so strong that when Magic trainer Joe Rogowski tested the team, Howard maxed out a grip strength machine at 90 pounds per square inch. (By comparison, most players measured in the 50s and 60s.) Says Rogowski, "That's like a dog's bite."

Now, granted, Howard doesn't fit the conventional psychological profile of a rebounder—that of the no-nonsense, utilitarian "dirty work" specialist. Rather, this is a guy who sings Beyoncé at the free throw line, who quotes not *Scarface* but *Finding Nemo,* whose idea of humor is ordering 10 pizzas to be delivered to another player's hotel room, or knocking on teammates' doors and sprinting off down the hall, giggling. He goofs around during practice, during press conferences and during team shootaround, for which Magic coach Stan Van Gundy has had to institute a no-flatulence rule because, as teammate Rashard Lewis says, "Dwight really likes to cut the cheese." During a photo shoot for an *SI* story last season, photographer Walter Iooss Jr.

had such a difficult time getting a serious pose out of Howard that he eventually told him to just do whatever came to mind. Unshackled, Howard launched into 20 minutes of antic posturing (including fake gangster poses and a Will Ferrell imitation), eventually producing so many fey faces that *SI* could now put out a coffee-table book titled *Dwight Howard: Dandy-At-Large.*

Still, when so inspired—which to be fair is most of the time—Howard is capable of getting just about every rebound in his general vicinity. To watch him in action is like seeing an eighth-grader playing against a bunch of fourth-graders on the playground, plucking balls off the boards as if they were low-hanging fruit. Here he is on a Friday night in January against the Portland Trailblazers. On this evening Trailblazers center Joel Przybilla, who stands 7' 1" and has his own set of coat-hanger shoulders, valiantly scrambles and pushes to get position underneath the basket. Yet, on play after play he is beaten to the ball by Howard. Not by some act of strategy but by sheer athleticism; when Howard leaps, he creates a one-man skyline above the basket, rising to snare the ball, contort his body for a tip-in or slap leather to palm in a majestic sweeping motion. As he plays, he accumulates rebounds almost effortlessly: six, then 10, and finally 13. Indeed, as he says nonchalantly, "getting 13 rebounds a game is easy, really." And the funny thing is that, for him, it may be. For his career Howard has never averaged less than 10 boards a game, and in one season he averaged more than 14. Which is to say that he has never known the frustrating feeling—call it gravitational impotence—of watching a larger, stronger player soar above him.

As with most players, though, Howard spends much of his time working on his shooting because that's where the glamour is. Rebounding is not sexy. There is no Nike Box Out VII, no *Come Board with Me* video. Little kids don't grow up wanting to be Reggie Evans, don't gaze up at vintage Larry Smith posters on their bedroom walls. And why would they? There's no glory in wedging your ass into another man's hip, elbowing him in the stomach, subtly anchoring his leg with your off arm and then grabbing a basketball that someone else has shot and, most likely, someone else will now requisition. Even the vernacular is utilitarian; rebounders "clean the glass," while scorers "light it up." Says Ben Wallace, who carries a career average of 10.3 boards a game, "For a kid, the last thing on his mind is to watch somebody and be like, 'Man, I want to rebound like him.' As a kid, I wanted to finish like Mike, pass like Magic, shoot like Bird and handle the ball like Zeke."

Yet elite rebounders are a rare and invaluable commodity in the NBA. It's no coincidence that each season the most successful teams can usually be found atop the rankings in rebounding differential (the gap between how many rebounds a team collects and how many it allows). In 2008–09 the Celtics, Lakers, Cavaliers and Trailblazers were all among the top five. Simply put, more boards equals more possessions. As Scottie Pippen said of having rebounder extraordinaire Dennis Rodman on his team, "It seemed like we were *always* on offense." To the casual observer, it seems a simple enough concept: *Just go get the ball.* But glass-cleaning is not so easy. As Wallace says, "It's really an art."

That's why, despite his prodigious physical talents, Howard is still not yet the rebounder he could be—and that, in turn, is a scary thought for opposing NBA teams. It's also why undersized men like Wallace or Charles Barkley can put up gaudy numbers. And it's why, despite their size and athleticism, some giants of the game find the act utterly confounding.

————————

Thirty and 40 years ago NBA players routinely grabbed 15 or more rebounds per game. For his career Bill Russell averaged 22.5, and during the 1960–61 season Wilt Chamberlain averaged an astonishing 27.2. For perspective, as of the end of the 2009 season, no NBA player had pulled down more than 27 rebounds in a game since 2002.

Part of the success of Russell and Chamberlain was due to skill, of course, but their spectacular numbers were also a product of a different game. Back then teams played at a faster pace and missed more of their shots, which may come as a surprise to those who speak wistfully of the good old days of "fundamental" jump shots. In Wilt's record rebounding season of 1960–61, as an example, teams shot an average of only 41.5% from the field (and this, remember, was with no three-point line). By comparison, the 2008–09 season average was 45.9%. As for pace, when Russell pulled down close to 25 a game in 1963–64, NBA teams not only shot a paltry 43.3% but, just as important, averaged more than 99 shots a game. During the 2008–09 season, when Howard led the league with 13.8 rebounds a game, teams shot a relatively scorching 45.9% from the field and averaged only 80.9

shots a game (and no, the difference is not made up in free throws; teams shot more of those in the '60s too). Using those numbers, one could calculate that the average game in 1963–64 yielded 24.8 more rebound opportunities than the average game in 2008–09. Naturally, fewer shots means fewer rebound opportunities, which, when combined with the advent of the three-point shot (which has led to more long rebounds) and taller guards (who are more likely to snag those long rebounds), means the days of 20 boards a game are in the past. "Today, it's a slow-down game, with more plays, so you don't see those numbers," says Hall of Famer Paul Silas, who averaged 9.9 rebounds during his 16-year career. Plus, he adds, "not too many guys are willing to make a science of it today."

Ben Wallace is one who has. An undersized center at 6'9", he combined, at his peak, the best attributes of his modern predecessors: the absurd jumping ability of Charles Barkley, the crafty skills of Rodman and the intense desire of Moses Malone, who once summed up his approach as, "If there are 100 shots in a game, then I go after all of them." (And he meant it. At Petersburg High in Virginia, Malone was so dominant that his teammates refused to feed him the ball inside. So he scored on rebounds, once pulling down 45 in a game. Later, with the Rockets in 1979, he grabbed 38% of the team's rebounds for the season, which is believed to be the largest percentage in NBA history, according to Alexander Wolff's *100 Years of Hoops*.)

In some ways Wallace was born into the job. Growing up in White Hall, Ala., with seven older brothers, the only way he could get touches at the local playground was to shag errant shots. "It was something I thought I had to do," he says. "I was under the impression that everybody went out and pursued the basketball like that, but I guess not."

He guessed right. Many NBA big men today are vertical rebounders, pulling in boards only in their immediate personal space and waving their arms at balls outside it, as if trying to flag them down. Especially in his prime, Wallace played a lateral game, jumping *to* the rebound. His M.O. was to create contact—to "hit first" in hoops vernacular— and carve out what he calls "a hole"; only then did he look for the flight of the ball. When he did jump, he had a tendency to do so with arms and legs at 45-degree angles, like an Afro-bedecked version of Da Vinci's Vitruvian Man, allowing him to simultaneously fend off would-be boarders as he snatched the ball or tipped it in from either side of the basket. Most important, though, Wallace tried for every rebound—what Przybilla calls "almost a suicide mentality."

To watch Wallace in his heyday, such as during the 2005–06 season when he averaged 12.6 boards a game, was to see his full repertoire of tactics on display. Consider his performance in one November game that season against the Sacramento Kings. In various pursuits of the ball he sneaked out-of-bounds then came back in under the basket; boxed Kings forward Shareef Abdur-Rahim in rather than out, pushing him deep under the rim; tipped the ball from his right hand to his left, as if playing one-man keep away; back-tapped the ball out of a crowd to Tayshaun Prince for an open shot; soared in for a two-hand follow dunk; and, in a single motion, snagged a defensive rebound and fired a baseball pass to Chauncey Billups to start a fast break. By the end of one quarter alone, Wallace had eight boards, the Pistons were up by nine and the Maloof brothers, the enthusiastic Kings owners, were slumped in their courtside seats.

For rebounders who don't possess Wallace's trampoline hops, the boarding battle is about power and positioning, a pursuit that can become, as Sixers forward Elton Brand calls it, "sadistic." Height matters, but not as much as width. Charles Barkley was only 6' 4½", but he was able to average 14.6 rebounds in one season and 11.7 for his career; as he once told *The New York Times*, "If I were 7 feet tall, I'd be illegal in three states." (At 270-odd pounds, there's a reason he was called the Round Mound of Rebound.) Likewise, Wes Unseld (14.0 per career) was only 6' 7", as was Danny Fortson (13.0 boards per 36 minutes—or starter's minutes—for his career). Fortson could leap about as high as the average hippopotamus but had another, meaty, advantage. "The best way to be a good position rebounder is to have a big behind," said Fortson, whose posterior is indeed formidable. "Your legs have to be big and strong, and you have to have some width on your frame. Jumping ability doesn't matter that much. If guys are long, you have to move them out of the way."

Doing so requires energetic boxing-out, a skill every player is taught at a young age but few ever master. As Brian Hill, the former Magic coach, explains, "Rather than just getting into a guy's upper body, you have to get low into his legs because then he can't really jump." Brand, the 76ers forward, is notoriously hard to box out, as he loves to slip out-of-bounds then come back in to establish position. (With Brand, opposing coaches talk about the importance of "hitting first.") For his part, Silas stresses the importance of "locking it in" when getting a body on a guy. "When the ball goes up, most guys have their front squared to the guy's rear, and that's a weak position," he says. "But if you turn your side, you can hold that position."

Of course, against some players it doesn't matter what you do. "The hardest to box out is Shaq," said Fortson. "He's so fucking big that it's not boxing out, it's pushing." On the other hand, Fortson labeled former Sixers center Shawn Bradley as the worst at boxing out he's ever seen—"Shawn's my man, but he was *terrible.*"

Once a rebounder has carved out position, the next step is to ascertain where the ball is headed. Talk to people around the league, and there are certain accepted truths—for example, that 75% of shots from the baseline carom long to the other side—and other learned ones. Some players take mental notes on their teammates' tendencies. While with the Bulls early in his career, the linguine-limbed Tyson Chandler learned that Chicago guard Ben Gordon shot a "soft ball," perfect for follow dunks, while Kirk Hinrich usually missed long, creating fast rebounds off the back of the rim that required a quick reaction.

There are subtle physical arts as well. Some players spin off defenders like running backs; others employ swim moves like offensive linemen. The less vertically inclined learn how to "ride the leg" of more athletic opponents, pinning it down so it's harder to jump, a trick Antonio McDyess told me he picked up after his knee surgeries robbed him of some of his athleticism. Howard learned to tap a defender on one side, then, "when they scoot to the right, I go to the left." Of course, there are other tricks, those of the, shall we say, less legal variety. Tyrone Hill and Charles Oakley used to step on opponents' feet; Adonal Foyle is adept at pulling an opponent's shorts. Alonzo Mourning says, "I'll grab a guy's arm and pull it behind his back to keep him from moving."

No one studied the craft like Rodman, who led the league in rebounding four times despite being only 6'8" and 215 pounds. He compared himself to a computer—the "software" being his knowledge of the game and the "hardware" being his body, which was in many ways perfectly suited to the task. Though relatively undersized, Rodman had freakishly long arms, and his wiry frame made him both difficult to box out and adept at slipping in between the cracks of opposing behemoths.

Whereas most players watch film to see how other players score,

Rodman studied the ways in which players *failed* to. When traded to the Bulls, for example, he would shag rebounds for Jordan and Pippen in practice to study their misses. Eventually he determined both men had a tendency to miss right, especially when shooting from the top of the key. So during games, whenever Jordan or Pippen fired a shot from straight-on, Rodman eschewed the mosh pit by the basket and slid to the right. More often than not, he got the board.

Sometimes his strategies were counterintuitive. After playing the Lakers a number of times, Rodman deduced that when Shaq missed from the baseline, his shot tended to carom back at him, due to the low (O.K., nonexistent) arc. So, instead of following the 75% rule and heading to the other side of the basket, Rodman ran *toward* O'Neal after he shot. And always, the Worm kept track of his prey, watching the ball—not the rim, as most players do—after a shot went up. In an *SI* story, Charlotte Hornets vice president of basketball operations Bob Bass once compared Rodman to Willie Mays, for the way he got a "jump" on the ball.

Unlike Mays, though, Rodman paid little heed to the obstacles in his path, regardless of what they might be. While with the Pistons he once knocked a sportswriter unconscious while chasing a ball. On another occasion Rodman was sued by a Detroit spectator after he flattened her in an attempt to keep a loose ball from going out-of-bounds. (The Pistons settled out-of-court.) Such was his single-mindedness that when Rodman was with the Detroit Pistons, the Bulls' Phil Jackson would tell the man guarding Rodman to shadow him, instructing his player that his job was not to rebound but rather solely to prevent rebounds by Rodman.

What people tend to forget about Rodman, amid all the cross-dressing and self-destructive behavior, was that he was a remarkable athlete. When recently asked the greatest athlete he'd ever coached, Jackson didn't answer Michael Jordan or Kobe Bryant but went with Rodman. (Bryant, responding to the *Orange County Register,* didn't put up a fight: "I do not disagree with that at all," he said. "You first think of Jordan, obviously, but Dennis as an athlete, he was a freak of nature in terms of his size.") During the off-season Rodman ran stadium steps, and during the season he lifted fanatically. "People think I just go get the damn ball because they don't take the time to really look at what I do," he once told *SI.* "Rebounding isn't brain surgery, but there's more to it than being able to jump higher than the next guy. A lot of the work is done before you ever even jump." He never did reach his goal of 50 rebounds in a game—his high was 34—but perhaps we're all better off for it; he claimed that if he got his 50, he'd tear off his uniform and run off the floor naked.

Rodman had an advantage many of his peers lack, though. Especially later in his career, he was allowed to roam free, at times leaving his man and running to the other side of the court because he "felt" a rebound was headed in that direction. By contrast, most players are tethered to the man they're guarding, meaning their rebounding opportunities are often controlled by factors out of their control, such as defensive matchups. Guard a post player, and you'll likely stay near the basket, where it's obviously easier to grab boards. But chase a shooter around the floor, or show on the pick-and-roll, and you're stranded far from the basket.

Team strategy also plays a role. It's hard to grab offensive rebounds when your coach insists that you sprint back on defense whenever a shot goes up (as Jeff Van Gundy used to dictate to all three of his "smalls"). On the other hand, playing for a Mike D'Antoni team means significantly more rebound opportunities, thanks to the sheer volume of shots produced by his Seven-Seconds-Or-Less offensive strategy. And playing for a Paul Westhead team was boarders' nirvana. Under Westhead during the 1990–91 season, the Denver Nuggets averaged 119.9 points a game and, for the season, attempted almost 2,400 more shots than the team with the fewest attempts, the Utah Jazz. That's a lot of potential easy rebounds.

When you consider all these factors together with the vagaries of shot caroms and the variable flow of the game, predicting rebounding success can be difficult. Not that it stops players from doing it. A few years ago I was talking to Chandler before a Bulls game, and during our conversation I asked whether he'd ever pulled down 20 rebounds in a game. He assured me he had and then made a promise. "You watch tonight," Chandler said. "I'm going to go get you 20."

"Just like that, you can decide?"

"Yup. Here comes 20," Chandler said with a grin.

I waited, curious. Chandler came out in the first quarter energized, flying around the court, but to no avail. By the second quarter, he had as many fouls (three) as rebounds. He finished the game with seven.

"O.K.," he said after the game, "so this wasn't the best night to get 20."

As naturally as rebounding comes for players like Howard (and, usually, Chandler), there are men out there—large, strong, athletic men—for whom the art of the rebound is elusive. The most notorious may be Eddy Curry, who is 6' 11" and 285 pounds but has never averaged more than 6.7 boards during his career. Even more enigmatic is Mark Blount, who has played with four teams during his nine-year career. To look at Blount, 7 feet tall, 250 pounds and blessed with imposing shoulders, one would expect him to swallow up errant shots. Instead, he often seems to jump in slightly the wrong direction, like a kid playing Marco Polo and grasping for unseen prey. During his nine-year career he's averaged 4.6 rebounds in 23.1 minutes per game (which translates to only 7.2 boards if he were to play starter's minutes—36). To understand how remarkably unremarkable this number is, consider that there were 115 NBA players in 2008–09 who played more than 500 minutes and had a better career rebounding rate per 36 minutes than Blount, including perimeter players Matt Bonner and Mike Miller. This, as one can imagine, is a bit frustrating for a coach. In 2005, when Blount was with the Celtics, he made a public plea for more shot attempts. Boston coach Doc Rivers responded by saying, "The next time someone asks for touches, tell him to go get the freaking rebound."

Maybe, however, it wasn't Blount's fault. Jim O'Brien said in an online Q&A with ESPN.com that when he was the Celtics coach, the team went so far as to make a study of Blount, bringing in former Kentucky athletic director C.M. Newton. Newton's conclusion, according to O'Brien: Blount doesn't have "the instinct" to rebound.

That analysis underscores what many believe to be true: Because timing, quick jumping and a space-consuming rump are difficult assets to acquire, you're either a rebounder or you're not, no matter how many tricks of the trade you learn. "What we found in looking over stats of players who played college ball and came into the league was that rebounders were pretty consistent: They were rebounders," says Del Harris, who has coached in the NBA for 35 years, most recently as an assistant with Chicago. "They didn't come into the league as shooters and then all of a sudden become rebounders. If you wanted better rebounders, you drafted rebounders."

Wallace concurs, arguing that the skill can't be taught because, as he posits, "it's a reaction. You can work with people on their form, shooting the ball, ball handling, all that," he says, "but for rebounding, you have to want to do it. If you don't want to do it, it's not going to happen for you."

Perhaps the desire is instilled early. Wallace had those seven brothers to fight off. Tyrone Hill, who averaged almost as many rebounds (8.6) as points (9.4) during his 14-year career, thinks of rebounding as a work ethic and traces his to his father, Eddie, who would rise at five every morning for his job cleaning oil drums. Jeff Foster, the Pacers' relentless (and offensively challenged) center, had an unusual incentive. As a teenager at Madison High in San Antonio, his coach told the then thin and tall Foster that he wasn't getting enough rebounds. So Jeff's father, Stephen, made a deal with him. Instead of an allowance, he'd be paid for his board work: $1 for every rebound he got in a game, $2 for each one above 10 and $3 after 15. Soon enough, he was cleaning his dad out. Though, considering Jeff's future, it was a bargain: In 2008–09, Foster made $6.175 million playing for the Pacers, or $12,156 for each of his 508 boards. (Jack Ramsey, when he was coach of the 76ers, also used an economic incentive, only it worked the other way: A player was fined $15 if his man grabbed an offensive rebound and $25 if his man was also the shooter.)

On the stat sheet a rebound is a rebound, but the true value of any given board can vary wildly. For an example, let's rewind to a midseason Lakers-Cavaliers game from 2006. As time expired, LeBron James missed a tough fadeaway jumper from the left wing that would have tied the game. Afterward, the broadcast discussion centered on whether James should have instead driven to the basket (Magic Johnson's analysis on *Inside the NBA*), whether he waited too long to start his move, or whether this was just a matter, as Steve Kerr, then with TNT, suggested, of James's not yet having the killer instinct of Kobe Bryant. (Though, to be fair, who does?)

What was lost was what happened immediately before James's missed shot, a play more impressive—and statistically improbable—than any Bryant or James made the entire evening, a play without which LeBron would not even have had a chance to shoot for the tie. With five seconds left James had missed a free throw, which caromed off to the left side. Charging from the right side of the lane, the Cavs'

Drew Gooden somehow got to the ball and called timeout, setting up the final shot. At the time Gooden's effort was briefly noted on-air by Kerr, after which the focus quickly shifted to what the Cavs would do with their final possession.

At a remove, however, let's stop and evaluate the magnitude of Gooden's board. Consider: At the time, the league leader in offensive rebounds after missed free throws was Mehmet Okur of Utah, who had 10 *the entire season*. Gooden was second in that category with seven. The chances that Gooden would pull down a board at the most crucial point in the game were minuscule (and coming from the other side of the lane, no less, with two players, Kwame Brown and Lamar Odom, assigned to box out and pinch down on him, respectively).

How does one quantify this type of play? Well, certainly, traditional stats can be misleading. "There are certain kinds of rebounds that are undervalued," says Daryl Morey, G.M. of the Rockets and one of the foremost practitioners of quantitative analysis in the NBA. "What you're looking for is a rebounder who increases the percentage of rebounds that his team is getting rather than the raw number." Antoine Walker, for example, put up some gaudy rebound stats during his career, but during the '05–06 season, for example, the Miami Heat actually garnered more boards when he wasn't playing than when he was (51.3% of those available to 50.7%). This suggests, as Morey put it, "that when he's on the floor, he's just grabbing rebounds that his team would have gotten anyway."

The most notorious stat-padding play is the opposite of Gooden's feat: the *defensive* rebound off a missed free throw. In most cases the defender doesn't have to fight for position, as he's already been awarded a prime space of real estate on the block, and often doesn't even have to fight off any opponents, as they run back on defense. Teammates, however, are sometimes another matter, and it can be a scramble to see who will snag the cheap board. (How often have you seen two teammates briefly wrestling over such a rebound, both loathe to cede the stat?) What's more, often two big men will box out their men only to watch a guard fly in for what Elton Brand calls the "pretty rebound." Says Brand, "Once in a while the big guys will yell at him, like, 'Hey, that's our stuff. We worked for that.'" (Is there actually a pecking order for such rebounds? When I asked Randy Ayers, who has served as head coach of the 76ers, he laughed. "You're the first person who's ever brought that up to me," he said. Then, after thinking about it, he asked me, "Does that count as a team rebound or an individual rebound?" The answer, as players like Brand know well, is the latter.)

So, clearly, Gooden's rebound was, potentially at least, far more valuable than a run-of-the-mill defensive board. But can we assign a number to it, or to any rebound? Flip Saunders, the Wizards coach, told me he'd researched the subject during his college days and determined that every offensive rebound is worth 1.5 points. At first, this sounds high, but I suppose it is possible, considering that a) most offensive rebounds are collected near the rim, where they can often be taken right back up for either two points or a free throw attempt; and b) since defenses by nature break down on a missed shot, the rebounder's teammates are usually open if he kicks it out.

Of course, the value of a board also depends on who is grabbing it; especially with offensive rebounds, a player's ability to go back up to the basket and score has to be considered. Or his inability: There is what I call the Nine-Year-Old Factor; that is, if you're in the NBA and a nine-year-old can shoot free throws better than you, then you really *shouldn't* be going right back up with the ball, inviting a foul. Even so, Brand doesn't think such rebounding specialists are necessarily undervalued. "Certain guys make a living doing just rebounding," he says. "Your free throws are terrible, you can't shoot a jumper, you can't shoot a jump hook. But if you can play D and get boards, you can make a lot of money. If you're shooting 50% from the free throw line and you can't hit a six-foot jumper but you're in the NBA getting paid millions, I don't think it's underrated. I think [G.M.'s and coaches] know that this guy gets boards, gets extra possessions, and that's why he's out there."

What Brand doesn't mention, of course, is that if you can do both—rebound *and* shoot, like, say, maybe Elton Brand—it makes you invaluable. For the specialists, however, those men who act as ball valets, tracking down the leather then cordially returning it to the hands of a shooter, there is an interesting conundrum. Sam Hinkie, an assistant to Morey with the Rockets, describes it as a showdown of sorts: When a team rotates away from a nonshooter like Reggie Evans (and they do), forcing him to take a jump shot at the end of the clock, the offensive coach has, in effect, lost the strategy game to the defensive coach, who can claim, "I found your nonshooter and made him shoot." But take Evans out of the game and replace him with a poor-rebounding big man such as Eddy Curry, and though Curry probably makes that shot, the team may get beat on the boards and lose that way. So who do you play?

Coaches tend to answer that question by essentially hedging their bets, strategically deploying the specialists, limiting their offensive exposure. Kendrick Perkins of Boston is a tremendous rebounder (who in the past has led the league in defensive rebounding differential, which is the percentage of available rebounds a team gets when a player is on the floor versus when he's not), but he's no more than a serviceable offensive player; he has averaged just 20.6 minutes a game for his career. Evans averages 19.6. Michael Ruffin of Washington treats offensive rebounding like a science; he has racked up some freakish numbers crashing the offensive glass, twice in his career averaging as many offensive rebounds as defensive rebounds. But he is flummoxed when it comes to putting the ball in the basket and averages just 14.6 minutes a game.

It's no surprise, then, that certain players don't want to be known as "just" rebounders. Wallace is the patron saint of the craft since the retirement of Rodman, the only other player of this era to become a celebrity based on defense and rebounding. But what Wallace really *wants* to do is score, as evidenced by those three-pointers he jacks up during practice. This may also explain why Gooden, despite his rebounding skills, can be frustrating to coaches. When I asked Silas about players who might be able to average 15 or 16 rebounds a game—a rarity in the last three decades—he mentioned Dwight Howard, Shaq ("if that was his focus") and then his former charge, Gooden. "He has the jumping ability, the timing, and he's strong," said Silas, "but Drew wants to score more than rebound."

Can you blame him? There is little glory, or thanks, in pulling down a board so that someone else can take the final shot. Consider: had James hit that final shot in the Cavs-Lakers game, no doubt the focus would have been on how he had "come up big in the clutch" and "willed" the Cavs to victory. Gooden, on the other hand, was just "doing his job," even if he was the reason the Cavs had a chance to win at all. It's something Fortson thinks should be rectified. "A lot of times you see a quarterback take his offensive line out to dinner," said Fortson, who retired after the 2007 season. "I think the NBA needs to have more of that—taking out their bigs. Because at the end of the day, we're guarding the star's back." Fortson paused, then made a harrumphing sound. "All I'm saying is, Take us out to a steak dinner, man."

Which, in a roundabout way, brings us back to Howard, for he is essentially both the lineman and the QB, pulling down boards but also scoring more than 20 points a game. What's more, Howard is grabbing *meaningful* rebounds. In 2008–09 Howard averaged 21.1 rebounds per 48 clutch minutes, with clutch time defined as play in overtime or in the last five minutes of the fourth quarter with neither team ahead by more than five points; Marcus Camby was a distant second with 18.8. Howard's raw rebounding numbers—12.5 per game for his career— are even more impressive when one considers that in recent years the Magic has often been near the bottom of the league in attempted field goals, and the shots the team does take are often three-pointers (leading to long rebounds).

Even so, Howard has the best chance of any current player to average 15 boards a season, something only three men have done since 1983: Rodman (who did it five times), Kevin Willis (in 1992) and Wallace (2003). Howard has the requisite athleticism and instincts, doesn't foul out often, isn't an offensive liability and is well-conditioned. Mark Bryant, who was an assistant coach with Orlando during Howard's first few years in the league, sees extraordinary potential. "Once he learns to sit down on people"—that is, box out on an opponent's knees— "I don't think there's going to be anybody. . . ." Bryant pauses and frowns emphatically. "I *know* there won't be anybody in the league who can stop him."

That may be true, but only if grabbing more boards remains his goal. When I first spoke to him about rebounding, in 2006, he was excited by the subject. He spoke enthusiastically about getting better, about raising his rebound average every year, about learning the tricks of the trade.

Three years later, when we spoke about rebounding again, in March of 2009, Howard admitted he no longer focused on the craft the way he used to. In the interim he had become Orlando's offensive and defensive anchor and an MVP candidate. Practice hours were now better spent developing his post moves—including an increasingly graceful running hook. And then, of course, came all those dunk contests and endorsements to attend to (none of which, it should be noted, were spawned by his rebounding numbers). As a result, there wasn't much time left over to work on the humble act of grabbing boards.

"Tapping someone on the hip, that kind of stuff, I forget to do that sometimes," he said.

Then there was the more elemental question of effort. If Moses Malone went after 100 out of 100 balls on any given night, Howard still only pursued 80 or 90 of them, something Orlando assistant coach Patrick Ewing harped on often. As Howard admitted, "That's the biggest thing for me. I have to learn how to play hard on a consistent basis. I do it for five or six games and then I might take one game off. Not that I take a game off, but I might take some possessions off, and I'm not as aggressive as I can be." Asked why, he frowned. "I don't really know. We had a game the other night in Philly, and I was so excited to play, I was amped up. But as soon as the game started, for some reason, my energy was gone. The whole game I was frustrated. I had a couple of fouls, I wanted to get myself going, but I couldn't ever do it."

It should be remembered that at the time Howard had just turned 23 years old, and already he'd pulled down 5,000 rebounds in his career. Know what Wilt Chamberlain was doing when he was 23? Playing in his rookie season.

In other words, there's plenty of time for Howard to become more serious, if not about life—and to be honest, I'm hoping that doesn't happen; his joy is refreshing for a pro athlete—then about chasing down missed shots. And even if he doesn't, he'll be the premier rebounder of his generation, a player who rings up double doubles nightly. But if he should start to really bear down and combine his physical prowess with the cunning and desire of a Wallace or a Rodman, then—well, then he could realize the dream of boardmen everywhere, as put best by Wallace: "to make rebounding cool."

The Dunk: Why We All Wish We Could Fly

It's the summer of 1989 and Chris Webber is about to dunk on my head. We're in Palo Alto, Calif., at something called the Stanford High Potential Basketball Camp, but it's fair to say the high potential designation applies to only one of us. Webber, a broad-shouldered, 6' 8" high school sophomore, is already one of the top prospects in the country; later in the week he will win the camp dunk contest by throwing down a leaning 360 that causes Stanford men's hoops coach Mike Montgomery to look as if he's just found religion. I, on the other hand, am a skinny, 5' 10" sophomore with a questionable left hand.

Webber catches the ball at the foul line and, using a screen, makes a power move to his right. I hear my teammate, the one who's supposed to be guarding Mr. Blue Chip Prospect, yell something that sounds a lot like "Switch!" So I do, stepping into the path of the oncoming Webber and preparing to . . . well, I'm not sure what I intend to do. I settle on a sort of half jump, half duck, as if bracing myself for a Gatorade shower.

Moments later I'm drenched, metaphorically speaking. And as I lie under the basket looking up at Webber, who is hanging from the rim, I realize something: In the instant before he leaped, Webber smiled. It was a gentle smile, one that seemed to say, *Relax, this won't hurt a bit*. I remember wondering, as I looked up, what it felt like to be him. Pretty damn good, I imagined.

Twenty years later I'm still wondering. Like a sizable chunk of sporting America, I remain captivated by the dunk, even if I'm not always sure why. After all, I've seen a million of them, replayed end-lessly on the highlight shows and dropped effortlessly through the net in NBA layup lines and shoved relentlessly down my throat by anthro-pomorphic mascots hurtling off trampolines. Yet I can't look away. A novelty in the 1960s and '70s, the dunk enjoyed a heyday during the Air-inflated '80s and, inevitably, became overhyped and overexposed. Still, there's something hypnotic about it. For men, it's like cleavage; we've seen acres of it, but that doesn't stop us from looking again. It's part instinct, part the lure of the unattainable and part the hope that we're about to see something *spectacular.*

This, it's fair to say, does not happen with an 18-foot jumper. There are no posters of scoop layups, no T-shirts of outlet passes. Mascots do not box each other out to delight fans. And teenagers do not spend countless hours jamming on Nerf hoops, then countless more trying to slap the backboard, then touch the rim and then, maybe, on just the right day, awkwardly squeeze one down all because they believe it improves their game. After all, what other shot boasts an entire lexi-con? Jam, slam, flush, throw down, cram, bang, windmill, stuff, rock the rim, 360, sky, posterize, facial, hammer, skywalk, boomshakalaka, talk to God and on and on.

The dunk is the easiest shot in basketball, really, but also one that relatively few can make, requiring a combination of height, youth, leaping ability and coordination. A 60-year-old can run a marathon, and almost anyone can get lucky and hit a hole in one or sink a half-court heave, but no one lucks into a dunk. Either you can do it or you can't. And considering that only about 4% of American males are taller than 6'2", there are an awful lot of can'ts out there. Even for those who can pull it off, dunking is a fleeting skill, generally possible only between the ages of about 17 and 34. Even making the NBA does not guarantee entry to the dunk club. Steve Kerr, the 6'3" former Chicago Bulls guard we met in Chapter 2, never dunked in a game. "When I would speak at camps," he says, "the first three ques-tions I always got were, 'What was it like to play with Michael Jordan?' 'What's your shoe size?' and 'Can you dunk?' It was always difficult to explain to kids that, yes, I do play in the NBA, and, no, I can't dunk." (Even worse is the plight of Jason Kapono, the Raptors sharpshooter who, through the 2008–09 season, had yet to dunk during his six-year NBA career—and he's 6'8". As Kapono explained when I asked him about it, "I choose the layup because there's a chance I could miss the dunk and get hung. So I'd rather go for the for-sure guaranteed two points.")

This is not to imply that Kerr or Kapono is among those who denigrate the dunk as "just two points." Jams are "incredibly fun to watch," Kerr says, adding that he and his high school buddies used to put up a nine-foot rim so they could throw down, which is sort of like PGA pros playing miniature golf to finally get that ace. But, hey, a cheap thrill is better than no thrill at all, right?

Some in the hoops community don't share Kerr's admiration for the slam. "It's very bad for the game," famed UCLA coach John Wooden once said. "If I want to see fancy play, I'll go see the Globetrotters." Such is the fate of the dunk: alternately celebrated and derided and, at one time, banned (from 1967 to '76, by the NCAA). Perhaps we're now entering the jam's postmodern period, when the shot itself no longer evolves but our feelings about it do.

Sometimes a dunk is more than a dunk. Think of Darryl Dawkins laying waste to a backboard, Julius Erving performing a flyby on Michael Cooper, Vince Carter leapfrogging Frenchman Frederic Weis on a jam so humiliating that his country's media dubbed it *le dunk de la mort* ("the dunk of death").

More recently it was the Golden State Warriors' Baron Davis climbing the ladder in Game 3 of the Warriors-Jazz second-round playoff series in 2007. Late in the fourth quarter the 6'3" Davis drove the left baseline as Utah forward Andrei Kirilenko, who is 6'9" and has arms like goalposts, soared in from the weak side. Davis launched off both feet, leaned into Kirilenko and threw down a righthanded hook dunk so nasty, so goddam-he-didn't-just-do-that electrifying that Kirilenko might as well have been bronzed in mid-slam with Davis's left elbow jammed into his nose and the statue shipped to the Museum of Historic Dunks, there to be enshrined in the Hall of Little Men Disgracing Big.

You'd have thought Davis's teammates had just witnessed a horrible car accident. Forward Matt Barnes turned away, hands to his head. Center Adonal Foyle scrunched up his face as if smelling rancid meat. The Bay Area was delirious. The next morning the *San Francisco Chronicle*'s headline read, ABOUT FACE! The story carried not one but three photos of the slam.

The half-life of a generic NBA fast-break jam might be one replay, but a transcendent dunk like Davis's lives forever. The NBA featured it in a commercial at the start of the '07–08 season, the Warriors reproduced it on a poster handed out at their home opener, and clips of it have been viewed millions of times on YouTube. Even a year later, wherever the Warriors went, people asked Davis about the dunk. "Kids, adults, everyone," he said. "They say, 'That's the guy who dunked on the big guy.'"

Here's the thing, though: Davis's slam was only one basket, and not even an important one. At the time the Warriors were up by 20 points with less than three minutes left. And the dunk had no lasting impact; Golden State lost the next two games and the playoff series. It was a beautiful moment, and even more impressive once you learn it was premeditated. (Davis says that after the previous play, when the Jazz had given him space on a layup, "I thought, I'm going to come back and do the same thing, only I'm going to dunk it this time.") But did it matter? Just as Darryl Dawkins's first backboard-shattering jam came during a loss, Davis's feat merely punctuated a blowout.

But then dunks have been eclipsing the rest of the game for years. That's why Vince (What Defensive Stance?) Carter was the leading All-Star vote-getter for four seasons, why Mars Blackmon sold all those shoes. Blame ESPN or Nike or whichever corporate entity you choose, but it doesn't change the fact that the slam is embedded in U.S. culture. So embedded, in fact, that some people want to dig it out.

Tom Newell has a revolutionary idea, insofar as any idea one's own father had 45 years ago can be revolutionary: Raise the rim to 11 feet. Newell has been an assistant with a number of NBA teams, as well as the head coach of the Japanese national team, and is the son of the late Pete Newell, the renowned former coach of San Francisco, Michigan State and Cal.

Tom's argument, and that of his father before him—as espoused in a 1967 *Sports Illustrated* cover story "The Case for the 12-foot Basket"—is that the dominance of the brute athlete is killing the game. Jack up the rim, whether to 11 feet or 12, and you spread the floor, empower smaller players and take away the ability of towering big men to score merely by dropping or tapping the ball in the basket, thus (theoretically) returning centers to their original role as distributors. In the summer of 2007 Newell the younger staged an exhibition at the University of Washington called For the Love of the Game in which two teams of collegians and low-level pros from the CBA and overseas teams played with 11-foot baskets, which made dunks prohibitive. Newell deemed the game a great success, but when you view the video, it's hard to get too excited. It's like watching an eighth-grade team: lots of standing around as clusters of players reach for rebounds like tossed bridal bouquets, then try to hoist the ball back up.

Still, Newell raises some interesting questions. Do we crave the dunk at the expense of more dynamic plays? (As Newell told me, "There's no skill in the dunk, yet we want to see it at every game in the NBA or college if possible.") And if the jam were rarer, would we appreciate it more?

On this last count, Newell has a wonderful suggestion: outlaw mascot trampoline dunking. Every time we see a stubby mascot perform a somersault jam, it cheapens the actual game dunks. (Similarly, an advantage to 11-foot rims would be that only certain NBAers could throw down, which would mean no more Rasho Nesterovic "dunks.")

Not surprisingly, NBA players scoff at the idea of raising the rims. "Ridiculous," LeBron James said when I proposed it. "That's like taking the deep pass out of football." Baron Davis concurred, saying, "The basket's already high enough, man." Even players who might be expected to welcome the idea—which is to say the nondunkers, which is to further say the short white guys—don't necessarily buy in. Kerr echoes James, calling the idea "unimaginable." And Steve Nash, when asked about the purists' perception that the league needs more play-the-right-way guys, doesn't entirely agree. "I think the truth is we need more of those, but we still want the spectacular finisher, the athlete," he said. "People say they want the league to have more [fundamental play], but if they're going to choose one, they're going to go with the badass dunks."

Ironically, it is sometimes the badass dunkers who downplay the slam, for fear the shot unfairly defines them, a concern that never troubled, say, Julius Erving. Ten years from now Davis may end up being best remembered for his jam over Kirilenko, just as fans remember John Starks (lefty slam on Jordan), Tom Chambers (surreal head-at-the-rim dunk) and Dominique Wilkins (who wasn't defined by one dunk so much as by all of them). "Once you get labeled a dunker, it's hard to get rid of the stigma," says Wilkins, who at 48 years old claimed he could still dunk when I asked him. "They start thinking that's all you can do." In 1996, when Wilkins was left off the list of the 50 greatest players in NBA history, it may have been partly because of his reputation as a jammer. "For me it's a travesty," he says. "You don't get 26,000 points on dunks alone." (Though for a while it seemed that Dwight Howard was trying.)

In today's NBA, being a dunker is not synonymous with being a star. Witness the 2008 Rising Stars Dunk Contest, won by Howard, a true star, but otherwise featuring a bunch of guys—Gerald Green, Jamario Moon, Tyrus Thomas—who won't be appearing in Hanes underwear commercials anytime soon. The following year Howard was joined by Nate Robinson, J.R. Smith and Rudy Fernandez, an equally undistinguished group. Jordan made his career on the jam; now James tries to make his career in spite of it. Shortly after entering the league, James was lobbied hard by one of his sponsors, Sprite, to enter the dunk contest, but he declined. "I just felt like I was in the NBA to showcase my talent and all phases of my game," he told me. (Nevertheless, LeBron did make an impromptu claim following the '09 dunk contest that he would compete in 2010.)

So we've come to this strange intersection: great leapers preaching *Dunk as I say, not as I do.* "I try to encourage [the complete] game," says Wilkins, now the Atlanta Hawks' vice president of basketball. "Dunking is secondary. That's just a tool I used for intimidation." Wilkins says he won't let his sons, Isiah, age 13, and Jacob, 2, dunk on lowered rims. Says the Human Highlight Film, sounding more like the Human Rec League Coach, "I tell my kids, 'You aren't able to dunk now, so you better work on other parts of your game.'"

Of course, there are plenty of men for whom dunking holds no stigma but rather represents an art unto itself. Once upon a time these jammers were playground legends, cats like Herman (Helicopter) Knowings and Earl (the Goat) Manigault and Demetrius (Hook) Mitchell, who at 5' 11" would do 360s over cars to win dunk contests. (The lore of such dunkers only grew with time. As Alexander Wolff wrote in *100 Years of Hoops* about the most famous schoolyard dunk ever, when the Goat threw down over two college stars, 6' 5" Vaughn Harper and 6' 9" Val Reed, at a Harlem gym, "Oral historians differ, but the shot is said to have begun at the foul line and included two full corkscrew revolutions in flight. 'I have personally never seen its equal,' Harlemite Bobby Hunter said. 'And I was in Detroit at the time.'") They were never more than legends, though, celebrated only by word of mouth. Men like the Goat had a rep; today playground stars have reps. Opportunity awaits them above the rim: join a street-ball tour, film DVDs, perform at halftimes and, of course, gain instant international fame on the Web. A nickname is still essential, so we have High Rizer and Elevator, and we've got Taurian (the Air Up There) Fontenette, whose surreal 720 jam has been viewed more than four million times on the Internet.

You don't even need to play street ball, or live near anything resembling "the streets," to join this act. In 2003, a 6' 6" high school player named Henry Bekkering from the woodsy town of Taber, Alberta (pop. 7,671), entered a dunk contest at a Canadian high school all-star game. Of course, someone had a camera and uploaded clips to the Web. They're amazing to watch: First Bekkering does a two-handed dip-it-between-the-legs reverse; on the next jam he sticks his arm elbow-deep into the basket à la Vince Carter; and on the next he leaps over another player standing a few feet in front of the basket. But the real holy-shit moment is Bekkering's final dunk, one never seen in an NBA contest: He takes to the air off two feet from just inside the free throw line, leans at a 45-degree angle and jams lefthanded. Adding to the unlikely nature of the spectacle, Bekkering is as white as Mitt Romney.

Soon enough, Bekkering was semi-famous. *The Best Damn Sports Show Period* bestowed upon him the 39th best dunk of all time, ahead of pros like Scottie Pippen, and invited Bekkering on the show. (The producers had him dunk over a seated Brian Bosworth and, to Bekkering's everlasting credit, he popped Boz in the side of the head with his knee.)

The dunk is not always a faithful mistress, though. Bekkering received a scholarship at Eastern Washington, but the coach didn't play him much. (He was also on the football team, assigned to the kick-blocking unit—"like a little circus animal, sent in to jump high," he says with a laugh.) Maybe the expectations raised by his dunking were too high. In 2006 he transferred to the University of Calgary, where in 2009 he averaged 20.2 points and two to three dunks a game as a fourth-year junior small forward. "I wanted to establish myself as a basketball player," Bekkering says of his decision to return to Canada.

"In dunking circles they were always saying, 'There's that white kid who can jump.' That's not everything about basketball."

Bekkering may not have NBA talent, but Ronnie Fields sure did. Fields was a star at Chicago's Farragut Academy in the 1990s, playing alongside Kevin Garnett on the '94–95 city championship team. As early as in the eighth grade he was competing in adult leagues and, in the words of his high school coach, William Nelson, the kid was "dunking on grown-ass men." His first two points as a freshman were on a 180 double-pump jam. Blessed with a 40-inch vertical leap, the 6'3" shooting guard scored 2,619 points in his high school career and tallied 372 dunks, numbers you can find alongside the giant mural of Fields on a wall in Farragut's gym, across from a mural of Garnett. The key difference in the two paintings is that Garnett is in a Minnesota Timberwolves jersey, while Fields wears his Farragut uni. You see, despite all his talent, Fields never developed a perimeter game. He didn't need one in high school, and he passed on college, where he might have broadened his skills. Lacking three-point range and playing tentatively for fear of aggravating a neck injury he suffered in a car accident in 1996, he never made the NBA, instead toiling for teams like the Pennsylvania Valleydawgs of the USBL. For what it's worth, though, Fields remains a legend in Chicago. Says Nelson, "All the shorties want to dunk like Ronnie."

––––––––––––––

Ah, the shorties—no one is more fascinated by the dunk. At the Basketball Hall of Fame in Springfield, Mass., there are rims set at six, seven, eight and nine feet. According to Matt Zeysing, the Hall historian, they are "probably our most popular element." There's a simple reason for this: Dunking is really, really fun. It's also very hard not to look cool when you do it.

Nowhere is this more evident than at Farragut. On a January night in 2008, the Admirals played Clark High, a magnet school they outclassed in size and talent, and a jam contest quickly broke out among Farragut players. The first play of the game was a backdoor alley-oop lob and jam. By halftime the Admirals had six dunks, three of them by 6'10" senior Michael Dunigan, who went on to play for the University of Oregon. By the end of the third quarter Farragut had a 30-point lead and 11 dunks. After one thunderous Dunigan follow jam, three boys ran screaming from the gym, as if they'd just seen a zombie, while women shrieked and danced, and the man on the P.A. roared, "Wow! Did you see that dunk?"

Feeling the revivalist fever in this gym, I could see how Fields got sidetracked. In neighborhoods such as the South Side of Chicago, the dunk is a kingmaker. "Everybody knows the kid who can throw down," says Nelson. "You forget who's the great passer, the shooter. Look at my boys—probably seven of the 11 dunk, but three of them can really dunk. Those are the three that people come to see."

One of the nondunkers is Isaiah Williams, a 6' 1" senior guard. In four years he's thrown down only once in a game. "People always tell me if I dunked more often, it would separate me from other players," he tells me, "but it's just not part of my game."

Part of his game? Go further down the hoops ladder, to boys in the seventh and eighth grades, and everyone expects dunking will be a part of his game. At Martin Luther King Middle School in Berkeley, Calif., all 14 members of the seventh-grade boys' basketball team raise their hands when I ask how many of them believe they will one day throw it down. This includes 4' 8" Mohammed Aledlah, a cheery 12-year-old with sheepdog bangs who is wearing a girls' uniform because the boys' are all too big (and his shorts still hang down well below his knees).

Like all seventh-graders, these boys have strong opinions. On dunking, this is what they believe: That it's the easiest way to score, because you can miss a layup but "you never miss a dunk." That they'd rather be able to slam in traffic than drain three-pointers, because throwing down "makes you more popular" and, well, it would be really fun (and here there is much acting out of tremendous jams). That Kobe no longer enters the dunk contest because it's called the *Rising* Stars Dunk Contest, and he's already a real star (duh!). That Jordan is the greatest dunker ever, and "didn't he once do it from half-court?" That Nash would be way, way more popular if he could jam. And that the idea of an 11-foot rim is really stupid—so stupid that "someone should get in trouble" just for proposing it.

When I ask them how one dunks, the boys all raise their hands, some jumping up and down. They expound strategies, from holding the ball with two hands to achieving the right balance to "getting lots taller." Finally, Mohammed asks his own question. "So," he says, earnestly, "are you going to tell us how to do it now?"

Shawn Kemp once described dunking as "better than sex." Julius Erving said, "When you feel yourself go up above the rim for the first time and put the ball through, there's nothing like it. You want to do it again and again and again." Wilkins says throwing down made him feel like a king. Dwight Howard so yearned to dunk as a youngster that he used to pull out a trampoline so he could work on his dunks. (He didn't have to wait long; he says he first dunked as a 5'8" eighth-grader.)

The year after that Stanford camp where I was posterized by Webber, I dunked for the first time. I didn't feel especially regal, but then again I relied on a slightly deflated ball and a half-court run-up. Soon enough, though, I had a repertoire of five or six dunks, and in the following years it's fair to say I practiced dunking often and implemented it rarely. At Division III Pomona College, I had a total of one dunk, and it was in a jayvee game. Against Cal Tech. And I traveled on the play.

Still, it was always something I took pride in. So in 2009, when, at 35 years old, it took me four attempts to weakly wedge one home, I found the feeling unsettling, a reminder of my athletic mortality. And I wondered, if a weekend warrior like me takes it this hard, how does a man for whom jumping is his livelihood, his identity, take it?

It is sad to behold the aging of an athlete, and no athlete declines faster than a leaper. Remember Erving, at age 42, in that shameless 1992 pay-per-view one-on-one game against 45-year-old Kareem Abdul-Jabbar, missing a one-handed slam? (If your answer is no, you're lucky.) Or how about the 38-year-old Michael Jordan—Michael Frickin' Jordan—clanging a wide-open breakaway jam in the 2002 All-Star Game? As Baron Davis puts it, "Your hops are the first thing to retire," and it happens before our eyes. Consider: In 2008–09 Nuggets reserve forward Linas Kleiza had only one dunk fewer (45) than Vince Carter. Is it any surprise that Carter wasn't voted on to the '09 East All-Star team? "When that jumping ability dissipates," says Wilkins, "you're just an ordinary guy."

So how do NBA players deal with it? Warriors assistant coach and former Indiana star Keith Smart—you remember him from his role in that hit movie *Baseline Jumper for the NCAA Title*—is now in his mid-40s, and he describes his last dunk with the mixed emotions most people feel watching a child graduate from college. "I was 37 years old, and it was a one-hand squeaker," says Smart. Once a high flier who threw down 360s, he felt his legs start to go after his playing career ended.

"When I became a coach, my goal was always to dunk by the first day of training camp," Smart says. "Then it was by the first game, then by the New Year. Finally, we played down in Florida [not long after New Year's], and I got warmed up and did it. That was the last one." The psychic toll was steep. Smart stopped playing even in pickup games. "I got frustrated not being able to do what I used to do."

In early 2008 the Cavs' Eric Snow wasn't there yet, but he knew the day was coming. The 6' 3" guard used to unwind some nasty dunks—windmills and the like—but at 34 he was on the downside of his career. After a winter practice, with ice on both ankles and one knee, he told me that he had a bet with then-teammate Damon Jones, also 6' 3": The first one to dunk in a game got dinner from the other. Said Snow, "That bet's been going for three years now." (Alas, neither would ever win it.)

It got so that Snow felt as if he were losing his rep. So when younger Cleveland players doubted him, he brought in a DVD of dunking highlights from his Michigan State days and stuck it on repeat on the TV in the locker room. "They thought I could only do those simple dunks," he said, "so I had to show them some proof."

At the time, though, he admitted that "there are only certain days I feel up to doing it [in practice]," but it remained important to him. "It's different if you're 6' 8" and 34 years old. Donyell Marshall is 6' 9". Dunking's not a big deal to him. It's only a big deal to me because I'm smaller." Snow paused, then looked out on the court and pointed. "I never could do that, though." There, at the near basket, James was ripping off a series of astounding dunks. He was shirtless, all corded muscle, the embodiment of youth and athleticism. As a crowd of teammates and reporters gathered, he rose again and again, each time delivering a ferocious finish: a 360, a two-hander off the backboard, a power one-hand extension, each accompanied by a prodigious *thunk!*

Later I asked James what he thought it would feel like when he could no longer jam. He talked about watching his sons grow up, then made a joke and finally said, "Maybe that will happen one day," as if he might ward off aging like it was just another weak double team.

———————

The dunk is important; it is unimportant. In the spring of 2008, after sitting out the first half of the season as a free agent, Webber signed with the Warriors. He was 34, with knees weakened from surgery. Never an outrageous leaper, he had become increasingly grounded.

I went to a Warriors practice a week after he signed. During a scrimmage he caught a ball on the break and headed toward the right side of the rim, uncontested. Up he went, but all he could manage was a finger roll (though, to his credit, it was an emphatic finger roll). Webber didn't look all that different from the way he looked at that camp in 1989: same grin, same cherub's face. But once he started moving on the court, slowly and methodically, it was clear this was not the same player. I was disappointed. Irrationally, I wanted him to remain lithe and springy, for if he did, maybe there was hope for me.

Afterward I caught up with him. He remembered the Stanford camp and the dunk contest. ("I think I tried to jump over some kid in a chair," he said.) He didn't recall dunking on me—why should he?—though he could imagine it. "I'm not surprised I smiled," he said. "I was probably just saying, Good effort, but I got ya."

The more he talked about dunking, the more nostalgic he became. "I remember leading the league in dunks a few years, and it just comes so easy," he said. Never mind that his claim is both hard to verify and unlikely—Shaquille O'Neal, for one, was in his prime back then—because after all, isn't getting older about remembering things the way we want them, not the way they were?

As for now, Webber said he still gets the itch to dunk, though he rarely scratches it. "When I look at a lot of the younger guys and see what they do, I say to myself, 'Man, I know what that feels like.'" He paused. "At the end of the day, your mind tells you you can do it even though your body won't let you."

And maybe that's the ultimate appeal of the dunk. Close our eyes, and all of us can imagine doing it. Most of us never will, though, so we live vicariously through those who can, reveling in their ability to make the impossible look easy. We wish we could become one of them. Inevitably, they will become one of us. Welcome to the club, Chris.

Free Throws: Standing in the Loneliest Place in the World

Maybe you remember the story, the one about the four free throws and how they changed one man's life forever. And if so, maybe you wince when you think about it. The year was 1995, and the Orlando Magic were playing the Houston Rockets in Game 1 of the NBA Finals. With 10.5 seconds left and the Magic holding a three-point lead, Orlando guard Nick Anderson was fouled. He stepped to the line, needing to hit only 1 of 2 to effectively end the game.

Anderson felt confident, and he had every right to. He'd had a great game—22 points on 9-of-17 shooting—and was a career 70% free throw shooter, not exemplary but certainly respectable. He was also, in many ways, the face of the franchise: the Magic's first-ever draft pick, an All-Star-caliber player (though he was never selected) and one third of a triumvirate, alongside Shaquille O'Neal and Penny Hardaway, that had Orlando on the brink of its first-ever Finals victory. If anybody deserved to finish this one off, it was Anderson.

All around him the Orlando fans began to celebrate wildly, whistling while they stood and twirled towels. On TV the camera panned to Houston coach Rudy Tomjanovich, who looked stunned by the turn of events—the Magic had just grabbed successive offensive rebounds leading up to the foul. A moment later, play-by-play man Marv Albert set the scene: "Nick Anderson making his first appearance at the line, usually a dependable free throw shooter."

Only, of course, Anderson was not dependable on this night. His first shot came up short, and then his second did the same. The rebound was tipped by Rockets guard Clyde Drexler and, as luck would have it, went right back toward Anderson. Taking one step, he leaped and grabbed the ball. He then tried to pass the ball off to a teammate before coming down to the floor, but he was fouled before he could do so. Which meant Anderson headed to the line. Again. And, again, he needed to hit but 1 of 2 to seal the win.

What followed was (and is, to this day) painful to watch. Anderson stepped up to the stripe, now with 7.9 seconds left, and followed his time-tested ritual: Three bounces, bend the knees, exhale, then release the ball, arcing it high in the air. Only this time he shot the first one long. Stepping back from the line, he laughed in disbelief. *This can't be happening,* he thought. And yet, remarkably, he could still finish off the game if only he could make this final free throw. *Just one,* he said to himself, as again he bounced three times, bent, exhaled and released. The ball seemed to hang in the air for a moment, then caromed off the back of the rim. The Rockets grabbed the rebound and called timeout, now afforded one last chance, while Anderson stood, frozen, staring up at the ceiling in despair, as alone as a man can ever be on a basketball court.

Now, if the Rockets had missed their next shot, we wouldn't have a story to tell; but, of course, they didn't. Instead, Rockets guard Kenny Smith sank a three-pointer to send the game into overtime, and the Rockets went on to win 120–118. And, naturally, the Magic were then swept by the Rockets and it took them 14 years to return to the NBA Finals. And while none of this is expressly the fault of Nick Anderson, if you talk to certain people, you might think it is.

————————

They were just free throws, right? Anyone can miss them. It is 13 years later, and Anderson is sitting at an empty desk in the Magic practice facility in downtown Orlando in the fall of 2008. He now works for the Magic's community-affairs department, attending events, rallying support. He enjoys being part of the franchise, being out there talking to people. He remains fit and muscular and, at 40 years old, can still dunk. He is, for the most part, happy with his life. If only people would stop talking about that game. Only the night before, he tells me, he was at a TGI Friday's in Orlando, having dinner with a friend. At the end of the meal, the waitress came over.

"Are you Nick Anderson?" she asked.

"Yes, I am," he said, smiling warmly, the way he always does when people ask him this.

"I called my boyfriend and told him you were here," the waitress said, "and he wants me to ask you why you missed those four free throws in that game."

Anderson, retelling the story, cannot believe it. He looks at me, eyes wide, and laughs ruefully. "This was yesterday. *Yesterday!* It's 2008!"

This is not an isolated incident. Anderson says someone mentions those free throws to him every couple of days, maybe even more often. He impersonates a fan: *"Man, I remember, man. I had money on y'all and you missed those four free throws."*

Anderson tries to stay calm when this happens, tries not to get angry the way some of us might. He realizes people don't always understand how sensitive the subject is, or that a lot else happened both in that particular game and in those Finals that could have changed the outcome. Still, he occasionally gets fed up. Once, when a fan brought it up, he snapped back, "Damn, is that all you remember about me?" and then the fan felt bad. "Oh, I didn't mean no harm," the man said. But, of course, the harm was already done.

How could it not be? Imagine if something you did nearly 15 years ago followed you around like a shadow. Not something illegal, not even a regrettable decision, just a momentary physical failure. You might put up some walls. Anderson certainly has.

As we talk about that game, it becomes evident that Anderson has created his own version of history. He blames the enduring public perception of his failure on "the media playing it up, like, Nick missed four free throws and it was a momentum change." He also downplays the significance of the shots by asserting that, "When I was shooting those free throws, there were six or seven minutes still left in the game," which is only off by six or seven minutes and is, when you think about it, a curious act of self-deception. (And even if we give him the benefit of the doubt and include five minutes of overtime in his calculations, there remains the unwieldy fact that there would have been no overtime without the misses.)

When it happened, back in 1995, Anderson claimed that the misses didn't affect him. A year later, though, it was clear they had, and profoundly. After shooting 69.2% from the line during the 1995–96 season, Anderson began the following year in a free throw funk. At 6' 6" and 250 pounds, he'd always relied on his ability to post up smaller defenders and bull to the basket, figuring he'd either score or get fouled, but now he was tentative, terrified of going to the line. Worse, his opponents knew this and were more likely to foul, in turn making Anderson even less aggressive, negating the reason he'd been so effective in the first place. Anderson had allowed his underlying fears to change his game completely.

During the first three months of the 1996–97 season, he shot an abysmal 36.2% from the free throw line. That meant that if you played on an opposing team and fouled Anderson on a shot, he would "punish" you by scoring an average of .72 of a point per possession. Considering that the league average is 1.1 points per possession, this was a pretty sweet deal for the defense.

At the time, shooting coach Buzz Braman, who worked with the Magic, said Anderson was beset with "demons," and it was hard to argue. Eventually, Anderson became such a liability that in January 1997, the Phoenix Suns intentionally fouled him in the second half even though he wasn't near the ball. Not long after, coach Chuck Daly stopped playing Anderson in the fourth quarter, afraid that opposing teams would purposefully foul him. Soon enough, he was removed from the starting lineup altogether. Even with a late surge, he finished the season with a free throw percentage of 40.4%, the lowest of any NBA player that season who attempted more than 70 free throws. (By comparison, Chris Dudley, a notoriously poor free throw shooter, shot 47.4% that season.)

For Anderson it was a daily struggle. He describes the missed free throws as "like a song that got in my head, playing over and over and over." He remembers sitting in an airport in Chicago a month or so after those fateful Finals, waiting to catch a plane back to Orlando. Looking up, he noticed that, right there overhead, the TVs were replaying the first Finals game. *His* Finals game. "And I'm sitting there, right, and people are looking, looking at the game . . . looking at me. And I'm like, 'Oh, God.' One would look, then another, then the whole damn airport, saying, 'That's Nick Anderson, sitting there!'" He remembers wanting to flee and hide, but he didn't know where to go.

Despite playing seven more seasons, Anderson's free throw percentage never again rose above 70% and was usually far short of that—twice below 50% and only 60.5% for the rest of his career. Likewise, he never averaged more than 15.3 points and played only five more years as a starter in the NBA (this from a player who'd averaged 19.9

in consecutive seasons only a few years earlier). Despite retiring as the leading scorer in Magic history, despite memorably locking down Michael Jordan in the 1995 Eastern Conference semifinals (including hounding MJ into an 8-of-22-from-the-field, eight-turnover performance in Game 1), Anderson remained That Guy Who Missed Those Free Throws. "It kind of messed with him," says Shaquille O'Neal, lowering his voice as if discussing the dearly departed. Steve Kerr goes further. "That screwed him up his whole career," he says, shaking his head. "It's sad that that's what he was remembered for. He was an All-Star type of player."

By any measure, the free throw is one of the easiest shots in basketball: an unguarded 15-footer. Technically, in fact, the shot is only 13'9", the distance from the line to the center of the hoop. (It's the backboard that is 15 feet away.) What's more, players can practice free throws exactly as they shoot them in a game, unlike most every other type of shot. To simulate a jumper, one must try to replicate the flow of an offense, perhaps coming off a screen, as well as the idiosyncrasies of a defender and numerous other factors. But a free throw is a free throw, and the language reflects this; after all, it is a "free" throw or a "freebie," one taken from "the charity stripe." You are expected to make it, and of course, this is the problem, the "expected" part—as Nick Anderson knows. (And here, so that poor Nick doesn't have to bear the burden of this chapter alone, it should be said that no account of infamous missed free throws can go without mention of Karl Malone, who on a Sunday afternoon, in Game 1 of the 1997 NBA Finals between the Bulls and the Jazz, missed a pair with 9.2 seconds left and the game tied. As he stepped to the line, Scottie Pippen reputedly walked over to him and said, "The Mailman doesn't deliver on Sunday.")

Put Shaquille O'Neal in a gym by himself, and he will hit, on average, 70% of his free throws, but in a game he's more likely to hit 5 of 10. (He's a 52.8% shooter for his career.) Same goes for Dwight Howard (60.1%). Perhaps the most inconsistent free throw shooter in history was Wilt Chamberlain. Consider: On Nov. 4, 1960, Chamberlain attempted 10 free throws in a game and missed all 10. (His team, the Philadelphia Warriors, won anyway.) That remains a record, but so is his performance on March 2, 1962, when he made 28 free throws (out of 32!). That feat occurred during his famous 100-point game, and the mark of 28 stands tied in NBA history for the most points on free throws in a game. How does a player go from being unable to hit 1-of-10 stationary shots to hitting 28 out of 32?

No one, it turns out, really knows. Sure, it has been studied—in physics books and in dissertations with titles such as *The Paradox of the Free Throw* (by Jim Poteet, a college coach for 25 years). Dallas Mavericks shooting coach Gary Boren identifies 41 common problems with free throw form—who knew 41 were even possible?—while Buzz Braman sells a videotape called *Buzz Braman Is Doctor Sure Shot* that claims to hold the free throw's easily learned secrets. Of course, if this were the case, all NBA players would be deadeyes from the line.

Instead, few acts in sports remain as perplexing as the free throw. After all, it is one of the only things in life you can practice over and over and get worse at. Golf comes to mind, and indeed this is the comparison most often made, especially to putting. A 10-year-old can be taught to consistently make five-foot putts, yet some pros have been run out of the game because they suddenly lost confidence on short putts, a case of "the yips."

A free throw shooter can suffer the same distressing decline. Despite years of repetition (and excluding a peculiar renaissance in 2008–09, which we'll come to later), Shaq's accuracy has actually gone *down* over the course of his career: During his rookie season, in 1992–93, he shot 59.2%. Over the next 16 seasons, only once did he top that mark, and often his accuracy was significantly lower (such as 42.2% in 2006–07).

Most every free throw miss is an important one. On average, nearly one out of every five points in an NBA game comes on a free throw. (The precise number was 19.1% in 2008–09.) That means that the difference between a team's shooting 65% from the line and a team's shooting 80% can be as many as five or six wins in a season, depending on the circumstances. And five or six wins can in turn be the difference between the playoffs and the lottery. Given how much the rest of the game has evolved—think of the intricate defenses and complex number-crunching and high-level conditioning—one would assume that teams would have made a science of free throws. But it hasn't happened. In 2007–08 the league average was 75.5%, or almost exactly what it was 20 years before, in 1988 (76.6%) and 10 years before that, in 1978 (75.2%).

All this despite the fact that, unlike most skills in the NBA, almost anyone can become an excellent free throw shooter. You cannot master the dunk or perform a wicked crossover dribble or consistently drain 25-footers without certain physical gifts. But you can teach just about anyone, at nearly any age, to shoot free throws.

For proof, I present Tom Amberry, a retired podiatrist who lives in Southern California. In 1993, at the age of 71, Amberry set a Guinness World Record by sinking 2,750 consecutive free throws. That is not a typo (though when I told Kerr about this, he said, "No way! That's *crazy*!"). Amberry accomplished the feat over the course of 12 hours at a health club outside Los Angeles, with 10 paid witnesses. What's more, the streak never actually ended with a miss; he only stopped when the gym needed to close for the night.

After his performance, Amberry went on to a certain amount of media fame—he shot free throws on *Letterman* and gave clinics— and even worked as a free throw consultant for the Chicago Bulls. He also won multiple free throw shooting championships at the World Masters games (which you probably had no idea existed— I certainly didn't), held biannually in locations around the world. In other words, if anyone can plumb the secrets of free throws, it should be Amberry. I arranged to meet with him on a weekday afternoon in the fall of 2008 at a coffee shop not far from his house in Seal Beach, Calif.

Amberry shuffled in, carrying a thick black leather briefcase. At 86 years old his posture is stooped, but he remains tall and thin—he was a 6' 7" power forward during his junior college playing days—with a full head of scrub-brush white hair. He is a regular at the coffee shop, where he meets a group of a dozen coaches and friends for breakfast every Saturday morning, and there is a framed photo on the wall of him grinning with Michael Jordan. (The inscription on the photo is not from Jordan but from Amberry, and it reads WORLD CHAMPION FREE THROW SHOOTER.)

Amberry was energetic, chatty and a bit corny. He made jokes like "I gave my girl a ring, and she gave me the finger," and when I asked what would happen if an NBA player practiced 500 free throws a day, year-round, he responded, "If I were a librarian and you came to me with that scenario, I'd say you'll find it under the fiction section."

These days, Amberry told me, he can't shoot as much as he'd like. Three years before my visit, he got both shingles and polymyalgia rheumatica, a muscle disorder that causes pain and stiffness in the upper body. Still, he said he practiced every Saturday and, though he only shot 25 at a time, he remained accurate. The weekend before I saw him, he'd hit all 25. At 86 years old.

Over clam chowder and grilled cheese sandwiches, he broke down his shooting philosophy, periodically fishing out artifacts from his briefcase, including a photo of Stephen Curry ("Perfect form!"), motivational flyers (a cartoon of Pogo saying, "We have met the enemy and he is us") and a Photoshopped graphic of Amberry reaching out and dropping the ball into the net, a visualization technique he preaches (the idea being that if you imagine dropping the ball into the net, rather than shooting it, it reduces your anxiety at the line, and as we know, anxiety is not the free throw shooter's friend).

As for Amberry's secret, if you can call it that, it really comes down to one simple truth: he practiced his ass off. He began shooting free throws in earnest in 1991. He'd recently retired from his podiatry practice and, being something of a workaholic, found himself rudderless. A friend suggested he take up an activity he'd enjoyed when he was younger. So Amberry, who'd been a junior college All-American at Long Beach City College during the 1940s and briefly played in the American Basketball League (an NBA precursor), headed to the local YMCA to play some pickup ball. It did not go well. "I barely got out of there alive," he told me with a chuckle.

So playing was not an option. Shooting, though, was a different matter, and he decided to see how proficient he could become. (As a player, a lifetime earlier, he'd been about an 80% free throw shooter.) He began going to a local health club during the peaceful early-morning hours, when the gym was empty. Starting at 5:30 a.m., with only a few breaks, Amberry, a natural lefty, would shoot nothing but free throws for two hours, noting his accuracy in a spiral notebook. Soon enough, he began entering competitions. But there was a problem: His body wasn't accustomed to the repetitive stress. Six weeks after beginning his training regimen, he blew out a tendon just below the elbow on his shooting arm. (It remains visible, like an egg bulging from his left forearm.)

Rather than give up, however, Amberry merely started over. *Shooting righthanded.* So when he set the Guinness record in that gym a year and a half later, he did it while shooting with his off-hand. Next time Shaq starts making excuses, he might consider that.

Technically, Amberry's free throw is more of a "push" shot than a traditional over-the-head jumper. He keeps his elbow tucked in to the side of his body as he shoots, puts his thumb along one of the black channels of the ball and points his middle finger toward the inflation hole. He believes this last bit with the inflation hole not only lines up his hand but provides him with something to focus on, an anxiety reducer if you will. For positioning his feet, he looks down and finds the nail in the middle of the free throw line—you probably never even knew there was one there—and straddles it. (At first he taped dimes to the court so he knew his toes would be aligned during practice.)

Then he enacts his seven-part mantra: *Feet square to the line. Bounce the ball three times. Thumb in the channel. Elbow in. Bend the knees. Eye on the target. Shoot and follow through.* Each element has a discrete purpose. Tucking the elbow helps eliminate missing left or right; the force of the push comes from bending the knees ("a little more than you think," he advises); eyeing the target sets his aim—not for the back of the rim but for the empty middle. Most important, though, he wants to shoot before his brain can get in the way. "Thinking is the worst thing you can do," he explains in his book, aptly titled *Free Throw.* "What's there to think about?"

By the time Amberry takes aim, he hasn't had a moment to ruminate upon anything else—like, say, the pressure of the situation or how many he's hit in a row or what he's having for dinner that night. He compares the act of looking up and focusing to "taking off the lens of a camera just before you shoot a picture." Before he set his record, Amberry even went so far as to embark on a "mental diet" for two weeks, reading and listening only to comedy and music. No news, no metro section, nothing that could upset him. While this may sound extreme, Amberry has a simple explanation: "I treated my mind the way most athletes condition their bodies."

Can Amberry's method work for real players? In researching his *Paradox of the Free Throw* dissertation at Oklahoma State University in 1999, Poteet decided to find out. He recruited basketball players from middle schools and high schools in the Oklahoma City and Jackson, Miss., areas and split them into two groups: a control group consisting of nine boys and one girl and an experimental group of 18 boys and two girls. Before the study, he had each test subject shoot 100 "pre-test" free throws. Over the next month, each group shot 30 sessions of 100 free throws in segments of one, two or three free throws (the point being to mimic a game situation, where one steps away from the line after each "segment"). Members of the control group, who continued shooting in whatever style they always had, improved minimally, from 77.2% pretest to, after a month, 79.9%.

Members of the experimental group, on the other hand, were given Amberry's book and video and attended a demonstration he gave. They were instructed to use his method, as best they could. At the end of the month, 19 of the 20 players had improved, with two finishing at about 90%. Overall, the group went from a 68.4% pretest average to 80.1% afterward. When I called Poteet to talk about his results, he told me the key to the improvement was the mental aspect: "I think psychological things happen to athletes when they step to the free throw line, and most of them are bad." Poteet told me he'd interviewed the athletes about what they think about when they stand at the line, and he got three common answers: a) I hope I don't miss ("which is self-defeating," Poteet said); b) I have to make this free throw ("That's a lot of pressure"); and c) I don't think about anything ("If the mind is not active and engaged, you're just going to chunk the thing up there"). The solution to the issue of too much thinking, Poteet believes, is to become "process-oriented rather than outcome-oriented."

In the interest of reader service (and because I was quite curious), I conducted my own—much simpler—test of Amberry's method. First, I decided to shoot around 300 free throws using my normal style—breathe out, two dribbles, bend knees, release—and I hit 90% of them (253 of 281), with a high of 42 in a row. In doing so, the first thing I learned was that it takes a really long time to shoot that many free throws, especially by yourself. Essentially I was shooting in "segments" of one, shagging my own shot after each attempt, and it took more than an hour to finish the session. That may not sound like a long time, but it certainly seems like it when you're shooting free throws by yourself. Which led to my second observation: It got really boring. I can't imagine how Amberry shot for two hours every day, for years. Perhaps this was his real secret: endurance. (My elbow was a little sore after doing it for two days.)

Next, I shot the same number using Amberry's method. In fairness, it took me the better part of 100 free throws to feel comfortable: I worried about whether my elbow was tucked in far enough, forgot to say parts of the mantra, felt weird bouncing the ball with two hands (as Amberry always does). The result: I hit only 63 of the first 80 shots.

After that, I became more comfortable with the routine. I sank 182 of the final 200 (91%), with a high of 34 in a row. (For perspective, this is still far, far below Amberry's level; he says that on 431 separate occasions he has hit 500 consecutive free throws—and who am I to doubt him?)

Obviously, mine was only an anecdotal study; but while my overall percentage didn't increase, I did feel like his method was helping me. For one, I felt more confident—more "process-oriented," to invoke Poteet—using the mantra. Second, my shot gained a bit of arc with his push method and thus the makes were, on the whole, cleaner. Would it help an NBA player? Well, that's a different question. Because, really, how many NBA players want to spend all that time in a gym, performing all those funny-looking dribbles? Perhaps predictably, Amberry had a hard time getting through to the pros. When Bulls coach Bill Cartwright brought him in to work with Jay Williams, the former Duke star who was struggling at the line, Williams wasn't especially interested. "He was the Number 1 draft pick, so he was busy doing commercials," says Amberry.

Ron Artest liked him, Amberry says; and Jamal Crawford improved by using his method but later reverted to his original form because he felt the Amberry style "looked funny." Says Cartwright, "I think guys were just stubborn and determined to shoot it their way, because the basic fundamentals of what he does are really good." (As proof, Cartwright notes that his own daughter uses the method, after picking it up as a girl from Amberry, and "she's shooting 86% at Northwestern right now.") In general, Amberry is horrified by what he sees when he watches the NBA: players walking to the line without a strategy, players who vary their form game to game, players who think it's cooler to shoot 70% with "manly" form than 90% with a polished, if slightly goofy, one. As Amberry said with a sigh, "Players don't want to do anything that other players think looks too different."

Ah, the importance of image. The most success Wilt Chamberlain ever had was when he briefly flirted with shooting underhand, "granny-style" free throws, à la Rick Barry. The problem? As he wrote in his 1973 autobiography, *Wilt,* "I felt silly—like a sissy." So he stopped looking like a sissy and went back to missing free throws. For his career, he shot 51.1%. Not to provide an excuse for players like Wilt, or Shaq, but there is a reason why it's harder for big men to shoot free throws. For starters, their hands are generally bigger, meaning the ball feels like a grapefruit, making it more difficult to have control over its flight. More important, physics are working against them. For an explanation, we turn to John Fontanella, a former college basketball player, professor of physics at the U.S. Naval Academy and the author of *The Physics of Basketball*.

The problem, Fontanella writes, is that the taller a player is, the smaller his "window" is to get the ball to the rim (which is to say that since he releases the ball from a higher point, he tends to put less arc on the ball to get it up and over the rim, making for a flatter and less-forgiving shot). The disadvantage can be rectified in one of two ways: by bending one's knees more or by putting more arc on the ball, neither of which most big men are taught to do. Together with the propensity of big guys to muscle the ball too hard to the rim—or in Fontanella's words, provide heightened "approach speed"—they lose the opportunity for a soft bounce on the rim. All of which makes the exemplary foul shooting of men like 7' 3" Zydrunas Ilgauskas of Cleveland (a career 78.2% shooter) and 7' 6" Yao Ming of Houston (83.2 %) even more impressive.

For the most part, though, elite NBA free throw shooters like Yao (and he is elite, even used by the Rockets to take technical free throws) or elite shooters of any size are unconcerned with how they look, as long as the ball consistently goes into the basket. Changes in form are made not for aesthetic purposes but for increased accuracy. Kerr, a career 86.4% shooter, spent his first five years in the NBA shooting with both feet up against the line, then made an adjustment and moved his left foot slightly back, in a staggered stance. (Paul Pierce might have the most exaggerated such stance in the league, looking as if he's about to throw a dart.) "The first four or five years, I leaned in a little bit," explains Kerr. "Once I brought the left foot back, I'd go straight up, and I was much more confident and my percentage went way up." Of course, that's a relative statement. Kerr was already a very good free throw shooter, in the mid-80% range, but after the foot adjustment he finished at 90% or higher in four seasons.

To shoot 90% during the game you need to be virtually flawless in practice, and Kerr was—he says he routinely hit 96 or 97 out of 100. His strategy was to try to shoot the perfect free throw every time. Literally. He'd select one free throw from early in the season that he felt was perfect—in form, release and finish—and then visualize it and attempt to replicate it every time. One year, his perfect shot came from a game against the Houston Rockets. "So the rest of the year, I'd get to the line, deep breath, one-two-three dribbles, then 'Houston!'"

Mo Williams, the shooting guard for the Cavaliers, professes not to think about his shot at all. Considering he finished at a stellar 91.2% in the 2008–09 season, he may even be telling the truth. When I asked Williams if he used a mantra, he shook his head. "No, not at all. It's like clockwork, like muscle memory. I'm so confident at the free throw line, I can joke with the other players. When you're confident and you know you can make it, that's all you need." (This is almost exactly what Rick Barry, the patron saint of the granny shot, believes. "There isn't any pressure when you have confidence" is Barry's aphorism.) On that same day that I spoke to Williams, in early 2009, in a game against the Warriors, he missed his first free throw, his first miss in three games. I had to wonder if, just by talking to me about it, he'd done exactly what he typically does not do: think about the shot. Of course, he would proceed to go on a run of nine games in which he didn't miss a free throw before he missed again.

Ask any good free throw shooter, and they'll agree on one thing: A rigid routine is vital, no matter how strange it might look. Reggie Miller dribbled the ball six times very low, as if petting a tiny dog, then looked up and shot almost as if in a hurry. Jerry Stackhouse bends his knees so deeply he looks as if he's in yoga class, while Rip Hamilton takes one dribble off to the right before shooting, as if he possesses a free throw sidecar. Gilbert Arenas goes around his back, Steve Nash begins by miming a free throw, and Patrick Ewing used to stare at the ball, as if it were about to speak to him, just before shooting it. Some send messages. Jeff Hornacek touched his right cheek with his right hand to say hi to his kids. Jason Kidd used to blow a kiss to his wife. Karl Malone whispered under his breath before every free throw and never divulged what it was he said. (When the *Salt Lake Tribune* hired two lip readers in 1997 to decipher his words, they determined that Malone was talking to his son, saying, "This is for Karl, Karl, my baby boy.") Perhaps there is something to be said for Malone's mumbling: Before he adopted this routine, he was a 54.8% free throw shooter; with mumbles, he shot 75.7%. Considering he attempted more free throws than any other player in NBA history, that's a pretty important statistical leap (2,560 points, to be exact, which, for example, is almost as many points as Chris Dudley scored in his entire 16-year NBA career).

Some players go so far as to rebel against the conventions of the free throw itself. At times, both Nick Van Exel and Rasheed Wallace shot their free throws from a good foot behind the line. Hal Greer shot 80.1%, even though he took each free throw as if it were a jump shot. Some players relish free throw opportunities; Ray Allen (89.3% for his career) told me that when he's in a shooting slump, he tries to get to the line because "it calms the body down." Others claim to loathe the line. "I don't like being out there," Dennis Rodman (58.5% for his career) once said, adding the dubious claim, "Too much attention."

Certain players detest the experience so much they prefer to opt out. During the fourth quarter of a January 2009 game, the Celtics began purposefully fouling Cavaliers center Ben Wallace, a career 41.8% free throw shooter, to send him to the line. So Wallace promptly air-balled the second of two free throws on purpose so he could be pulled from the game before being fouled again. As Wallace told Brian Windhorst of the *Cleveland Plain Dealer,* "I mean, I didn't want to be there all night."

It's one thing to be a bad free throw shooter who rarely shoots them, like Wallace; it's another to be a poor free throw shooter who has no choice but to be there all night. Which brings us back to Shaq, the foulest foul shooter of his generation. Like it or not, O'Neal knows he'll spend quality time at the stripe every game he plays. Six times, he has led the league in attempts. And eleven times he has led the league in misses. (If not for injuries, it would undoubtedly have been more.) To put this in perspective: O'Neal has missed more free throws in his career—5,145 and counting—than Larry Bird *attempted.*

Over the years O'Neal has worked with myriad coaches and specialists and once even took advice from his agent. He has claimed a variety of excuses, including that he can't properly follow through on his shot due to a childhood injury that left him with a short tendon in his right wrist (an injury that apparently doesn't affect him during practice). His struggles even led to a whole new coaching philosophy, the Hack-a-Shaq, that O'Neal has labeled "cowardly." Of course, Shaq has always been unable to do the one thing that would stop those "cowards": hit his free throws.

Until, that is, he did. In a remarkable metamorphosis, O'Neal suddenly began sinking shots from the line midway through the 2008–09 seasons. Not just occasionally, but habitually. During the month of January, he hit nearly 70%, and his season percentage rose high enough that he flirted with 65% for the season, unheard of territory for the Big Bricklayer. At one point he hit 12 in a row, inspiring O'Neal to dub himself Shaqovic. As he explained to reporters, "If you go down the league, anybody with the last name [ending in] *vic* is a great shooter. Radmanovic, Vujavic . . . all those Viches."

O'Neal's renaissance was so impressive that he impacted the perception of NBA free throw shooting at large. An editor at *SI* remarked to me in February 2009 that it seemed we were in a golden age of free throw shooting, citing the then league average of 77.1%. And he was right; if that percentage held up, it would be the highest in more than 30 years, since 1973–74, when there were only 17 teams in the league. Certainly this sounded impressive. At least until I ran the numbers and found—and this is pretty crazy—that the increase in league-wide foul shooting percentage could be attributed *entirely* to O'Neal. Had he taken the same number of free throws and been shooting his usual 52% instead of 61.7%, the league average would have been . . . 74.9%, or lower than the previous year and historically average.

This Shaqovic phenomenon was something I needed to investigate. In February I caught up with O'Neal after a Suns shootaround and asked for the secret to his (relative) success. As is his nature, he prefaced his response with a delightfully illogical philosophy. "I've never really believed in percentage, because my thing is how many guys have you seen shooting 90% who miss the one they're supposed to make?" he said. "So what you do is throw those percentages out of the way. I've been known to hit the ones I needed to hit."

Next O'Neal asserted that he was hitting more free throws simply because he was motivated to do so—that he wanted to end up in the "top four or five" in scoring when his career was finished, and so he was "concentrating more."

Finally, though, he got to the core of it. "I went back to my old high school form," he said. "I think I broke a golden rule by changing what was taught to me by my father. That's what I tell all kids, Whatever the method is you learned, stick with it. A lot of people have different forms, and they've become masters of what they do: Shawn Marion, the kid from Sacramento"—here O'Neal mimicked Kevin Martin's herky-jerky shot. "I just went back to the way I shot in high school."

Really, what Shaq was saying was that, finally, he was doing what Amberry and Mo Williams and all the other great free throwers espouse: shooting the ball rather than *thinking* about shooting the ball.

Just as Shaq prepares to leave the league, his successor has already arrived. It is the legacy of dominant big men and free throws; one hands the torch—or perhaps tosses it without arc or backspin—to the next. And now it is the age of Dwight Howard.

Despite Howard's abundant physical gifts, no one wants to emulate him at the line. His career free throw percentages look as if they could just as easily fall under his FG% heading: 67.1%, 59.5%, 58.6%, 59.0% and 59.4%. In fact, for two years in a row, from 2006–07 to 2007–08, Howard shot better from the field than from the line. In the past two seasons, like O'Neal before him, Howard has led the league in both free throw attempts and misses.

And, like O'Neal, Howard's form can be unsightly: a hitch at the top, a weird elbow-too-high release, wildly variable height and spin. In Orlando, some of the media jokingly explain his uniform number— 12—as standing for "1 of 2." And his nickname for a while was "Fitty," not as in the rapper 50 Cent but as in "fitty *per*cent."

In January 2009, I met up with Howard the morning before a game in Sacramento. At the time he was still smarting from criticism leveled a week earlier by his coach, Stan Van Gundy. Just after New Year's, Howard had scored 39 points against Toronto in a game the Magic had nonetheless lost, by six points. Afterward, Van Gundy was upset with Howard's 11-of-18 performance from the line. "That's about what he shoots, but it's not good enough," Van Gundy told reporters. "Sixty percent at the free throw line makes it tough. We've got a tremendous advantage down there. They couldn't guard him at all, but they get to the fourth quarter, and they just foul, and it's 1 for 2 every time. Then you're coming to the other end, and it's 2 for 2. That's a big difference."

When I asked Howard about whether it's frustrating to score *only* 39 points because of some missed free throws, he frowned. "I was kind of upset about that comment that I could have made more, because it wasn't like I was trying to miss them on purpose," he said. "I know sometimes you're going to make free throws and sometimes you're going to miss them." He paused, then shrugged. "Can't do nothing about it."

The issue, of course, is that conceivably he can. And just as with O'Neal, everyone has a suggestion. Dennis Hans, a self-styled shooting guru and freelance writer, wrote on his blog that the problem was "a premature unhinging of the flexed wrist of the shooting hand" and compared Howard's motion to the way golfers get in a bad habit of "hitting from the top." In case we didn't get the point, Hans also called Howard's form "a sickly shooting motion," "lousy" and a "monstrosity."

Dan Barto, a trainer at IMG Academies in Florida who has worked with prospects such as Joakim Noah and Corey Brewer, offered an even more technical diagnosis. In suggesting Howard switch to a push shot, Barto explained on the IMG website: "Dwight is in the most difficult segment for shooting form improvement. His high-hipped, long-armed build makes him all extremity. If you watch him shoot free throws, you can see his knees pop significantly earlier than he releases the ball. He never extends his ankles, pushes his hips forward, extends his back, brings the ball above his head and sends a variety of ball flights toward the rim." In other words, he's doing almost everything wrong.

Last year, Howard even received advice from an unlikely source: Nick Anderson. Seeing Howard struggle, Anderson took him aside. He told him there was nothing wrong with his mechanics, that it was mental, and that of all people he understood—he'd been there. "I told him, 'You start telling yourself you can't do something, and you start to believe it,'" says Anderson. "I was there once, mentally, telling myself, 'Well, you're not gonna make this free throw, you're gonna miss this free throw' and I was believing it. I can see the same thing with Dwight. He's believing what people are saying." Anderson paused, becoming very serious. "This is something you've done your whole life. You were good at it, and all of a sudden you get into a funk. Come game time, he lets all the outside stuff affect him. I tell him all the time, you have to stay in the game."

There are encouraging signs, however. Patrick Ewing, the former Knicks center who works with Howard in his current role as Magic assistant coach, told me that Howard is a work in progress. Ewing's big goal is merely to get Howard to follow through on his shot, something most nine-year-olds have already mastered. Still, at the end of each practice Howard must make 10 in a row, and surprisingly, according to Ewing, "he usually does." "Dwight has enough ability to become a very good shooter," Ewing said. "It's just repetition, repetition, repetition—and believing in it."

Or, more to the point, believing in it at the right time. Howard told me that in practice he is money. "It's crazy, dude. When I shoot free throws in practice, I can go for 20 straight, 15 straight," he said. "And then I get in the game, and I might miss 1 of 2. I think the thing is, blocking out everybody trying to tell me how to shoot free throws and just shoot it. I don't need a million shooting coaches or all those people saying, 'Hey, shoot this way.'" He paused. "My new thing is, I just go up there and shoot." (Howard is also trying to drown out distractions and has adopted a novel strategy: singing Beyoncé songs at the free throw line. As he explained, "I need to block stuff out because what people don't understand is you can really hear everything that goes on in the crowd—people saying stuff, saying, "Bend your knees!" or "Follow through!")

Thus, at least in theory, Howard understands what needs to happen. He calls himself a "willing listener and learner" and noted that, "a lot of people are talking about how they could get my free throws up to 85 percent or this magical way of getting my free throws up, and the only thing I can do is keep practicing. That's the *only* way." Then he said something that, for such a young man, was quite wise. "That's the way you get better in this league. By practicing and having confidence in your game to do what you did in practice. It's not about having the best shooting coach, it's just practice." Not coincidentally, this is the same philosophy espoused by men like Amberry, who is fond of saying, "Practice is like a leaky bucket that you have to keep refilling. If you don't do it, one day you'll lose something."

So Howard knows what to do but can't do it. He doesn't want to shoot free throws, but he must. After my conversation with him, and before the Sacramento game that night, the Kings' center, Mikki Moore, told me that the team's strategy for the game was to hack Howard whenever he got too close to the basket. "He's long and he can jump high, so we'd rather he be shooting free throws than dunking on anybody," explained Moore.

And foul they did. It took all of 34 seconds for Howard to go to the line for the first time, smothered on a successful reverse layup. As always, he put his right toe forward, breathed out, took two dribbles, then pulled the ball back toward his hip briefly before taking a third dribble. He raised the ball up, released it with nice rotation—if a bit forcefully—and . . . swished the shot. To be honest, it looked almost beautiful. Nice rotation, nice arc. Less than two minutes later, he was back at the line for two free throws. He rattled the first one in, then sent the second shot rocketing off the back of the rim. I settled in for a long night of painful free throwing.

Only it didn't continue. Maybe it was because Arco Arena, home to the struggling Kings, was less than half full, so the pressure was minimal. Maybe he was just feeling it. Whatever the reason, Howard suddenly turned into Steve Nash. He nailed two more, then two more. By the end of the night, a blowout Magic victory, Howard had hit 9 of 11 from the line.

In the locker room afterward he was ebullient. He joked, "I'm going to tell Coach to let me shoot the T's!" then mimicked a free throw in my direction. "What did I tell you?" he said. "It's because I was just shooting them, not doing what everybody tells me to do."

As he was boasting, J.J. Redick, the former Duke star and 87.1% career free throw shooter, stopped on his way to the shower.

"What'd you shoot tonight?" Redick asked.

Howard beamed like a proud father: "Nine of 11!"

Redick looked mildly shocked, then provided his blessing: "Atta boy!"

And just like that, in one night in Sacramento, Dwight Howard had cured his free throw ills.

I am, of course, kidding. The next game Howard hit 9 of 16 and, over the course of the following weeks put up a 12-for-18 night and a particularly unsightly 5-for-12 night. Van Gundy did not ask him to shoot any T's and Redick had no words of praise. Five months later, Howard would step to the line at the end of Game 4 of the NBA Finals with a chance to ice the game. The Magic led 87–84 with 11.1 seconds left and, with the win, could even the series at two games apiece. Everything about the situation felt eerily familiar. The fans were giddy. The Magic were again led by another young, dominant center. And the game could be won at the line with one of two free throws. Howard dribbled, exhaled, looked up and then . . . rattled one in and out. A thousand nightmares began to hatch as he lifted the ball for the second shot. This time it went long, bouncing high off the back rim and into the hands of the Lakers. What happened next seemed inevitable: of course, L.A. came back to send it to overtime (this time it was Derek Fisher playing the role of Kenny Smith by hitting a long three-pointer). And of course the Lakers won the game—Howard missed another crucial free throw in overtime—and, later, the title. It left many to wonder what might have been had Howard been able to hit but one free throw, a task that had seemed so easy for him on that January night in Sacramento.

It is a struggle some people can never win, and the most vexing thing about the free throw: one night it's the easiest shot in the world an the next it is the hardest. Which is to say that while everyone *can* make free throws, it's *when* you make them that matters. Or when you don't. Just ask Nick Anderson.

Point Guard: Steve Nash
Can See the Future

Before Steve Nash became an NBA All-Star, before he won two MVP awards, before he racked up 7,500 assists (and counting), before he set new standards in shooting accuracy, before he caused countless teenagers on countless courts across the country to grow their hair out and tuck it behind their ears, before he became *the best point guard of his generation,* he was just a skinny Canadian teenager with an aversion to the easiest shot in basketball.

How Nash went from there (unknown Canuck with layup issues) to here (35 years old and a six-time All-Star) tells us a lot about what makes an effective point guard, for inside his story is the blueprint for a great floor leader.

"Stop dribbling so much."

It's 1991, and Ian Hyde-Lay is watching the new kid run the offense. Hyde-Lay is the head coach at St. Michael's high school in Victoria, B.C., and he has certain core beliefs about what works on a basketball court. Fancy dribbling, no-look passes and breakneck fast breaks, for example, are not to his taste. He prefers to slow it down, bang it into the post and make the simple, easy pass.

Thus Hyde-Lay is trying to break the colt in his new point guard, a highly touted senior named Steve Nash who transferred in from a nearby school. Hyde-Lay first saw Nash play as an eighth-grader and immediately noticed that the young man saw the floor in ways other kids did not. It was as if Nash were playing soccer, cutting and reading angles and looking for teammates to make "runs," just as a midfielder would. This shouldn't have been all that surprising, as Nash was a gifted soccer player, and his father, John, played semiprofessionally in England and South Africa. Still, rarely have those skills translated to the basketball court so seamlessly. "He made anticipation plays that you just went, 'Whoa!'" remembers Hyde-Lay. "A lot of his passes weren't completed because the receiver wasn't ready."

The problem at St. Michael's, however, is that Nash prefers to make these passes while racing downcourt or swooping in semicircles under the basket, neither of which qualifies as slowing it down or banging it into the post. So Hyde-Lay reins him in, day by day. And, to his credit, Nash goes along with it, even if in hindsight it seems a peculiar decision. "We had two pretty effective power post players, a lot of motion and a lot of screening, but it wasn't on-ball screening," says Hyde-Lay. "We didn't really run that much, which sounds laughable given Steve. In retrospect I might have shackled him a little bit."

Not that this suffocates Nash's game. He averages a near triple double as St. Michael's goes 50–4 and wins the British Columbia high school championship. Along the way the team becomes exceptionally close, in part because Nash goes out of his way to make everyone feel equal. "Whenever our team was struggling, even though he would not be at fault for a play that went wrong, or a bad pass, he would always have his hand up, saying, 'That's on me,'" says Hyde-Lay. "If he penetrated and kicked out for someone who wasn't ready for a pass, it was never, 'Get ready!' It was more like, 'My fault that pass wasn't on the money. I gave it too late.'"

It's a team-building tactic Nash will find invaluable in the years to come, as the egos get bigger and the stakes higher. A decade later, playing on a Phoenix Suns squad stacked with players not lacking in self-regard—in particular power forward Amar'e Stoudemire, who chooses the jersey number "1" and gives himself the nickname STAT (for Standing Tall and Talented)—Nash volunteers himself for blame whenever he feels the team is in danger of fraying. "I'd be in the middle of talking to the team," says Mike D'Antoni, who coached the Suns from 2003 to '08, "and he'd come into the locker room and say, 'Hey, guys, I screwed this one up; I wasn't sharp tonight. It's on me. Let's do it next time.'" D'Antoni pauses. "Do you know how much easier that makes your job when you're the coach?"

"What kind of layup was that, Steve?"

It's near the end of Nash's senior season at St. Michael's, and Hyde-Lay is wondering what the hell his point guard is doing. Approaching the basket, Nash has an open lane for an easy righthanded layin, but he instead veers across the basket to shoot a lefthanded floater, a significantly more difficult shot.

It is something the coach has noticed on numerous occasions: Nash doing everything possible to avoid jumping off his left foot for a simple righty layup, even though this is the dominant leg for a right-handed player. One time Nash cuts middle, the next he uses his left hand, or jumps off his right foot and uses his right hand, a move both difficult and unnatural. (Just try it sometime.) "It was ironic because he was so good at everything else," says Hyde-Lay. "But he was never good at the traditional righthanded layup."

For Nash, the difficulty began when he was a 10th-grader. He'd sprained his left ankle and, gym rat that he was, never let it properly heal. As a result he found it increasingly difficult to leap off his left foot; whereas he'd been able to dunk off his left leg before, he no longer could. Thus every drive became an adventure. "It really made it much harder to finish with my right hand," he says. "I'd make most of them, of course, but I had to really concentrate." As a result, Nash became, as he puts it, "basically lefthanded around the basket."

What is initially a weakness will later become a strength (and this is to become something of a theme in Nash's basketball career). Watch Nash now, playing in the NBA, and you'll notice he still rarely goes off his left foot for a righthanded layup. Rather than hindering him, however, this actually makes him more difficult to guard, as defenders can neither anticipate nor time his unconventional moves, which include floaters and scoops and all manner of flip shots that appear to have been concocted in a particularly crazy game of H-O-R-S-E. Similarly, because Nash doesn't focus on elevating to the rim, he is able to better protect the ball. "A lot of times I try to jump that way"—and here Nash points on a horizontal plane—"rather than up."

Paired with a change of pace, this creates a devastating combination. Watch closely, and you'll see that when Nash beats a defender, he often does something counterintuitive: He slows down. This not only throws off the timing of the defense, but it also creates contact. Now Nash can extend the ball out rather than up and release a protected shot from waist level, essentially using his back to create an umbrella around the ball. Like most elements of his game, it is a conscious decision. "If I just run and put it straight off the glass, [the defender] can beat me in pretty easily," explains Nash. "But if I dictate when the race starts and stops, I have a chance to beat him." Furthermore, because Nash has slowed down the play, he doesn't have to commit to going to the basket, which keeps his passing angles open and, at the same time, makes it harder for a help-side defender to take a charge.

Are these moves awkward looking? Sometimes. But they also serve to mask Nash's disadvantages (his height, his lack of explosiveness and length, his bum left ankle) while providing him with the advantage of unpredictability. "You'd never teach a 13-year-old to do a lot of what he does," says Suns coach Alvin Gentry, "but it sure does work."

"I'll offer you a full ride, but I've got to tell you that you're the worst defensive player I've ever seen."

Now it is the end of Nash's senior year, and St. Michael's is playing in the first round of British Columbia's senior boys' AAA championships. Watching from the stands is Santa Clara coach Dick Davey, who has flown in to see Nash for the first time. After the game Davey approaches the young guard and offers him a scholarship (along with a little constructive criticism about his lack of D). Incredibly, it is the first offer he has received from a school in the United States, though not for lack of effort from Nash. Over the previous year Nash and Hyde-Lay have sent letters and videotapes to more than 30 schools. Most dumped them right in the trash. As Pepperdine coach Tom Asbury told *SI*, "When you're at Pepperdine, you get 300 letters a year [from prospective players]. And for a white guard from Canada, you're probably not going to do a lot of follow-up."

At the time Nash was disappointed in the lack of interest, but in retrospect he sees that it was an advantage in his career. Since he didn't grow up in the U.S. amateur basketball circuit, where top prospects are shuttled to high-profile tournaments and showered with gifts, some less legal than others, he never developed the overinflated sense of self-worth of so many U.S. prep stars. He was confident, sure, but he also saw himself as just a guy who liked to play sports. He likens his upbringing to that of his good friend Dirk Nowitzki, another down-to-

earth All-Star. "I think we were both brought up in very humble surroundings where there was no room for being bigger than your team
or bigger than your boots," says Nash. "Whereas a lot of guys who
come from humble beginnings don't necessarily come from humble
surroundings. The culture we were both brought up in was one of,
'Take it down a notch.' Especially in the Canadian hockey culture,
you're called out right away if you put yourself ahead of the team or
think you're too cool. It's the same with British soccer culture, and
those were what I grew up with."

"I'm going to keep picking you up full-court. Every single time, baby."

It's Nash's freshman year at Santa Clara, the fall of 1992, and he is
being absolutely hounded by John Woolery, the incumbent starting
point guard. It's one of the team's first scrimmages, and Nash is having
a difficult time even getting the ball past half-court against Woolery.
Time and again he tries to advance the ball, and time and again Woolery—tall, athletic and strong—strips him unceremoniously. If Nash
tries to go right, Woolery beats him to the spot; if he spins back left,
Woolery is there. As Woolery will later say, "To be honest, I was trying
to break his confidence because I didn't want him to take my starting
spot. I don't think he'd played against real athletic guards before. He
wasn't used to that pressure."

Day after day this happens, and what is interesting—besides the
fact that a future MVP point guard was a frustrated ball handler as a
college freshman—is how Nash responds, at least externally. Rather
than acting embarrassed or seeming to lose confidence, it's as if Nash
has stumbled upon some fascinating discovery. *Interesting, he's taking
the ball from me!* After practice he pulls Woolery aside and interrogates him, curious as to how, exactly, he is stealing the ball so easily.
"I think he actually liked it," says Woolery. "He'd want to work on it,
and I could feel him getting better. It wasn't like, 'You ripped me, so
I'm not going to dribble.' It was more like, 'You're going to have to rip
me every day, every time, and I'm going to keep coming. And eventually I'm going to figure it out.'"

Not that Nash was immune to the experience. "Well, he *was* killing me," says Nash. "There were times I'd go back to my room and be

like, 'I want to be a professional one day, and I can't even get the ball to half-court against somebody I've never heard of?' I wasn't going to give up though."

On the contrary, Nash harbored grand dreams. Sitting around one night with Woolery and a few teammates talking about life goals, Nash says his is to be drafted into the pros. "I said, '*Ohhhh-kayy,*'" remembers Woolery. "Then I saw him working, and I said, 'Maybe.' He was the hardest-working player I've ever been around." (This wasn't the first pro ball proclamation from Nash; when he first visited Santa Clara, he matter-of-factly told people he was headed to the NBA.)

Not only did Nash show up early before practice to work on his game, but he also had a key to Toso Pavilion and would ride his bike to the court at one or two in the morning to do extra shooting. During the day he dribbled a basketball everywhere he went on campus until he decided that was too easy—so he started dribbling a tennis ball. "Some of my family members said to me [when Nash made the NBA], 'You used to start over Steve—what happened?'" says Woolery, who now works for a medical diagnostics company and coaches at Antioch High in the Bay Area. "I told them he just worked harder than me. He just worked his ass off over the years."

"I think we're seeing something unique here."

It is the WCC championship game in the spring of 1993, Santa Clara versus Pepperdine, and broadcaster Kareem Abdul-Jabbar, a man not given to hyperbole, is astonished. A spindly Santa Clara freshman reserve with a horrendous haircut—it looks like a bowl cut that has been shaved clean from the top of the ears on down—is taking control of the game. Nash has come off the bench and is hitting driving layups (lefthanded, of course) and knocking down three-pointers. First one, then another until, if you include the previous game, he has hit seven threes in a row. "He's a baby-faced assassin," shouts play-by-play man Steve Physioc, who also likens Nash to Isiah Thomas (for his part, Abdul-Jabbar at one point refers to Nash as "a foreign ringer!"). Behind Nash's 23 points and his perfect night from behind the arc, Santa Clara, picked at the beginning of the season to finish last in the conference, wins 73–63 to advance to the NCAA tournament. (A week later the 15th-seeded Broncos, who are listed at 800 million-to-1 odds to win the championship, will pull off one of the biggest upsets in tournament history, beating second-seeded Arizona [7-to-1 odds to win it all] behind six straight free throws made down the stretch from Nash.)

It is odd to watch a tape of the Pepperdine game years after the fact and see Nash, the consummate point guard, in the role of pure scorer. So focused is he on being a spot-up shooter that, by my count, he finishes the game with a grand total of one assist

It shouldn't be so surprising, though. People have spent so much time during Nash's NBA career admiring his passing abilities—and rightly so, given his career average of 9.3 assists a game—that his shooting skill has often been overlooked. Since the three-point shot was introduced to the NBA in 1979, only six players have accomplished the vaunted 50/90/40, and only two have done it more than once. One is named Larry Bird (he did it twice) and the other is Nash (three times).

"You have to take at least 10 shots a game."

It's 1999, and Steve Nash is in his third season in the NBA, playing for the Dallas Mavericks. Don Nelson, the Dallas coach, is so frustrated with his point guard's unrelenting unselfishness that he has decided to mandate a certain minimum number of shots per game for Nash. Nelson chooses 10, but that ends up being an optimistic goal, as Nash ends up averaging only 7.9 field goal attempts for the season. (It drops to 6.5 the following year.) "He wants to pass first," Nelson later tells *SI*. "I guess it's O.K. to be that way on a certain kind of team, but I needed him to get 15 points every night. It went against his grain, I guess."

This is true. Though he'd been a scorer in his early years at Santa Clara, Nash sees his role in the NBA, and in basketball at large, really, as a distributor. After being chosen in the first round of the 1996 draft by Phoenix, he spent two seasons apprenticing under then Suns point guard Jason Kidd before Dallas acquired him in a draft-day trade in 1998. Inserted into the starting lineup by Nelson, Nash couldn't bring himself to look for his own shot. "He overpassed," remembers Randy Winn, the San Francisco Giants outfielder who roomed with Nash at Santa Clara and remains one of his close friends. "You could see it. He wouldn't even shoot 10-footers."

In the years to come, even as Nash blossoms into an All-Star, he will retain his reputation as a reluctant shooter, despite proving himself capable of prolific outbursts when necessary. After Nash has rejoined the Suns, and Phoenix is playing Dallas in the 2005 Western Conference semifinals, the Mavericks' game plan is to force Nash to beat them by scoring. Almost grudgingly, Nash obliges by scoring 48 points in Game 4, 34 points in Game 5 and 39 points in Game 6 as the Suns prevail 4–2 in the series. "I could have scored 20 points for a season a number of times, but I just don't shoot enough," says Nash, whose career average is 14.4 ppg. "But it's not really always the best route for us to win."

He's right, of course, though some think he takes it too far—and others pick up on this. Despite Nash's success against the Mavericks in that playoff series, some Dallas players continued to believe the make-him-shoot strategy remains the wisest. "He's just going to pass the ball," Jerry Stackhouse said. "He feels like if he's getting 30 points, it's almost too much. He's going to force passes to the point where he can be baited into having a big turnover game just because he's going to pass the ball."

Nash takes issue with this characterization. And what's striking about his argument is the acknowledgment that while he may indeed be a better scoring option, that doesn't necessarily mean the best thing for the team is for him to score. "I think there are intangible benefits to passing up some shots, especially early in games," he tells me. "[The payoff is] the confidence my teammates will gain by shooting rather than me, regardless of whether I'm a better shooter or not. It's not just a refusal. It's more of an instinctive thing. I want everyone to feel good because in the long term of a full 48 minutes, I think that comes back to you somewhere along the line."

"Where the hell did Steve go?"

It's a few weeks before Mavericks training camp is to begin in the summer of 2003, and Nash is out to lunch with Mavs athletic trainer Al Whitley and another buddy. It is a beautiful day, and the guys begin badgering Nash to have a beer. Reluctant to alter his preseason training routine, Nash says he'll do it on two conditions: They drink one beer per bar, and they have to run between bars. "So we finish our beer and then take off jogging," remembers Whitley, who grew up with Nash in Victoria, "only Steve immediately sprints way ahead of us. By the time we got to the next bar, he was finished with his beer and telling us the name of the next bar." And so it continues, through the McKinney area of Dallas, from the Taco Diner to TABC bar to The Quarter, Nash racing ahead and his friends straggling behind. All the while startled passersby wonder if the local NBA team's star has embraced an unusual new workout regimen. After running close to six miles, Whitley and his buddy are gassed. They stumble up to the final bar, which happens to have an outdoor pool attached, and walk in. Unable to find their friend inside, they look out back, only to spot Nash in the pool, doing the backstroke. "He smiled and waved," says Whitley, "like it was the most natural thing in the world."

It is quintessential Nash: accomplishing two seemingly incongruous goals simultaneously. He maintains his training program, *and* he hangs out with his buddies. He gets in a run, he and his friends have a memorable afternoon, and many beers are consumed. It is, in a way, multitasking of the highest order. Which, when you think about it, is what being a point guard is all about. *Keep everyone happy, be efficient, have fun, achieve the end goal.*

Granted, every point guard leads in a different way. Some, like Allen Iverson and Nate Robinson (if we can call them point guards), play like the former option quarterbacks they were in high school. The ball stays in their hands, they make the decisions and dish only when it appears their own scoring options are cut off.

Chris Paul of the New Orleans Hornets goes with a combination of lead-by-example, castigation and babysitting. I remember spending a few days with Paul when he was a rookie guard with the Hornets, who at the time were playing in Oklahoma City. I was surprised to find that part of Paul's daily routine was to pick up teammate J.R. Smith every morning. If Smith wasn't awake yet, Paul would honk his horn, call Smith's phone and, eventually, use the garage code to enter and wake the slumbering 21-year-old. Now *that* is a point guard.

Then there are players who lead by being the loudest, most confident guy in the room. Denver Nuggets point guard Chauncey Billups describes it this way: "My teammates can look at me, and they can draw strength from my demeanor." Jameer Nelson, the Orlando Magic point guard, thinks it's an innate quality, saying, "A lot of people don't want to be the guy that tells somebody what to do, no matter how old they are." Baron Davis is so comfortable being that guy that when he would play in high-level summer pickup games at Pauley Pavilion in Los Angeles while still in high school, even though he was significantly younger than his college and pro teammates, he had no problem handling the ball and ordering people around. "His presence was just so big," says Woolery, who played in those games with Davis. "Even though he was playing NBA guys, he was still the most vocal guy on the court. Some of those guys just have it."

Nash, on the other hand, is an assimilator. He sees the sacred duty of the point guard as "to never lose the trust of your teammates and maintain a sense of team unity." This makes him a spiritual descendant of Celtics great Bob Cousy, who once said, "The playmaker has to be a respectable shooter, but scoring is not his real function. He has to keep the other four guys happy. He has to pass out the sugar."

"Nashie dunked it!"

It's the winter of 2006, and it's relative mayhem at Phoenix Suns practice. Coaches are smiling, players are whooping. Moments ago, at the urging of Raja Bell, the team's short, white, thirtysomething point guard leaped off two feet, caught an alley-oop pass and jammed it down. He then rose up off his right foot and threw down a one-handed dunk.

The how-did-he-do-it jokes in response to Nash's rare dunks are something he is accustomed to and an indicator of the most pervasive stereotype about him: that he is an overachieving nonathlete who's made good purely on smarts and hustle (the "short white kid from Canada"). But to suggest that Nash isn't a good athlete is to define the term in the most narrow fashion. In many regards he is one of the best athletes in the NBA. Growing up, he was the best baseball player in his town, excelled at lacrosse and hockey, and was named the player of the year for all of British Columbia high school soccer. As a 10th-grader the spindly Nash even won the provincial discus championship, and at St. Michael's he was so good at rugby that Hyde-Lay, who was also the school's rugby coach, thinks he could have played professionally. "He was the best placekicker I've ever seen, professional or amateur in any sport, and I'm counting guys in the NFL too," says Hyde-Lay. "He could kick equally well with both feet, and for a placekicker that is unheard of. That just does not happen, even at pro-level rugby."

Whitley, the Mavs trainer and Nash's friend, is used to his versatility by now. "He pretty much wins at everything he does," says Whitley, who despite being a college athlete himself (basketball), lists arm wrestling and beer chugging as the only two events in which he can take Nash. "Ping-Pong, tennis, whatever. He won't pick up a golf club for nine months, and then he'll shoot in the low 80s. His hand-eye coordination is amazing."

"Did he really just make that pass?"

Now it is April 2007, and the Suns are playing the Mavs in front of 20,000 at U.S. Airways Center in Phoenix on a Sunday afternoon, their matchup beamed to millions more via ABC. It is the height of D'Antoni's reign as Suns coach, during the heyday of the Seven Seconds or Less offense, and Nash is pushing the Suns at their typical breathtaking pace. As usual, in doing so he makes a handful of passes that, if he were anyone but Steve Nash, would give a coach a coronary. A couple in particular stand out.

Early in the first half Nash grabs a rebound and sprints up the floor. Seeing a cutter on the opposite side of the court, he unleashes a lefthanded scoop pass from outside the three-point line. The ball skips through a crevice in the defense, like a putt on a miniature golf course sneaking by the cycling arms of the windmill, and into the hands of a teammate, who lays it in. It is a ridiculously difficult pass, but Nash makes it so often that assistant coach Alvin Gentry even has a name for it: the Southpaw Slinger. Explains Gentry, "What's most impressive about that pass is he can start it, and if the defense sags to the middle, he can pull it back."

A few minutes later, Nash is dribbling along the right wing when, without breaking stride, he slices a righthanded backdoor bounce pass to Suns guard Leandro Barbosa for a layup. The play appears to occur almost instantaneously because Nash doesn't change anything—the height of his dribble, his speed, the position of his body—to ready the pass. He continues dribbling and then, merely by moving his hand from over the ball to behind it, redirects it to Barbosa. In doing so he throws the ball not to where Barbosa is, but rather to where he *will be*—seeing not just the court but, in a sense, the future. Woolery uses a photographic analogy. "It's almost like he takes a snapshot when he gets the ball in transition and then he can anticipate where that picture is going to be in two or three dribbles," says Woolery. "I've never seen anything like it."

That both of these passes are made with one hand is not surprising. During the game, by my unofficial count, 47 of the 68 passes that Nash throws are essentially one-handed. When I report this number to Nash, he is a bit surprised ("Really? *Forty-seven?*"), but he explains that, like those unconventional wrong-footed layups, it's a matter of adapting to the situation. "If I could make every pass with two hands, I would," he says. "In this league, with the length of the athletes, the spaces close so quickly. So if I gather with two hands every time, that just cuts down exponentially the amount of avenues and openings on the court."

Nash has had such success with the one-handed pass that he has altered the perception of this once-frowned-upon play. David Thorpe at the IMG academy (Chapter 8) now instructs his pro prospects to fling one-handers, yelling out, "Make a Nash pass!" It's an acceptance D'Antoni has been campaigning for for years. "Sometimes we're slow on teaching things," he says. "Most coaches teach you to put two hands on it, and to be honest with you, we probably need to teach kids to throw with one hand. Sometimes I think we limit."

Then again, there are probably only certain players who possess the hand-eye to consistently and effectively make such passes. (Larry Bird sees plenty of players who fall prey to the Magic Johnson effect. "Magic was bad for basketball in one way," Bird, then the coach of the Pacers, wrote in *Bird Watching*. "He made all these great passes, and then everyone else started trying to do it. You have to be special to thread the needle the way he did, or fire off those no-look passes. Magic knew how to do it. Most players don't.") When I ask Barbosa, the Suns' backup point guard, about the Nash slice pass, he shakes his head. "He has talent no one can get," Barbosa says. "I know how to catch that pass, but to throw it is tough."

"He missed the layup!"

It's the spring of 2009, the Suns are playing the Magic in Phoenix, and the announcers are astonished that Suns backup forward Jared Dudley has muffed an easy one.

It has been a rough season for both Nash and the Suns. New coach

Terry Porter installed a slow-down, bang-it-inside offense at the beginning of the year, causing Kevin Arnovitz of TrueHoop to describe Nash as looking "like a hummingbird trapped in a sandwich bag." Porter was then fired at midseason, replaced by Gentry, and the team, full of mismatched parts, has yet to jell. Nash clearly pines for the days of D'Antoni.

Yet as always Nash remains positive, at least around his teammates. In this case, Nash drives baseline at the end of a closely contested first half, elevating and sneaking a pass around the defense to Dudley, who needs but reach up and lay the ball in. Only Dudley flubs the gimme. Fortunately, reserve center Robin Lopez is there to follow it, but *he* misses the tip from a foot away. The halftime buzzer sounds, and Dudley and Lopez are both visibly angry at themselves, the former swearing and the latter shaking his head. Before either can react further, however, Nash sprints over and slaps hands with Lopez, then pats him on the back and whispers something in his ear before hurrying to do the same to Dudley, extending his hand for a quick high five.

It is one of dozens Nash will dispense on this night. In fact, he does more high-fiving than just about any other NBA player, though it's not your traditional high five, thrust in celebration, but more of a five-digit pat on the back, a raised hand in acknowledgment. It says, *I see you* or *Nice play* or, more often, *We'll get them next time,* a recurring connection between point guard and teammate that is both verbal and physical.

Naturally, this type of support endears Nash to his teammates, who speak almost reverently about him at times. To talk to Barbosa is to receive the equivalent of a Steve Nash infomercial. Barbosa speaks earnestly about how Nash is his "best friend," how he takes tapes of Nash back home to Brazil in the off-season so he can study them and how "in hard times and good times, Steve is always there."

Woolery says he's never met another player who makes people feel the way Nash does. "He's just a good guy," he says. "I know that's trite, but when I see him, he welcomes me like we were best friends in college, and we weren't. We were teammates and worked hard together, but he welcomes me like we're family. He's a better friend to me than I am to him, and *he's* the NBA guy. I mean seriously, he is."

With a bit of prodding from me, Nash attempts some self-analysis. "It's my nature to be good to people," he says. "It's almost a negative thing, to want to be liked, to want to be accommodating. At the same time I think that's a positive to try to live that way. I try to be good to people, especially those that mean a lot to me. John [Woolery] was not only a good friend but a great opponent to learn from."

In light of this I suggest that, if we boil it down, perhaps the secret to being a great point guard involves something as simple as wanting to be liked. Just as Kobe Bryant would not make a good point guard because he doesn't give a damn what people think of him, Nash is successful because he does. "Of course that helps me as a point guard, having those qualities," Nash says, nodding. "Wanting everyone to have a good time, wanting everyone to feel good about themselves, the assist thing, wanting to set up my teammates." He pauses. "Those are natural instincts that other guys might not have. It feels *good* for me to get in the paint and set up a shot for someone else. It feels *good* for me to see that person have a chance to do something good."

Thus, you could say that by being so unselfish Nash is, in a way, being selfish. He is doing what he wants (passing), and that happens to result in what his teammates want (receiving passes). Nash nods at the thought. "If it didn't feel as good, I probably would shoot more, and then I'd be a different player."

It occurs to me that the way Nash runs the Suns' offense is much like the way a masterly CEO runs a company, not only keeping the enterprise humming with a tidy profit margin but also inspiring employees and boosting morale. The renowned business author Peter Drucker once wrote an essay titled, "What Makes an Effective Executive." Based on six decades of studying corporate leaders, he found the successful ones were all over the map in terms of personality. But they almost uniformly followed eight practices: They asked, "What needs to be done?"; developed action plans; asked, "What's right for the enterprise?"; took responsibility for decisions; took responsibility for communicating; focused on opportunities rather than problems; ran productive meetings; and thought and said *We* rather than *I*.

It's an imperfect analogy, obviously—Nash gets no golden parachute if he ever gets cut, for instance—but it's noteworthy that so many similarities exist between Nash and a successful CEO. Nash plays a team-first game (what's right for the enterprise/*we* rather than *I*), holds himself accountable (takes responsibility for decisions/communicating), remains positive with teammates and turns his weaknesses into strengths (focuses on opportunities rather than problems) and thinks strategically about how to win games (develops action plans). Indeed, in most every regard Nash fits Drucker's idea of a good CEO, save one. Drucker believes that to be an effective leader one needn't be liked, whereas Nash believes this is paramount. Which is just another reason why little boys idolize basketball players, not Wall Street tycoons.

"We're talking about a pickup game?"

It is a cool evening in Phoenix in April 2009, and Nash is sitting in a leather chair in a coaches' room in the lower level of U.S. Airways Center, talking about leadership. I've posited to him an (unlikely) hypothetical: He walks into a gym for an impromptu pickup game, and a regular guy (like me or, perhaps, you) joins his team. How does he integrate the new guy? Or does he?

He thinks for a moment. "Well, the first thing I'd do is find out what position you play and where you like to get the ball."

Once he does that, however, he would not pass it you. Not yet, at least. First he'd "observe your skill level," as he puts it, like some anthropologist of the hardwood. "I want to see if you can play or not and if you should get the ball, and how much."

If you earned a shot and made it, Nash would try to pump you up, though not necessarily in the interest of having you shoot again. Rather he'd want to "give you confidence and energy and encourage you, so you'll play harder defensively and hustle." He pauses. "But if you make your first shot and it looks terrible, even though it went in, I'm going to try to avoid having that happen again."

Now, let's say your first shot not only looked horrific but missed badly. Like side-of-the-backboard badly. And let's say that, even so, you refused to stop shooting. His hand forced, Nash would first try diplomacy, saying something like, "Look for me when you get the rebound and get me the ball so I can get us a good shot." If this didn't work, then Nash would have no choice but to employ the nuclear option of any point guard: He'd freeze you out. "What can you do?" he says with a sigh. "If you're stuck with a guy who just doesn't get it or is selfish, it's tough at any level."

Then I ask him about the reverse of the situation. This is even less credible as a hypothetical, but let's say Nash showed up to play a pickup game and, by some strange occurrence, nobody knew who *he* was. In this case the regulars would probably look at him and—let's be honest here—not exactly be blown away. Let's see: He's six-foot-very-little and about a buck-eighty, max.

So how would the short, oldish white guy take control of the game?

For the answer to this, we turn to D'Antoni, who knows Nash better than just about anyone in the league. "He'd be the guy who would just move the ball," says D'Antoni. "When you play with a guy like Steve, you automatically throw the ball to him because you know he's not going to just jack it up, and he'd be setting picks for other guys and getting them open. The game would become very simple, and the players playing with him would be like, 'Oh, it's really easy.' You just come off a pick and the ball will be right there and you just shoot. They would just gravitate to him, and unconsciously or not, the ball would go to him and he'd do the right thing."

So Nash would make all of the YMCA dreamers feel good, setting them up for open shots and propelling the squad to a high level—"making the game fun," as D'Antoni puts it. And then, if it were close at the end? D'Antoni grins. "Then he'd probably score the last 10 points and win the game."

The Defensive Specialist: Stranded on Kobe Island with Shane Battier

Pity the perimeter defender.

Often referred to as a "stopper" or a "lockdown defender," he is nothing of the kind. Assigned to guard the opposing team's best player, he knows before the game begins that he will likely get torched. This is not baseball, where a pitcher can strike out a batter four times and be done with him; in basketball, a star scorer can miss his first 10 shots yet still have time (and license) to hoist 20 more. As such, no matter how effectively our man does his job, he's going to be scored on, and usually in ways some might find embarrassing. Slippery drives, crazy step-back jumpers, perhaps a vicious dunk or two. The reality of the NBA is that there are certain offensive moves that are unguardable. If Kobe Bryant wants to take a fadeaway 25-foot jump shot, he can, and he may well hit it. If Ray Allen runs off of five screens, chances are he's going to eventually get open for a three-pointer—and all the TV audience is going to see is our guy flying in at the last minute, flailing at the shot, too late to stop it.

A good night for the perimeter defender really comes down to one question: Did his team win? If the answer is yes, then the point total of the opposing star is irrelevant. The defensive specialist will gladly—O.K., perhaps grudgingly—live with a 40-point night if it requires the star to take 35 shots in a losing cause. Regardless, there is little glory for our man afterward. But that's not why he plays. "You're never in the limelight and you've probably been that way most of your career," explains Nate McMillan, the Blazers coach who spent his 12-year NBA playing career as a defensive-minded guard for the Seattle SuperSonics. "You don't need the attention to go out and play. You're caught up in your own little game, your own little world, and whether you get recognized or not, it doesn't make a difference because if you needed that attention, you would have stopped doing it long ago."

While the value of a player like McMillan is fully apparent to his teammates—who adore him like that guy who's always willing to loan you money—it isn't always clear to casual fans, who see his typical stat line and find it mystifying: 36 minutes, five points, three rebounds, two assists, one steal. That guy, they say, isn't doing much out there.

And when he *is* in the limelight, it's often for the wrong reasons.

Remember Craig Ehlo? To a certain generation of basketball fans, let's say roughly those age 25 and under, Ehlo's name probably doesn't register. Unless, that is, they're familiar with his one (rather spectacular) cameo in NBA history. It lasted about three seconds and took place at the end of a deciding game in the first round of the 1989 Eastern Conference playoffs, in a series pitting the Cavaliers against the Bulls. It began with Ehlo, a 6'7" small forward then playing for Cleveland, sprinting toward the sideline in pursuit of his man. Reversing direction, Ehlo then hustled back to the middle of the court, where he arrived just in time to leap at a certain lanky, tongue-baring Chicago shooter. As Ehlo flew in, however, the shooter merely hung in the air, patiently waiting for Ehlo to clear his airspace before rattling in a 16-foot jumper from near the free throw line. Afterward, the two men headed in opposite directions: Michael Jordan into the air to celebrate and Ehlo to the floor, where he covered his face, as if he'd just been teargassed. Two decades later, when ESPN named the top 10 plays of Jordan's career, the network deemed this moment No. 1, for it perfectly captured the rise of MJ, signifying the Bulls toppling of the Cavs as Eastern powerhouse. Of course, it also immortalized Ehlo, who remains frozen in time as That Guy MJ Left Flailing. (What no one remembers is that the Cavs player who hit the shot to give Cleveland the lead just before Jordan's famous shot was . . . Ehlo. "It was the best playoff game of my career," Ehlo says with a laugh. "I scored the last eight points for us. But ask anybody about that game and what happened, and they say, 'Cleveland scored [before MJ hit the jumper],' and I say, 'Yeah, but *who* scored?'")

Most fans, when they think of the play, remember Michael's greatness. Jordan, it is assumed, just sank a tough shot because he is a superior player. Because *that's what he does*. And to a certain extent, that's correct. Though it's been 20 years, Ehlo says people still come up to him almost every week to talk about it, and most say the same thing: *Hey, you were in great position*. And in response, Ehlo will say, "I appreciate that," then shrug and say, "There was nothing more I could do." Deep down, though, Ehlo knows this isn't true. "When Michael got to the wing, I was running instead of sliding; that was the problem," he explains. "If you look at it, Michael stops on a dime and goes straight up, and I go flying by him. In my own mind I think, 'Oh, man, if I hadn't been out of position, I could have stopped that shot.' I had a hand in his face but only for a split second. But people still say, 'Hey, you were in great position.'" Ehlo laughs. "Maybe they're just ignorant."

Perhaps. And this is part of what makes the defensive specialist's craft so exacting; he is at times applauded for things he does wrong (like gambling for high-risk steals) and blamed for things he does right. But he can never lie to himself. Plenty of times Ehlo played perfect defense on Jordan yet still gave up a bucket. Ehlo remembers Jordan once coming off a down screen in the triangle offense. Reading the play, Ehlo stepped out into the passing lane, only Jordan instinctively countered him by stepping back, where he caught the ball, changed direction and hit a jump shot.

"How did you do that?" Ehlo asked as they ran back down the court. "I totally had you covered on that one."

Jordan shrugged his shoulders. "I don't know, Craig," Jordan said. "It just happened."

Of course, nobody ever figured out how to stop Michael Jordan when he was Just Happening. Many were the nights when Ehlo would spend 40 minutes shadowing MJ only to surrender four-dozen points and secure goat status in the eyes of Cavs fans. Cleveland trainer Gary Briggs knew better. Says Ehlo, "After the game, Gary would look me dead square in the eye and say, 'He may have scored 45 points, but you were dead in his shit all night. You were on him all night.'" Ehlo pauses. "And that was all I needed to hear."

When it comes to guarding an elite scorer like Jordan, there are various ways to prepare for the challenge. On one end of the spectrum we have Stacey Augmon, the 15-year NBA veteran who earned the nickname Plastic Man for his freakishly long arms and his ability to use them defensively.

At the U.S. Olympic Basketball Trials in 1988, Augmon was a relatively obscure, wispy-thin college sophomore at UNLV. During scrimmages he was assigned to guard Hersey Hawkins, the reigning NCAA scoring champion and a man with a vast repertoire of offensive moves. To the surprise of the U.S. coaching staff, Augmon not only held his own against Hawkins but was the only player during the trials who proved effective in slowing him down. This was no mean feat, as the group assembled included future NBAers like Sean Elliott, Mitch Richmond, Rex Chapman and Alonzo Mourning. At the end of the week one of the U.S. assistants approached Augmon and commended him. "You did a great job on Hawkins," the coach said.

Replied Augmon: "Who's he?"

Today, Augmon could never get away with such blissful ignorance. Coaches in college and the pros alike hammer their players with information—Cavaliers coach Mike Brown calls it KYP, as in Know Your Personnel—believing it a crucial tenet of team defense. To walk into most NBA locker rooms before a game is to see a small snowfall of scouting reports draped over players' chairs, many full of arcane stats.

For most players this is a lot to take in. But for Shane Battier, the Houston Rockets forward and defensive specialist extraordinaire, scouting reports are just one element of an approach to perimeter defense that is so comprehensive as to be almost scary. Battier memorizes the top 20 or so plays of every opposing team and, upon recognizing these plays during the game, calls out the "action"—say, a pick-and-roll coming left or a clear-out to the right—to alert his teammates. Sometimes he picks up the play as soon as the opposing coach calls it out. Some coaches, such as Gregg Popovich of the Spurs, have taken to trying to shield their calls from Battier, using a clipboard or an angled palm at the lips, but it does little good; he usually picks them up regardless. Battier's knowledge of the opposition is so keen that, were he to be traded, he says, he could credibly step in midseason for any team in the league on a moment's notice. "I could be traded to Utah tonight and go in tomorrow morning and have a very loose interpretation of how to run their offense," he says. "I could go to San Antonio—they've been running the same stuff forever. I could run their offense. Stick me in the game, and I could do O.K. after no practices." Told of this, Warriors forward Stephen Jackson, a defensive specialist himself, raises his eyebrows. "Now *that* is impressive," Jackson says. "Over the course of a game I might pick up a play or two, but knowing them beforehand? Damn."

But this is how Battier's mind operates. Here's a guy who, at age 14, began making a list of 10 goals per year and has continued to do it ever since. (No longer, however, does he include "Building a giant city out of Legos," an item from his first list.) His evolution from all-around player to defensive specialist, though, has been a gradual one. As a senior at Detroit Country Day High School in 1997 he was the Naismith player of the year. At Duke, he was a star on both ends of the floor, setting school records for blocked shots and finishing eighth on the school's alltime scoring list while receiving the Naismith and Wooden awards as national player of the year as a senior. Early in his NBA career he was a capable scorer, averaging 14.4 ppg as a rookie for Memphis; at 6'8", 220 pounds, he was versatile enough to play multiple positions. The longer he played in the league, though, the more he realized that he was built for D. (He hasn't averaged more than 10.1 ppg since that rookie season.) "I don't have an offensive mind," he explains. "Some people are brilliantly creative offensively. I'm not that way. I can't see how plays develop on offense, but I can see how plays develop defensively and what the rotation should be, two to three passes from the current point during the play."

Thus Battier has embraced defense and become *that* guy for the Rockets, the one assigned to guard the opposing team's best wing player. One night it's LeBron James, the next it's Kobe Bryant. For a "breather" he will face Danny Granger or some other up-and-coming gunslinger. For the most part he has been unheralded, only making the All-Defensive team twice (he was selected to the second team in 2007–08 and 2008–09) and finishing third in voting for the Defensive Player of the Year once in 2007–08. Yet every season, no matter where he's played, Battier has made his team better on defense. His team consistently allows fewer points with him on the floor than off it, sometimes dramatically so. (Per 100 possessions, the difference by year in his seven seasons has been: -1.5, -1.4, -6.1, -7.0, -3.7, -0.9, -1.6.) Those whose opinion matters most—that is, NBA coaches— know how effective he is. "He has size and strength, but he's also got the intelligence," says Mike Malone, the Cavaliers' lead defensive assistant. "A lot of guys have the ability but not the desire. You have to say, 'I'm going to shut this motherfucker down.' You have to *want* it, and Shane wants it."

Battier's preparation is meticulous, his approach to each game minutely detailed. "He's become a student of it to where he's damn near perfected it, in the sense that he's gone to this next level of preparation, really getting into the scouting reports, studying teams' tendencies, players' tendencies," says McMillan. "There aren't many players who've ever committed to defending like that."

I headed to Portland in November 2008 to meet up with Battier with the goal of deconstructing his approach to the game. The Rockets were in town to play the Trailblazers in an early-season game, but Battier was on the shelf, still recovering from a bruised left foot, and it was driving him bonkers. (At one point he told me, only half in jest, that he was actually angry at his foot for letting him down.)

Over beers at a hotel bar Battier broke down his defensive philosophy, his tactics and his feelings about the game. He was surprisingly open. Some defenders, namely Spurs forward Bruce Bowen, are loath to discuss their strategies. When I approached Bowen during the 2008 playoffs to talk about how he guards Kobe, I mentioned a couple of the little tricks he used. He pretended not to know what I was talking about. When I told him it was Bryant who'd clued me in, he acted as if I was speaking Romanian. Even when I offered to go off the record, because now I was just curious, Bowen smiled and promised he knew not of which I spoke.

Battier was quite the opposite. It became clear during the conversation, however, that to truly appreciate Battier's skills, I would have to do more than listen to him—I would need to watch him in action. We made plans to meet up again in Houston later during the season, when he was healthy.

In the interim, a curious thing happened: At 30 years old, seven years into his career, Battier finally, and suddenly, got his due. In mid-February, Battier appeared on the cover of *The New York Times Magazine,* alongside the headline THE NO-STATS ALL STAR. The story was written by Michael Lewis, author of the acclaimed baseball book *Moneyball.* As one would expect from Lewis, his Battier story was excellent, focusing on the way Rockets general manager Daryl Morey used statistical measures to provide Battier with small advantages as a defender. The story was widely discussed, at least on sports blogs. One enterprising writer for *Slate* even attempted to apply the Battier principles to his own pickup game, wondering What Would Shane Battier Do? (Alas, he got tired too quickly to find out.)

So when I headed to Houston in late February to see Battier again, I assumed that the unheralded forward would now be heralded. And he was. Sort of.

He said he'd heard from plenty of people about the story. Old Duke teammates, friends, college professors.

But within the NBA?

"Not a single person mentioned it," he said.

"Not even Elton Brand?" I asked, figuring Battier's old Duke team-mate would have had something to say.

Nope.

Any Rockets players?

None.

While I think the indifference of his peers bothered Battier a bit, it also meant that most hadn't read the story, and that meant he retained his competitive advantage. If they hadn't learned anything about the tactics he was using, then he'd have no trouble continuing to use them.

He'd need all of those tactics and more during the two games I watched on my visit. Each presented a dramatically different challenge. First Houston hosted the Portland Trailblazers, featuring All-Star shooting guard Brandon Roy. Two days later the Cleveland Cavaliers and LeBron James came to town, meaning Battier's man-to-man coverage (against Portland) would be just as valuable as his help-side defense (against LeBron).

Tuesday, February 24: Houston Rockets vs. Portland Trailblazers

10 a.m. The Rockets meet for morning shootaround at the Toyota Center in downtown Houston. As the team walks through plays, Battier occasionally stops coach Rick Adelman with questions, asking about a rotation here, a potential mismatch there. He does this for his own benefit, of course, but also for his teammates. "NBA players are no different from high schoolers in chemistry class," Battier says. "They're afraid to ask questions because they're afraid they'll look stupid."

One might think Battier could come off as a bit of a know-it-all, but he is smart enough to frame questions and suggestions as team issues, not personal ones. "He is a perfect teammate," says Rockets center Yao Ming. Then, to stress the word, Yao says it again. "*Teammate*. He could fit in on any team tomorrow."

5 p.m. Battier arrives at the Toyota Center for the 7:30 game and heads to the hot tub in the training room. For 15 minutes he soaks his feet as he works through the night's 48-page scouting report. Whereas the rest of the Rockets receive the same standard scouting reports, Battier gets his own special printout of information from Morey and assistant G.M. Sam Hinkie. Tonight's provides an in-depth breakdown of Roy, who is an especially tough matchup for Battier. Unlike many NBA players, who have obvious preferences and known weaknesses, Roy is remarkably well-balanced as a player. He is equally effective going left (scoring .91 points per possession) and going right (.92), though he shows a slight preference for driving left (54% of the time to 46% of the time). He is above average as a spot-up shooter, three-point shooter, in the post and in the pick-and-roll.

As he soaks and reads, Battier formulates his individual game plan— "within the team framework, of course," as he puts it. The overriding goal is to limit the other team's field goal percentage. Battier, a big football fan, likes to compare it to rushing yards in football; average more than 4.5 a carry and a team usually wins. "It's the same thing in basketball," he says. "If you're able to hold your opponent to under 44 percent shooting, you're in a pretty good position to win. Hold them to 43 percent or 42 percent, and you've got a great shot to win." Doing this, of course, starts with the top scorer, who may well take one third of his team's shots. On this night, peering at the numbers and remembering his past encounters, Battier decides he is going to encourage Roy to drive left. He has his reasons.

6:02 p.m. Taped and dressed, Battier jogs from the locker room to the court to go through his pregame shooting routine. It is the only time during the day that he will focus on his individual offense, cycling through a handful of post-up moves, mid-range jumpers and three-pointers, making 10 to 12 from each spot before moving on.

For the Rockets, everything Battier contributes on offense is essentially gravy, so long as he can swing the ball and drop in an occasional open three to keep the defense honest. This is not to say he doesn't have standards. His "barometer," as he puts it, has long been to be a "170 guy"—40% on threes, 50% from the field and 80% on free throws. It has so far proved an ambitious goal; the closest Battier has come was his second season in the league, when he went 39.8%/48.3%/82.8%.

6:16 p.m. As he does before most every game, Battier sits down with Hinkie, the assistant G.M., in this case on a couple of chairs courtside as the arena slowly fills with fans, to pepper him with questions. Affable and unassuming, Hinkie is a Stanford MBA who specializes in quantitative analysis and is, for Battier, the link to all those numbers. Sweat beading on his shaved skull, Battier interrogates Hinkie about details that concern him, saying things you don't usually hear on a basketball court, like, "I was confused by this perceived contradiction."

Most of what Battier asks about is information that falls into a gray area. "He's very smart, but he gets nervous and anxious before games," explains Hinkie. "So if there are two low-percentage options, he'll want to know which one he should choose. And the sample size might be 11 on one and seven on the other, so I can't tell him one way or the other." The solution? "I might say, Do whatever keeps Yao out of foul trouble." Hinkie laughs. "Shane's like me. In general, he wants rules. 'If A happens, then do B, and then C. . . .'"

In the case of Roy, Battier is curious about what to do on pick-and-rolls. He asks Hinkie whether it's worth going under the screens sometimes instead of over them ("Not a bad idea; try it a few possessions," is Hinkie's take) and about sending Roy right instead of left on occasion ("Not advised," says Hinkie).

6:24 p.m. Jogging back to the locker room, Battier stops to sign autographs along the side of the stands, as he does before every game. He jokes, grins, holds a fan's camera up to get a shot of the two of them together. Battier has a philosophy on this, as he does on most everything. "I like to sign autographs for people who actually buy a ticket to an NBA game," he explains. "It's like 'You help me, I'll help you.' It's like going up to someone and saying, 'Hey, give me 20 dollars.' Why? 'Because you have it and you should.' No! It's like, 'Sign this ball.' Why? 'Because you should.' No, it doesn't work that way. If you want to come see a game and support the NBA, I'll support you."

After signing eight autographs—he varies between seven and 10 or so depending on the night—Battier continues his jog toward the

locker room, slapping hands with fans and fist-bumping Dikembe
Mutombo, the 41-year-old backup center who moves as languorously
as Battier does hurriedly, each methodical step making him look like a
jersey-clad Imperial Walker.

Watch Battier long enough, and you'll realize that he runs just about
everywhere. From the locker room to the court. From the court to the
locker room. From the huddle to the game. From the game to the huddle. It's as if he is engaged in his own strange, inter-arena decathlon. He
says he does it in part to keep loose, a practice he learned at Duke, but
mainly because he is something of an efficiency obsessive. "It's such a
long walk, and I just want to get there," Battier explains of traipsing the
75 yards or so from the court to the locker room. "I'd always rather do
my work early and then relax. Versus procrastinate, procrastinate, procrastinate, then work. Just do your work early and play later. That's the
way I am. I take that to the extreme, running off the court each time."

Asked about it, Hinkie laughs. "His routine is so meticulous that if
the trainer answers a phone call while Shane is getting his ultrasound,
Shane tells him to get off. His thought is, 'It's 92 minutes until game
time. This is my time.'"

6:28 p.m. As Battier stretches in the training room with David Macha,
the team's strength coach, twin monitors nearby cycle through various
esoteric stats, each meant to motivate the Rockets.

One screen shows turnovers forced per 100 possessions, highlight-
ing a Houston weakness. (The Rockets are 29th in the league at 13.9
per.) Another ranks Rockets players by percentage of shots taken that
are "high quality"—defined as three-pointers, free throws and shots
in the lane. Not surprisingly, Battier leads the team at 79%. Near the
bottom is star wing player Tracy McGrady, who is close to the league
average of 63%. On this night, as he has been for much of the season,
McGrady is hurt.

7:20 p.m. After a pregame team meeting, Battier is back on the court
for layup lines. While other players practice crowd-pleasing dunks,
joke around and chat with players on the other team, Battier runs his
layups with precision, claps his hands and, inside, quietly dies. This,
he says, is by far his least favorite part of the night.

Part of the reason is that Battier dislikes the fraternizing. "I want to
play the game and go home," he says. "If I have one of my boys there

Kobe Bryant's need to win is obsessive; says a teammate, "He can't turn it off, even if he tried."

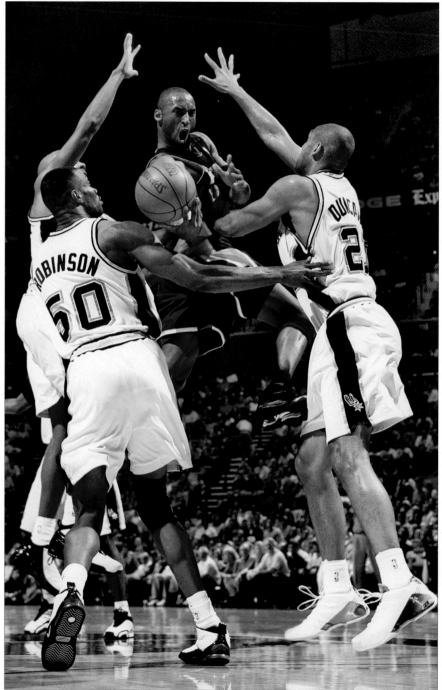

When Kobe "goes off," it's a mesmerizing thing to watch; like the man himself, it's never subtle.

JEFF HAYNES/AFP/GETTY IMAGES

GENE LOWER/SPORTS ILLUSTRATED

In the third quarter of a 2003 playoff game, Steve Kerr entered the game cold and swished 4-of-4 three-pointers.

The author challenged Kerr to a shooting duel with hopes for an upset, but the master schooled the pupil.

The math says more rebounds equals more possessions, but, says Ben Wallace, "It's really an art."

The perfect rebounding specimen, Dwight Howard has a chance to set a lofty benchmark: 15 boards per game.

JOHN BIEVER/SPORTS ILLUSTRATED

The ease of a Shaquille O'Neal dunk has led some to suggest the basket be raised to 12 feet, a notion scorned by NBA players.

In a 2007 playoff game, Baron Davis rose for his ferocious facial of the taller
Andrei Kirilenko—and the rest is dunking history.

In an infamous failure at the line, Nick Anderson missed four consecutive free throws, and fans have never let him forget it.

Bedeviled by the game's simplest shot, Shaq has missed more free throws in his career than Larry Bird attempted in his.

Steve Nash's preference for passing caused one coach to demand that he shoot at least 10 times a game. It didn't work.

Craig Ehlo's name is etched in NBA history for one play: a 1989 playoff shot by Michael Jordan that Ehlo couldn't defend. Game over.

Shane Battier took on Kobe Bryant in the 2009 playoffs; Kobe got his points, but Battier burnished his reputation as an elite defender.

Yao Ming presents the Rockets with a medical dilemma: How to keep a body of such massive size from breaking apart.

Is the blocked shot a dying craft? It's a skill of underappreciated difficulty, but Emeka Okafor, with his 88-inch wingspan, is a modern master.

Alonzo Mourning, demonstrating his shot-blocking technique on Dirk Nowitzki, says, "Jumping isn't even important. It's timing."

LeBron James likes to keep his actual weight a secret—250? 260? 270?—but when he sets a pick, his amazing body is punishing.

Already a physical "freak," LeBron got even better with Lasik eye surgery in 2007. "It's cool," he says, "because I can see stuff."

from Memphis or Duke, I'll talk to him after the game. Before the game is not really the time to do that stuff."

What irks him more, though, is the empty time. For a man who runs to the locker room to save 45 seconds, 10 minutes of going through the motions is an eternity. "If I could just come to the gym, read my scouting report and then play, I'm happy," he says. "There's so much dead time. We shoot layups for like three minutes, and from 15 minutes to five minutes [counting down on the clock], it's free shooting. I'm already warm, I got my shots up, I'm ready to play." Battier pauses. "I calculated it. At 90 games a year, that 10 minutes of dead time means I've wasted hours and hours of my life just waiting for the game to start. To a person who values efficiency, it just kills me. By the time the game tips at 7:35, it's like, 'All right, finally.'"

First Quarter

11:55 on the game clock As planned, Battier starts the game on Roy, though he will occasionally switch with Ron Artest, the burly Rockets forward and former Defensive Player of the Year. Together, they give Houston the best pair of perimeter defenders in the league, especially considering that the two employ such different styles. While Battier is cerebral, playing percentages and angles, Artest relies on instinct, strength—at 6' 7", he weighs 250 pounds—and anticipation to bully opposing players and create turnovers. This gives the Rockets the option, as Houston assistant coach T.R. Dunn puts it, of switching between "fundamental" (Battier) or "aggressive" (Artest) at any moment. In the case of Roy, Battier is the better choice most of the time, as his attention span is, shall we say, longer than Artest's. "Ron doesn't like to run through all those screens, and I don't mind," says Battier. "I'm not saying I'm great at it. But I can sort of dictate and make the guy catch in the area where he doesn't want to catch."

It's easy to get a first impression, when watching Battier in action, that he's not really doing much. He crouches in his stance and shadows Roy, but he neither crowds nor bumps him. Indeed, in general Battier doesn't wave his arms, or slap the floor, or sprint back and forth, or gamble for steals, or any of the stuff that typically makes it *look* like one is playing defense. This ties in to the common perception that defense is really just a matter of effort, so can't anyone do it if he tries hard enough?

As you might imagine, this really pisses off Battier. "I tell little kids that defense is a matter of playing hard, but you also have to play smart," he says. "You have to understand what you can do and can't do. I'm not doing a service to my team if I'm running around like a maniac and fouling all over the place. When you foul a lot, that's bad defense because it allows the most efficient shot in basketball: the free throw. So much more goes into defense, and especially individual defense, than just playing hard. I've played plenty hard lots of times, and I've gotten torched on defense. That's just the way it is."

A fitting analogy might be racquetball. When people first play the game, they consider it a tremendous workout, primarily because they are going about it all wrong. Sprinting around the court, they whack the ball as hard as possible, sending it caroming off two or three walls, then rush back and forth from the front wall to the back to retrieve their opponent's shots. The better players, however, learn that the key to the game is a combination of shot placement and defense, with the goal being to spend as much time as possible anchored to the center of the court, where one can control the game. Similarly, Battier strives to occupy the most advantageous position at all times.

9:48 Roy gets the ball at the top of the key and drives to his left, seemingly right past Battier. To the untrained eye—hell, to the trained eye—it looks like Battier just got beat. But the defense was by design. "He rarely gets beat left or right," explains Hinkie. "If a guy is going left or right, it's because Shane wants him to go left or right. Now, he might have made the wrong choice, but it is his choice. In an iso situation, he fails in what he tries to do about five percent of the time."

In this case, it's something of a counterintuitive strategy. The numbers told Hinkie and Battier that Roy prefers to go left. So why are they letting him do what he wants? "Taking a player where they don't want to go isn't always the plan," explains Hinkie. "Sometimes, having them go where they're comfortable helps us because they might be more likely to self-destruct." By this Hinkie means that when a player has more shot options, odds are some of them won't be good ones (just as we all have a running hook or an ill-advised fadeaway in our repertoire that, if we're feeling good enough, we might pull out). "So he's more likely to feel comfortable and go to his full arsenal, whereas if he's uncomfortable, he might go to only one weapon, but it could be a really good one."

(As you can see, the task of interpreting statistics is never-ending. For example, if Player X has a low efficiency move—say a baseline fadeaway—is it because the player's not good at that particular move or is it instead because when the pressure's on, Player X *prefers* to go that way and often ends up taking that shot against a double team? Which in turn means that when there's not a double team, it could be a high efficiency move. Such are the questions that keep Battier and Hinkie up late.)

In this instance, Roy keeps charging to the rim, but, finding Yao awaiting, has to pass back out to Steve Blake, who misses a jumper. Battier fights for the rebound, tipping it to himself on the left baseline. For one play at least, the strategy worked.

7:43 Roy comes off a screen on the right wing and rises up for a jumper. Battier fights his way through the pick and leaps at Roy. For an instant it appears inevitable that the two men will collide, and if you were watching Battier for the first time, you might deduce that he is reckless. Then, in a feat of midair coordination, Battier turns sideways, his right leg leading the way, and he skims just past Roy, like a dance partner. Simultaneously, Battier extends his right hand so that it is inches from Roy's face, the fingers spread to obscure his vision. The shot sails left, caroming off the rim.

This is something of a calling card for Battier; as Hinkie says, "his greatest skill, by far, is contesting without fouling." Some defenders try for blocks on the perimeter (a risk), and others are content to "just get a hand up" while staying stationary; Battier has spent years honing this strange-looking leap. The goal is not to block the shot but rather to distract the shooter and make him think he is about to be fouled.

Depending on the situation, Battier has a whole arsenal of ways to contest a shot. When following a player around a screen toward the basket, he will come from behind and reach around the waist of the shooter, then bring his hand up from below the shooter's arm and in front of his face. (Battier demonstrates this to me during one of our conversations, and it is disquieting. It seems impossible that he won't hit you on the chin—akin to someone walking up behind you and surprising you with a bear hug.) In another variation, which I witness two nights later against Mo Williams of Cleveland, Battier leaps and jabs as if he's going to punch Williams in the stomach, then pulls his fist back at the last second.

Some players, frustrated by Battier's invasion of their personal space, lean or move to try to draw the foul. But when this happens, Battier feels he has the advantage. As he says, "Then I know they're reacting to me instead of focusing on the basket."

7:05 With the Blazers holding an early 10–6 lead, Battier runs back on defense, and as usual, his eyes are on Blazers coach Nate McMillan. The moment McMillan calls out the play—this time it's a simple Roy pick-and-roll with forward LaMarcus Aldridge—Battier starts shouting at his teammates.

"Coming to you, Luis," he says to Rockets forward Luis Scola. "Pick-and-roll, left side."

In calling out plays, Battier is sometimes interpreting a name—such as "horns down" or "motion strong"—while other times it is a number. (When Avery Johnson was the coach of the Mavs, for example, any play with a 7 in it was a pick-and-roll—37, 75, etc.) Or it can be a gesture; when the Clippers call fist up or fist down, it is a high pick-and-roll.

By yelling out both the play and what action is coming, Battier is accomplishing a number of things. First, he's preparing his teammates, who now know where to help. Second, he's preparing himself. And, perhaps most valuable, he is throwing off the offense. It's a trick he learned at Duke. "Even if I don't know the other team's plays, I'll call it out anyway," Battier says. "All of a sudden, if you have five guys saying, 'Oh, they know what we're running,' that puts them back on their heels a little bit."

So if a team calls, "red five," Battier will start yelling it—"RED FIVE, RED FIVE, RED FIVE"—even if he has no idea what it means (which is rare). "It's sort of the same as yelling, 'Ball ball ball ball' or 'Help, help, help,'" he explains. "If you hear that as an offensive player, you're much less apt to dive into the teeth of a defense. If you're around basketball, you know that when a team's getting its butt kicked, the players are silent. They're *passive*. That's why I try to be aggressive even vocally. I think it has a psychological effect."

In some cases, the greatest beneficiary of that psychological effect may be Battier himself. Says Rockets forward Chuck Hayes: "He'll call the action, but a lot of times he's guarding the best player, so the action is going at *him*."

6:56 On an isolation on the left wing, Battier again pushes Roy left, hoping to goad him into a baseline fadeaway, but Roy makes a nice step-through and gets to the rim, only to be met by Yao, who swats the shot off the board.

This is a luxury Battier didn't have early in his career. When Battier was in Memphis, the Grizzlies had no shot blockers inside, so, as Battier puts it, "I got stuck out on Kobe Island a lot of times." Explains Battier, "I knew I couldn't foul him because I had to stay in the game, and I didn't have much help behind me, so I had to be superpassive."

Battier pauses. "I'm lucky to have a guy like Yao. He's not the best shot blocker, not the fastest, but he's there. Chuck Hayes is an unbelievable help-side defender. It wasn't until I got better help behind and better interior defenders that all of a sudden my reputation as a defender grew. Is it a coincidence? I don't think so." He laughs.

"Not to take away from the great perimeter defenders in this league," he continues. "I think Ron's one of the best, I think Bruce Bowen's one of the best, I think Tayshaun Prince is one of the best, I think Kobe is one of the best. But they usually have guys behind them that make their job a heck of a lot easier."

Battier has never enjoyed what he calls the "mano a mano aspect that drives some defenders," preferring to play within a team scheme. But for some players the mano a mano attitude is the only way to survive. When I spoke with Nick Anderson, he of the four missed free throws, he told me that his strategy against Michael Jordan on the wing was to pretend the two of them were on the court alone. "I always looked at it like my help wasn't there," said Anderson. "I couldn't rely on help. Help might be there, help might not. I looked at it as if we were playing one-on-one."

Battier, who is ever aware of his help and will take teammates to task if it's late arriving, shakes his head when told of Anderson's strategy. "I think the opposite. I don't want to be on Kobe Island, I've been on Kobe Island enough in my career—it's not a fun place to be. I'm trying to get *off* Kobe Island."

Second Quarter

2:36 During a Rockets timeout, Battier leans in, sweat dripping, nodding along with Adelman. If Battier sees something he thinks is hurting the team defensively, he has license to speak up, an unusual privilege for a player. This has been the case his entire time in Houston. When Jeff Van Gundy was coach, he sometimes presented his game plan, saying something like, "If they do this, we rotate here, and if they do this, we rotate here, but if they do this, then we're screwed and that's on me. But I'm betting they're not going to do that." And sometimes Battier would offer a solution. "With most players, Van Gundy would have ignored them, or worse," says Hinkie. "With Shane, he'd go over it, and if Shane was right, he'd change the defense. It was like Shane was his partner."

29.6 With the half winding down, Roy drives left—toward the base-line and the help defense—but this time Battier can't keep up with him, and Houston teammate Von Wafer is forced to foul Roy to pre-vent the easy layup. Roy steps up to shoot his third and fourth free throws of the night (one of the first two was a technical), and Battier is visibly upset, slapping his hands together and murmuring, "Damn!"

In this instance Battier didn't want to foul, but this isn't always the case. Say he's face-guarding a player, hands up in his opponent's eyes as described earlier. On occasion Battier might tap him on the head when he contests, even if it leads to a whistle. "Every now and then I'll just take a foul," he says. "I'll hit the guy on the wrist or the elbow or even the face just to put that thought in the offensive player's mind. Because the offensive players, they don't like contact. Those are shoot-ers. They *do not* like to be touched. And anything I can do to keep a guy off guard and keep him guessing as to what I'm going to do, I'm going to do."

Moments later, the Rockets go into the half up 60–43. Roy has 12 points but has taken 13 shots, right in line with Battier's general goal against elite scorers: to limit free throws and field goal percent-age so they score one point or less for every shot they take. As he says, "Twenty-five points on 25 shots, and that's a good night for me."

Third Quarter

6:18 Seeing LaMarcus Aldridge spin to the middle, Battier helps off his man and pokes at the ball. It's the kind of quick, barely there play he makes dozens of times in a game. This time, however, he gets whistled for it. Battier turns to referee Scott Foster, amazed.

"You either have great eyesight or you're lucky as hell," Battier says. "You made an unbelievable call. I mean, I *never* get called for that."

"You got him," Foster says.

"You're right, I did," Battier responds, "but I don't think many people would see that."

Of all the things I see Battier do, this is one of the more impressive. There is a primal response men have during a basketball game when called for a foul. We feel wronged. We complain about it. We are, frankly, obnoxious. But in the heat of the moment, Battier is able to somehow push two very different agendas: voice his displeasure with the call and compliment the referee.

Of course, it's all part of a larger plan to curry favor with the refs by maintaining a civil dialogue. So, later, when Brandon Roy kicks out his leg on a jump shot, Battier makes sure to point it out to Foster, once again being diplomatic. "Hey, we both know Brandon Roy is not a dirty player," Battier says to Foster. "But by the rule, that's an offensive foul."

Later, Battier explains his strategy to me. "I'm just planting seeds in his mind," says Battier. "It's amazing if you just notify the refs, 'Hey, look for something,' how you're much more apt to get the call because they're already thinking about it."

2:51 The Blazers are closing the gap, down 12, when Aldridge steals the ball and passes it ahead to Portland forward Nicholas Batum, a long, rangy second-year player. Batum races off for a fast-break layup. Despite starting on the opposite side of the court and behind Batum, Battier is the only Rocket who gives chase.

In this situation, if you are the player who has the ball on the break, Battier is the last guy you want to see closing in. He has a unique ability to jump *with* an offensive player in transition rather than at him. This is confounding because generally on a fast break a defender takes one of three courses of action: go for the steal, let the guy go and fight the next fight, or foul him. But, as Hinkie says, "since Battier never takes the cheap foul, he puts it on the ref to make the call."

To watch clips of Battier in these situations, as I later do, is to note that he always appears under control. He runs with the offensive player, like a cornerback on a wide receiver, and once airborne, rather than trying to block the shot, Battier merely keeps his hand in front of the ball for as long as possible. It's a counterintuitive move—you want to stop the play, right?—but offensive players aren't ready for it and are often forced into an awkward shot as they wait and wait for the foul. "What we see is an unusual number of missed shots near the rim," says Hinkie, citing Rockets data. "It's a subtle difference, but it's there. It might move the percentage from a really high chance of making the shot to just high, but that might be 80 percent to 60 percent. And that's a lot of points over the course of a season."

Naturally, Battier sees it as a matter of efficiency. "When I make those plays in transition, when I jump back, what am I doing?" he asks. "I'm challenging a shot, which brings their field goal percentage down. I'm not fouling them, so that raises efficiency because the guy's not going to the line. Basically I'm doing things that are consistent with how I would guard a guy in the half-court, but I'm just doing it in a transition element."

Knowing this makes what happens next all the more surprising: Battier chases down Batum but, concerned about the young forward's athleticism—"I didn't want him to take off and dunk on my head," Battier explains later—he gets caught in what he calls "the dread in-between," going for neither a steal nor a block. Rather than elevating, Batum stays on the ground and opts for a layup, and Battier feebly reaches across his body, grabbing his arm. It's the worst case scenario: a made basket plus the free throw on a soft foul. Battier slaps his hands together, then walks to the sideline and, in what amounts to a wild display of emotion for him, tosses his gum to the floor. "Those are the kinds of plays that drive me crazy," he tells me after the game. "That's the kind of play that keeps me up at night."

1:46 Roy is starting to heat up. He hits consecutive jump shots, and Battier is becoming concerned. All game he's been going over the screen on the pick-and-roll, allowing Roy to step into a 15-foot jumper; now Battier sees that Roy recognizes this, so to give him a different look, Battier instead goes under the screen a couple of times.

At the same time, Battier is noticing a second troubling trend: Roy is better going left than anticipated. Instead of heading into the teeth of the defense, Roy is using a step-back dribble to create space when he drives left. "And if he creates space, then I have to come out and contest the shot," Battier says. "And if I come out, he can go by me, which means I'm more prone to fouling him and he can see the court better because the space has been created. That's a big advantage."

In the flow of the game, Battier doesn't have time to make a drastic adjustment, but it is something he will file away for later use. "The mental book on a young guy like Brandon Roy, who's an All-Star and getting better every year, is constantly changing," he tells me. "You have to constantly update it, and I did tonight."

Fourth Quarter

6:08 With the Rockets holding a 13-point lead, Battier walks over to inbound the ball on the sideline near the Blazers basket. Before he does so, he takes two extra steps and extends his hand to McMillan, the Blazers' coach.

"Congratulations on the medal," Battier says, referring to the gold medal won in the summer of 2008 by the U.S. Olympic team, for which McMillan was a coach. Battier had been on the national team from 2006 to '08 but didn't make the Olympic cut. As McMillan tells me later, "That's a classy move." It is about as fraternal as Battier gets with the opposition.

3:25 Portland closes the gap to 91–86 on a three-pointer, and the Houston crowd starts to fret. Coming out of a timeout, Battier switches onto Batum so that Artest can take Roy.

Choosing which elite defender to sic on Roy is an enormous luxury for the Rockets. Before Artest's arrival in the summer of 2008 as a free agent, Battier had no true defensive "backup." This in turn meant Battier had to conserve energy (and fouls); and when he did sit, he could barely bring himself to watch, lest his opponent get hot in his absence. (This is a common fear of defensive specialists. The Spurs' Bowen visibly festers on the bench. "I've never seen a guy get mad like that when he's on the bench," says Malik Rose, the Hornets forward who played on the Spurs with Bowen for many years. "When we'd play Kobe, Bruce would do a great job on him. Then when Bruce would get subbed out, he'd be yelling at his backup to 'get up on him' and 'do this' and 'do that,' because he didn't want Kobe to get hot. Because *nothing* is worse than coming in against a hot player.")

In crunch time situations the Rockets' coaching staff now leaves it up to Battier and Artest to figure out the matchups. In this case Artest feels it is time. "Once a guy starts heating up, I make the switch," he tells me after the game, adding definitively, "At the end of the game, I go on the best guy." Then, since he is Ron Artest, he contradicts himself by adding, "I always go ask permission from Shane first."

Battier knows he must treat the situation diplomatically. On the one hand, he's done a good job on Roy much of the night. On the other, he's a better help-side defender than Artest, so he can be just as valuable off the ball. Plus, he is the more willing of the two to cede the matchup. "It's not an ego thing to me. I don't care," Battier says. "I don't need to be on the top guy to prove I'm a good defender."

Besides, as Battier points out, it's a nice change of pace from the previous years. "It's better than Tracy McGrady," he says. "I'd be on one side of the court and he'd be pointing, 'Pick him up! Pick him up!' So I'd have to run all the way across the court to guard a guy like Kobe. It's gone from one extreme to another."

16.1 After a few scary possessions—Artest loses Roy on a screen for a layup and then allows him to drive by for a dunk—Roy misses a tough three-pointer on the right wing, and the Rockets hold on to win 98–94. Afterward, Artest will look at the stat sheet and, despite only guarding Roy for a half dozen possessions during the game (and relatively poorly at that), announce, "He had 24 points on 23 shots. I can't be too upset about that."

10:30 p.m. The game is over but Battier's second shift is just beginning. Win or lose, injured or healthy, effective or ineffective, Battier faces the cameras and microphones. It's a role he assumed as a rookie in Memphis and has maintained ever since. He's been given three NBA sportsmanship awards and, if there were such a thing, he'd be a perennial member of the NBA All-Interview Team.

His one rule is that he get dressed from the waist up before the cameras click on. Thus the viewers in Houston, and across America, see Battier in a crisp button-down shirt addressing the camera sagely and saying all the right things. What they don't see is that he's wearing a towel around his waist, has bags of ice taped to both knees and both hamstrings and has his feet immersed in a yellow Rubbermaid mop bucket full of ice.

Battier is eloquent—and not just "for an athlete" eloquent. He even employs the politician's trick of posing questions for himself to answer. For instance, in discussing Roy: "Are there things I could have done better? Yeah, but you say that about every single game."

For years Battier has been considered a natural for public office once his playing career is over. When younger he was often compared to Bill Bradley, the Knicks forward who went on to become a senator, and, more recently, to Barack Obama. His agent, Lon Babby, loves to rib another client, Grant Hill, by saying, "Grant, you're going to be head of the President's Council on Physical Fitness . . . in the Shane Battier Administration."

Once the media leaves, Battier huddles with Hinkie for a final breakdown of the night. The pair go over what worked and what didn't, focusing on the strategy of pushing Roy left, where he was supposedly less effective and less efficient. While he generally liked the strategy, Battier says that Roy's step-back dribble was so good going left, putting him at a disadvantage, that he wonders if pushing him left isn't always the best idea. Hinkie agrees. Unspoken is that both men know Roy is a tough matchup for Battier. When I later ask Battier about his five toughest covers in the league, he includes Roy alongside Dwyane Wade, Bryant, Manu Ginobili and James. (Honorable mention goes to Paul Pierce and Kings guard Kevin Martin, whom Battier deems the best in the league at getting to the foul line.)

Once he and Hinkie are done, Battier heads home to have a beer and relax, believing it's crucial to let the game go as quickly as possible. This is why he won't watch film the next day—"I already know what I did wrong anyway," he says with a chuckle—or review it with assistant coaches. "I look at it more like a factory worker," he tells me. "You just put in your work. I do the scouting report before the game, I play to that scouting report and I play as hard as I can and I live with the results."

Wednesday, February 25, Rockets Practice

12:45 p.m. The Rockets have finished practice, and discussion has already turned from the previous night's win to the impending matchup with the Cavs and James. Battier spends much of the media session praising James—"With him, it's pick your poison, lethal injection or firing squad"—and downplaying his own physical attributes.

The latter is an old Battier trick. Read enough stories about Battier from over the years, and you can't help but notice how many of them include self-deprecating quotes. He makes fun of his jumping ability, his speed and his quickness, saying things like, "I'm not feeding my family and my dogs on my athletic ability and my highlights and dunks." Naturally, this is just another part of his strategy; as you've no doubt noticed by now, everything Shane Battier does is on purpose.

"The reason I say things like that is I think it gives me a psychological advantage," he says. "When guys think I'm some sort of chump and I'm slow, and then I play pretty good defense on them, they get mad. They think they should do much better. But, in fact, it's not about my athleticism, it's about my preparation, knowing what you're going to do, what your weakness is. I know I can't rely just on speed. If I get beat off that first step, I'm in trouble and I put my team at a disadvantage. I have to know my job better and I have to concentrate on every play. And I think that's my strength. My strength is concentration. I can focus on every single play."

Engelland, the Spurs's assistant, has known Battier for years and thinks it's all a matter of definition. "Maybe Shane isn't athletic in the traditional sense but he is *defensively* athletic," Engelland told me. "His feet are quick. He covers ground to block a shot. He gets across the lane quickly. If you're not athletic, you wouldn't be able to do those things. Bruce Bowen was the same way. It's just that neither guy *looks* that athletic."

Rockets vs. Cleveland, February 26

7:30 p.m. Game night, and the LeBron buzz in the Toyota Center is palpable. Despite it being a Thursday evening in a down economy, the game is a sellout and, at 18,399 fans, the Rockets have drawn the sixth-largest crowd in team history.

In the locker room before the game, the chair of each Rockets player holds a scouting report titled EXECUTIVE SUMMARY, suggesting the level of seriousness with which the Rockets treat such matters. Included are a number of bullet points on James, including the following:

- LeBron wants to drive left two thirds of the time.

- He scores more efficiently going right. He drives to the rim 59% of the time (versus only 42% of the time going left).

- Overall he shoots 23% worse on jumpers versus drives.

Unlike Roy and his balanced game, it doesn't take a Stanford MBA to interpret these stats: Make LeBron shoot jumpers. The challenge, of course, is how.

Tonight, Adelman has opted to use Artest as the primary defender on James, mainly for reasons of size; Artest is the only wing player in the league who can match James in bulk and strength (if not explosiveness). This means Battier will start on shooting guard Delonte West and be expected to key the team defense. Even with the size factor, Hinkie tells me, he'd prefer to see Battier on James—he feels Battier is better at forcing players into low-percentage shots. Of course, being a numbers guy, and a Battier fan, Hinkie would rather see Battier on *anybody*.

The game begins, and Artest immediately signals his intent to treat the paint like a line of scrimmage, bumping and slapping at James whenever he gets within 15 feet of the basket. Meanwhile, freed from being "zoned-in" on the main guy, Battier is seemingly everywhere on help defense. Late in the first quarter James turns the corner on Artest, but Battier slides over and places his hand on the ball. Just as with his transition defense, Battier doesn't try to strip down or hack—he just keeps his hand there, as if feeling for a pulse. James can't bring his arms up and, as a result, the ball goes out-of-bounds, to Cleveland.

This tactic might best be termed the "ride-along steal." As Battier sees it, when players are driving past you to the hoop, they're going to finish with their protected hand. In so doing, though, very few guys—other than the All-Stars—hide the ball on their protected side as they stride to the hoop. "A lot of guys bring it right in front of your face, and if the ball is right in front of my face, all I try to do is keep my hand right on top of the ball and not swipe. If I just get a hand on it and disrupt the timing, he's probably going to miss the shot." Battier's logic is that it's easier to stay with the ball than to try to strip it. There's also a significantly lower risk of a foul call. (It's not as easy as it sounds, however. Hayes, the Rockets power forward, has tried to adopt the ride-along, but as he says glumly, "I always end up swiping.")

This leads us to one of Battier's pet peeves: He believes this hand-on-ball disruption should be scored a blocked shot. It is in the act of shooting, he argues, and he has his hand on the ball. But the official scorers usually only count a blocked shot when the ball is released above the head (though the official NBA scorekeeping guide does say, "A shot can be considered blocked even if the ball was not in flight before being blocked. For statistical purposes the act of shooting shall be considered any upward and/or forward motion with the intent of trying for a goal"). Instead, the call is often a jump ball. "A jump ball is nothing," Battier says, becoming animated. "No stat, no blocked shot, no steal. And if I swipe it, and he loses it and my teammate picks it up, *he* gets credit for the steal. I kid you not. I've done that four or five times in a game, and I'm like, 'Oh, yeah, I got four blocks or four steals depending on how they score it.' I look at the stats and I have one, and I'm like, 'You got to be kidding me!' So that's my crusade when I'm done playing: to change that rule to *anything* that's in the act of shooting should be a block. Or . . ."—and here, in the middle of his soliloquy, Battier stops and looks at me—". . . what do you think? Should that be a block or a steal?"

"Well," I say, "I'd think it should be a steal."

"But it's in the act of shooting," he counters.

"You're right," I say. "But I think you're expecting a lot from the scorekeepers."

With the first quarter winding down, James gets an iso up top and goes at Artest, driving left. Upon reaching the paint, James spins middle, violently swinging through. Battier has beat him there, though, coming over from the weak side. It is an easy charge call, and it accomplishes a few things. First and foremost, it gets Houston possession of the ball and, as Nate McMillan says of being a specialist, "You're out there to get possession of that ball, and that is the reward—to get the ball for your team and then give it to somebody who can do something with it."

Second, the charge is a foul on James, forcing him to be more cautious. And, perhaps most important, now James has it in his head every time he drives that if he spins he might run smack into Battier, ready to tumble backward again.

Certainly, there is no glamour in the charge. Shaquille O'Neal has spent his career deriding "floppers," while TV announcers like Bill Walton often admonish big men for trying to take a charge when they could try to block a shot. But that's overlooking the ripple effect of the play. Especially for big men who are shot blockers, occasionally taking a charge provides a significant psychological advantage; next time down the offensive player has to be wary of a repeat. "And that second of indecision might be the difference in the guy making the play or missing the play," says Battier. "So when I take a charge, half the time I don't really care if I get the call or not. Even if they call the block, the opponent knows that I'm going to step up and take the charge, and that puts something in his mind."

Though not on a level with Derek Fisher, who led the NBA in charges taken in 2007–08, with 58, Battier is usually among the league leaders. (He finished 11th in the league in '07–08.) A few minutes after taking the charge on James, Battier draws another one on the Cavs star, sending him to the bench with three fouls. It will not show up as a stat in the box score, much to Battier's chagrin, but the effect on the game is profound.

———

Now it is the third quarter, and Battier is guarding James on the wing after a switch. It reminds me of what Battier showed me when I asked how he would guard someone in a pickup game. Standing a few feet away from me in an empty room at the Toyota Center a day earlier, one foot forward, he put one hand in the air and said, repeatedly, "Shoot it. Go on, shoot it."

Battier is now essentially doing the same thing to James, who is only the best or second-best basketball player in the world. James, seeing the space, takes the bait and launches a 20-foot fadeaway jumper, which is of course exactly what the Rockets hoped he'd do. As usual, Battier leaps at him and contests, sticking his hand into James's face. Perhaps because the two men play in different conferences, or perhaps because Artest has been on him all night and he's not accustomed to Battier's trick, James looks visibly affected upon finding a hand flying at his eyes. He misses the shot badly.

Even if he had hit it, though, the odds are against James over the long haul on such plays. As most players know, the most efficient shot in the NBA is a layup, followed by the corner three (because at 22 feet it's shorter than other points on the arc), followed by any other three and, finally, a mid-range jump shot. This holds true with only a few exceptions. "There are always some outliers, guys like Deron Williams, Dirk Nowitzki, Rip Hamilton," explains Battier. "I think there are 10 guys in the league [for whom] a two-point shot is as good as the league efficiency at other spots on the floor. Basically there are 10 guys who can hurt you shooting two-point jump shots. But even then, you live with it."

(Not every coach goes along with that strategy. When he played for Hubie Brown and Mike Fratello in Memphis, two old-school coaches, Battier says with a laugh, "You'd give up a two-point jump shot and they'd yell, 'You got to try harder!'")

Thus, Battier's advice to players in a pickup game is to concede the mid-range J. (Take note, all ye YMCA regulars.) "If you're not in the NBA, or you didn't play college basketball, chances are you're probably not a very good two-point jump shooter," Battier tells me. His logic is that the rec-league regular may be able to stand alone, unguarded, and knock down shots, but in a game situation, with a hand in his face, he's going to start tossing up bricks. "Just don't let the guy drive," warns Battier, "and if he makes a few jumpers, then worry about it. But over the long run you will stay on the court longer." Then Battier qualifies his remarks with a word of caution about one category of pickup player. "You *do* have to worry about the old man who can't move, who has knee braces and rec specs but has an unbelievable J," Battier says. "I call it Old Man Game. They don't miss any open shot, and they can just shoot it." So how to defend this crafty if arthritic opponent? "You're out of luck," says Battier. "You run into the Old Man Game, what I do doesn't apply. That's a whole different book."

(It turns out there is also an Old Man Defensive Game, at least when it comes to defensive-minded men like Battier—and Craig Ehlo. Most guys who keep playing into the twilight of their athletic lives survive by honing their jump shots, living for those mid-range set shots. Not Ehlo. Though 47 years old, he still regularly plays against men who recently played in college. Of course, Ehlo still wants to guard the best player. And of course, that player wants to take it at the ex-NBA guy, so they isolate Ehlo and have at it. Often enough, he holds his own. "It doesn't do it for me to play with guys my age," Ehlo says. "I'm still competitive, even if it's only in my mind. It makes me feel alive is the best way I can think to describe it." To which I say, amen, Craig, amen.)

———————

Battier and the Rockets dominate the second half and finish with a rousing 93–74 blowout win, the worst loss of Cleveland's season to date. James has a few moments on offense but is largely ineffective, scoring 21 points on 7-of-21 shooting with one rebound and, for the first time in his career, zero assists. Battier, for once, receives his due and is credited with four blocked shots. And, other than one unlikely play when the slow-footed Cavs forward Wally Szczerbiak drove right by him for a righthanded floater, Battier didn't get beat all night.

Afterward, he sits in his familiar spot at his locker, feet in the Rubbermaid bucket. He smiles for the cameras, reiterates that it is "just one game." If he's excited about holding James to zero assists, he's not showing it. He does become animated, however, when I bring up the Szczerbiak drive.

"He usually doesn't drive," Battier says, incredulous. "Only 31 times all season in the half-court. *Thirty-one!*"

He pauses, shakes his head. "That's an example of the scouting report not translating to the actual game."

Then again, the scouting report on James worked to a tee. Not that everyone on the Rockets is buying it. Ten minutes later, as the players are preparing to leave, Battier turns to Hayes, the power forward and his good friend (and something of a defensive nerd himself), who sits two lockers down.

"So, Chuck," says Battier, "do you acquiesce to our game plan?"

Hayes looks up, frowns. "No, no. I think he just missed shots tonight."

Battier is incredulous. "Those were the shots we wanted him to take."

"No, those were open looks. When you were on him, you contested, but Ron didn't contest all night. Those are rhythm jump shots, a guy like that, you can't let him shoot those. Those are high-percentage shots!"

Battier opens his eyes wide. "That's the point. They *aren't* high percentage. He shoots 38 percent on two-point jumpers."

Hayes looks up from buttoning his shirt; he is having none of it. "These were different. He was open. They were rhythm jump shots."

"You'd rather have him go to the basket?"

"Yeah."

"In the lane where he shoots 67 percent?"

Von Wafer, the young Houston guard dressing nearby, hears this and pipes up, "No way! You're dead! Dead!"

"Fuck that," says Hayes.

"So you're saying," says Battier, lacing his voice with sarcasm, "that you'd rather have him do what he did in Cleveland, where he went 11 of 23 and got to the basket? We *want* him taking those jump shots."

Hayes remains steadfast. "He's the second-best player on the planet, and we all know who's Number 1, and you're going to give him open jump shots?"

Battier looks at Hayes in disbelief, then looks at me and shrugs his shoulders. There is only so much one man can do.

Training: Preparing Like the Pros (and Feeling Their Pain)

How fine is the line between NBA starter and the guy who spends the rest of his days talking about being the last cut? You be the judge.

When Sacramento Kings guard Kevin Martin was a freshman at Western Carolina University in 2001, he had one exceptional skill: He could shoot. Good thing too, because he disliked contact, wasn't all that effective off the dribble and was a subpar passer, averaging 1.5 assists per game for the season. Hoping to remedy these weaknesses, his coach, Steve Shurina, sent him to see a man named David Thorpe. At the time, Thorpe was a high school coach in Clearwater, Fla., and just beginning to work as a trainer for pro prospects. His early clients included Udonis Haslem, who went on to play for the Miami Heat, and Josh Powell, who went on to sign with the Golden State Warriors.

That summer, Martin drove from North Carolina to Thorpe's base in Clearwater, Fla., where he roomed with one of Thorpe's other players. And for one week Thorpe killed him. Conditioning, shooting drills, ball handling, all without a hint of coddling. At the end of each day, when Martin would drive off in his car, Thorpe would announce to the rest of his guys, "Say goodbye to Kevin. That's the last we'll see of him." But every morning Martin returned.

A few months later, in the first game of his sophomore season for Western Carolina, Martin scored 46 points. If he'd had any lingering doubts about the value of his trip to Clearwater, they evaporated right there on the court. He was now sold on Thorpe, and each summer afterward Martin headed back to Florida. In 2004, after averaging 24.9 points as a junior, Martin declared for the NBA draft. It was a risky move. At 6'7" and only 175 pounds, he didn't have the prototypical NBA build, and Western Carolina wasn't exactly a hot spot for NBA scouts. In June, the Kings chose Martin with the 26th pick of the first round—five more spots, and he would have dropped to the second round. The margin for him to make the league was uncomfortably small; hundreds of players of his stature fall through the NBA cracks and spend years playing in hoops outposts from Belgrade to Iowa City.

Perhaps Martin's skills and drive would have led him to the NBA regardless. Perhaps not. "If I hadn't known David, I think I'd have been one of those seniors that got lost in the shuffle as a great college player," Martin says. "He really pushed me."

His rookie year with the Kings, Martin barely played. The next season he averaged 10.8 points. Thereafter, he increased his scoring average each season, from 20.2 to 23.7 to 24.6 points per game in 2008–09. Throughout, he continued to rely on Thorpe, who remained valuable, only now in different capacities.

When I caught up with Martin in the spring of 2009 at a Kings game in Oakland against the Warriors, he was enduring what could only be described as a ruinous season. Not personally, necessarily— after returning from an early injury, he was averaging 24.1 points, the highest of his young career. But the Kings were a whopping 41 games below .500, playing to a nearly empty home arena and had held a mid-season fire sale that saw Martin lose his two most effective teammates, former All-Star center Brad Miller and swingman John Salmons.

Martin could have been forgiven had he been pessimistic, and to a certain extent he was. Which only made Thorpe's job more important. In previous seasons Thorpe and Martin would talk a couple of times a week. Now Martin was calling his trainer before every game, on his way to the arena, and the two spoke after every game. Against the Warriors, for instance, Thorpe had given Martin two pieces of advice (by BlackBerry in this case). First, because Golden State, unlike many teams that keyed on Martin defensively, was almost indifferent to his scoring, Thorpe told him to look for his shot early and, if the climate was right, take aim at a 40-point night. Second, Thorpe advised him to attack the rim, since Golden State was missing its best inside player, Andris Biedrins. (You could say the strategy worked: Martin went on to score a career-high 50 points, 23 of which came on free throws.)

These were day-to-day, game-to-game concerns though. Longer term, Martin and Thorpe were looking ahead to the summer, when he'd return to Bradenton. Only this time, instead of working on his physical skills, they would be working on his leadership skills. "Kevin has reached the point where he's a 25-point scorer, but now he needs to learn how to be a charismatic and vocal leader," Thorpe told me. "I don't think he got that before, but now he's been the best player on a bad team for three years, and he gets it." Thorpe's solution was to put Martin in a position of authority. So rather than running through drills, Martin would serve as an assistant coach as Thorpe worked out a number of pro prospects. "He'll be the highest-paid assistant I've ever had," Thorpe said with a laugh.

Then, once his coaching stint was over, after a couple weeks, Martin would hit the gym to refine his game as he does every summer, undergoing grueling workouts for weeks at a time.

I'd always been curious how it is that players like Martin make the leap from borderline prospect to NBA mainstay, and the role that men like Thorpe play. Not just generally, but specifically. What happens in those summer workouts? How much better can a player get? Well, now I understand on a different level. Six months before I watched Martin torch the Warriors, I had traveled to Florida, in the fall of 2008, to spend four days training with Thorpe at the IMG Academies. Accompanied by eight other media types, I went through (mostly) the same program that Martin and Tyrus Thomas and Luol Deng of the Bulls follow during the summer. Same coaches, same drills, same searing leg cramps at 2 a.m. Or maybe only I got those.

The goal was twofold: first, to get an understanding of what goes into the making of an NBA player; and, second, to examine (or debunk) the enduring perception that, of all athletes in the major U.S. sports, basketball players are the ones most capable of getting by purely on natural talent. Sure, in rare cases this may be true—Allen Iverson would be happy to tell you his thoughts on the efficacy of practice—but by and large it's an antiquated notion. In today's NBA, summer has become the season when careers are shaped, new moves mastered and physiques honed.

So I expected to be impressed at IMG. What I didn't expect was the extraordinary attention to detail. All those moves that look like crazy, lucky shots in an NBA game? You know, when a player double-pumps and then fades away and somehow makes the shot? Well, some of them are crazy, lucky shots. But a lot of them are well-practiced. I know because we practiced them. We also practiced dunking with our opposite hand and running "Reggie Millers" to work on our shooting and a lot of other things I never imagined doing. But I'm getting ahead of myself. Let's start at the beginning, on a Monday, fresh off a cross-country flight.

Day One: Evening Session

We've been on the court for 30 minutes, and already I feel like I'm wearing a wet dishrag. One thing about training in this part of Florida: You sweat in ways you never knew possible. Even though it is fall, the air is as heavy as a lover's breath, and the slightest exertion summons rivulets of perspiration. This makes warming up tired muscles surprisingly easy. It also means we surround the water jug like a bunch of addicts jonesing for a fix. Still, I can see why it's a great place to train— you always *feel* as if you're really working.

We begin with basic dribbling and shooting drills on the two NBA-sized courts. As if by way of apology, at least half a dozen times coach Mike Moreau, director of the IMG Basketball Academy and one of our two main instructors (along with Thorpe), tells us, "Don't be insulted by the simplicity of what we're doing." His point is to focus not on *what* we're doing but *how* we're doing it. So when we yo-yo the ball back and forth with one hand during a dribbling drill, we're to do it as hard as possible—*"HAMMER NAILS!"* Moreau shouts, like some crazed foreman—and until we go so fast that we lose the ball. The idea is to simulate a game situation, when a defender is crowding you at full speed. "If you don't lose the ball, you're not going hard enough," Moreau shouts. *"MAKE YOURSELF LOSE IT!"* It's a totally unnatural sensation, like speeding up a treadmill until you wipe out. It requires a concerted effort, perhaps even more so, I imagine, for NBA players conditioned to feel that losing the ball is a sign of weakness. Once accomplished, however, the drill is quite liberating. Rarely does one get to screw up and be praised by a coach.

And what emphatic praise it is. As head of the academy, Moreau has the wired intensity required to command a teenager's attention. (He coaches the high school kids at IMG.) He often speaks in italics, whether commanding us to hammer those nails or *"KILL THE GRASS!"* during a ball handling drill. Thin and wiry, with a buzz cut and intense eyes, he moves like a boxer and seems to genuinely delight in our small victories.

Thorpe isn't as intense as Moreau but is just as serious. Built like a fullback, he has the clean, tanned look of a politician or the most popular dad at the PTA meeting, with short hair and a thick jaw. In the span of 15 years, he has risen from Florida high school coach to NBA trainer and analyst for ESPN.com. He's not only fluent in the you-can-do-it motivational patois required of any good trainer but is also capable of unleashing three motherfuckers in a single sentence when the moment calls for it. As his clients know, he's also a good listener, on his cellphone so often that he has two Bluetooths and carries a corded headset for when his batteries inevitably peter out. (Depending on the personality and experience of a client, Thorpe says he varies his ratio of talking to listening: He estimates that with Deng, he does the talking 30% of the time, while with Tyrus Thomas it is 50% and with Courtney Lee, the Orlando Magic rookie, it's closer to 90%.)

With us, Thorpe alternates between encouragement, gentle ribbing and clinical assessment. The latter comes quickly. He watches me take all of two jump shots before concluding, "You've got nice form. It's a little flat, but it's compact and easily replicated." Later, while I'm performing jab-step-dribble-drives from the wing, he instantly notices that I'm sliding my right leg back before going forward, like a tiny unnecessary dance step, wasting a split second. It's the kind of detail that, in 20 years of playing the game, I'd never even thought to consider. His solution is simple: Practice the move with a chair behind your right leg; the bruises will tell you how you're doing.

Day Two: Morning

IMG is like a sports factory, or perhaps an athletic Disneyland: 300 acres of fields and gyms and courts where tiny Sharapovas and little boys in wicking shirts train year-round at everything from soccer to basketball to baseball. This is where Nick Bollettieri runs his tennis program, where Freddy Adu honed his dribbling, where off-season NBA players spend their days shooting jumpers and chugging chalky protein shakes. To walk the campus, with its man-made lagoons, emporium-sized weight room and roaming packs of long-limbed athletes, is to feel like you've stepped into a Nike ad.

Breakfast is at the cafeteria, near the eastern edge of the IMG campus. And it is a campus, with dorms (girls on one side, boys on the other), a functioning K-through-12 school and even, each spring, a prom. The manicured grounds stand in stark contrast to the surrounding area of Bradenton, which, best I can tell, consists primarily of auto dealerships, condo complexes, liquor stores and fast-food parlors. It's not what I expected—where are the posh resorts and Botox'd women in their Beamers? On the drive in from the airport I even began to wonder if I was lost (and indeed, the relative isolation of Bradenton is why some NBA players choose not to train here, preferring the "entertainment" options of working out in Vegas or L.A.). But then I saw the gates, large, white and imposing, as if the academies are some enormous fortress or nature preserve, which in some ways I guess they are.

The tight security is provided for good reason. It's not cheap to send your kid to IMG; the annual tab runs around 60 grand for academics, training and room and board, and can run upward of $80,000 depending on how much personalized instruction is involved. This means that millionaire off-season athletes are joined by millionaire's progeny. New Jersey Nets owner Bruce Ratner's son, for one, was on campus for a couple of weeks. To vet the place beforehand, Ratner had a friend visit and report back on the security measures, which are impressive. During the night, for example, staff members check on students every three hours or so, shining a flashlight into each room, which, IMG recruiting coordinator Anthony Macri tells me, "the kids get used to pretty quickly."

When NBA players train at IMG, they endure no flashlight checks, usually renting a nearby condo or staying in one of the villas at the rear of the compound. (Bulls forward Thomas rents a four-bedroom place, just for him and his manager.) By contrast, most of us stay at the adult lodge, which offers small, tidy rooms. We eat communal meals and do so with alarming ferocity. Chicken Parmesan, turkey filet, yogurt, potatoes, salad—we shovel it all in, trying to replenish calories our bodies aren't accustomed to burning. Over the course of four days, a couple of my peers lose close to 10 pounds.

On this morning, as we inhale scrambled eggs, we talk about two things: hamstrings (how tight they are) and sleep (how blissful it was). There is a good vibe to our crew, which includes bloggers (like Henry

Abbott of ESPN's True Hoop), stats gurus (Roland Beech of 82games .com) and even one agent (Jason Levien, who was hired as assistant GM of the Sacramento Kings two months later). We scan our schedule for the day:

9:30–10 Stretching and Warmup

10:00–11:00 Basketball Strength and Conditioning

11:00–12:30 On-Court Training

12:30–2:00 Lunch

2:00–3:00 Mental Conditioning/Attitude

3:00–5:00 Communication Training

5:30–6:30 Dinner

6:30–8:00 On-Court Instruction and Games

8:30 Film Breakdown with Coaching Staff

Actual basketball takes up only three hours, and even so, a chunk of that is spent listening. Both Thorpe and Moreau are believers in quality over quantity, dismissing the boasts of players who claim to work out "six hours a day." "If you're working hard, you can't go six hours a day," says Moreau. "We get our guys through in a little over an hour for each session, and they're gassed."

Everything here is functional. When we stretch and lift, it's by mimicking basketball moves. Instead of a slow-and-heavy bench press, which builds mass, trainer Corey Stenstrup favors speed work, whether it's cable pull-downs, box jumps or hitting the "jammer," a weight machine that mimics exploding from a squat up toward the basket. The goal is not to get bigger but to build lean muscle; Stenstrup says he strives for a "remodeling effect." Tear up too many muscle fibers on a Monday, he explains, and you can't lift on a Tuesday. Much of his job is aimed at the psychological. "If you can get NBA players to do conditioning, then you're good," he says.

We are willing pupils. Our problem is coordination. Much of what Stenstrup stresses involves core work, which in turn involves balance. So when we jump rope, we not only do it forward and side-to-side but backward. (Try it; it's totally counterintuitive.) We topple off balance boards, lose our grip on heavy balls and wobble while doing one-leg hamstring lifts. It's becoming increasingly clear that the stereotype of lazy, it-all-comes-naturally NBA millionaires is unfair. The reason it looks effortless when Kobe Bryant adjusts in midair is because he's worked his ass off so that he can adjust in midair.

Our work on the court is similarly focused on applicability. During dribbling drills we not only switch speeds—going through five "gears" while handling the ball, to mimic the way a guard like Chris Paul changes tempo—but we try to keep our eyes up and aimed downcourt. Not just anywhere, either; we are to rotate looking at four imaginary teammates, thus keeping the equally imaginary defense off guard. (Apparently, Martin gets so into this drill that he calls out the names of his Kings peers as he goes. I decide that as long as it's my imaginary team, I might as well be the guy taking all the shots, so I envision an all-defensive-specialist lineup of Joel Przybilla, Bruce Bowen, Quinton Ross and Jeff Foster.

Day Two: Afternoon

It's time for mental conditioning, which I can summarize as follows: Hey, man, you're *really, really* good!

Even elite athletes, it turns out, need love, and lots of it. As Thorpe says, "When they play well and win, they don't need me. They need me when they're down."

So for each NBA client the IMG team creates a personal highlight reel, which players can dial up on their iPods before games or whenever they need a shot of self-confidence. We watch the reel for Lee, the Magic rookie guard. It begins with keyboard-heavy instrumental music—think Alan Parsons Project—and what follows is five minutes of Courtney Lee, Super-Frickin-Star. We see Lee dunking, we see him draining threes, we see him soaring over an opponent and blocking a shot out-of-bounds. Six times we hear a broadcaster intoning, "The Sun Belt Conference player of the year!" Interspersed are clips of Michael Jordan, Allen Iverson and sprinter Michael Johnson doing incredible things.

By the time the video finishes, I feel like *I'm* the Sun Belt Conference player of the year. I can only imagine how pumped Lee must get. (And I can't help but wonder what the counterpart would be for my line of work: maybe shots of me triumphantly hitting the RETURN button cut with slo-mo footage of Frank Deford pounding a typewriter?)

Of course, after you build players up, you must break them down. So IMG provides a written analysis of every game its clients play. We check out a critique of Daniel Santiago, a former NBA reserve now playing in Spain, from October 2007. The breakdown is by half and is by turns encouraging ("Free throw stroke looked good") and constructive. For example, regarding an early entry pass Santiago doesn't get to: "Don't just hold position back on your heels and hope the pass is perfect. Go get it if you have to—especially from [teammate Marcus] Haislip. Expect a bad pass!"

Then later, referencing a botched move to the basket: "On the first drive when you got jammed, you tried to force a pass to the baseline and turned it over. Always look diagonally opposite in that situation. You had No. 7 wide open ready for the jumper. . . . Look to make the easy play, which 90% of the time will be diagonally opposite."

So, after any game, when Santiago may or may not have received feedback from his coach in Spain, he can later sit in his apartment and pore over a complete deconstruction of his play from a dedicated coach half a world away. And this, more than anything, is the lesson of the week at IMG: You can't do it alone. If you're an NBA player, and if every NBA player is essentially his own small business, then, like any company, you need your own tech support and oversight. And the focus has to be overwhelmingly, constantly on you. What you eat, how you train, what you think. No detail is too mundane. No wonder pro athletes seem selfish and egotistical. To succeed, they pretty much have to be.

The challenge, of course, is to not come off in public as an egomaniac. And that is the purpose of our next session, communication training, which teaches athletes how to deal with people like me. The program is run by Steve Shenbaum, an actor, comedian and, as he likes to say, "recovering narcissist." His clients have included Pete Sampras and Greg Oden, and his goal is simple: make athletes seem like human beings. So he tries to teach "honesty, humility and humor." Much of this, it turns out, is about feeling comfortable.

To get a feel for it, we run through a series of improv games, learning to vary our tone and presence. For example, during one game I'm on an "expert panel" with two other media guys. Our expertise, we're told, is as lobster hunters; we then take questions from the audience, trying to read one another's cues as we go. For us, the exercise is surprisingly enjoyable, even quite funny. But we're all journalists, accustomed to talking for a living. For an NBA player, wary of the media and perhaps not comfortable in front of a camera, the process can be both novel and valuable.

A good example of Shenbaum's work is Oden. When the then Ohio State center arrived in New York for the NBA draft in June 2007 he was an unknown quantity as a personality, but he quickly charmed with his humility and wit. He told *The Washington Post,* "My face isn't made for movies, so I'll probably do the cartoon route—*Shrek 5,* holla at me." When asked why he was marketable, he broke into a robot dance. The reaction from the sporting public was surprise, if not shock, at this relative eruption of charisma.

It was a calculated performance. Before the draft, Oden's reps sent the young center to work with Shenbaum. To begin, the two worked on improv games and "punching a joke." For instance, when reporters asked about a draft showcase that Oden elected not to play in, Shenbaum had prepared a line. "My first thought was to say, 'It went great. I didn't miss a shot,'" says Shenbaum. "I don't know if that's funny funny, but when Greg would say it, people would go crazy. My friends that write on *Will & Grace* would scoff at me and say these aren't very good jokes, but everyone loves them."

Of course, that everyone loves them says something about everyone, in this case sports fans and media. "It's not like Greg is doing high-concept, off-the-wall humor," says Shenbaum. "He's just showing that he's quick."

It seems simple enough, but if so, why don't more athletes do it? Kobe Bryant, for example, has spent years trying to connect with fans but has never had much success beyond his play on the court. "That, to me, is Kobe's ego getting in the way," says Shenbaum. "Because he's one of the greatest basketball players ever, he also thinks he can be his own media coach. He's going home thinking, 'I can kill it here.' It takes humility to say, 'This isn't my skill set.'"

Day Three

The alarm bleats. I consider rolling onto the floor then crawling to the shower. It's not that my joints are sore—amazingly, due to the extensive stretching and strength work, they are not. But my hamstrings feel like they're attached to a winch that won't stop turning. I head to the gym early to loosen up. This, I find, is a great luxury. As a 34-year-old father, my basketball these days usually comes in frantic bursts, and aside from a hasty quad stretch here and there, it is focused 100% on playing. Show up, go full speed, race home. To have the time to warm up properly, using a rolling pad to loosen muscles and performing a variety of exotic stretches, makes a huge difference.

There's even greater luxury in the recovery time. Icing down after each workout, naps in the afternoon, a veritable Gatorade IV. And, this afternoon, after our morning session, an ice bath. It's something Deng does every day in the summer, and I see why. Aside from the initial shock of entering 50° water, it's quite nice. During two-minute sessions, it feels like this: *COLD!, cold, cold, cold, cold, cold, bliss.* Afterward, I feel like I've just unwrapped a new pair of legs.

It turns out I need them. In the evening session we practice finishing strong at the rim, always overhand rather than with a scoop or finger roll. ("Remember Patrick Ewing," warns Thorpe, invoking Ewing's heartbreaker of a missed finger roll in Game 7 of the 1995 Eastern Conference semifinals.) Then, after practicing coming off picks—drills Thorpe refers to as "Reggie Millers"—we pair up, a guard with a big man, and work on ball screens, turning the corner and, my favorite, running the "pinch post." If you've watched many NBA games, the play is familiar. First, the big man comes to the foul line extended to receive a pass from the guard, who's at the top of the key. The guard can then cut past the big man's hip and receive a handoff, his defender getting picked off in the process. Or, the big man can fake the handoff and then hit the guard with a dump down pass as he continues looping toward the basket. Or, finally, as Chris Webber used to do so often for the Sacramento Kings, the big man can fake the handoff, then spin and shoot the jumper from the free throw line.

The night ends with a scrimmage that is most notable for the fact that no one gets injured.

Day Four

In deference to our conditioning, Thorpe put this morning's workout last. "Had we done it on Monday, you'd all be done for the week," he says.

We arrive in the gym to find the baskets lowered to various carnival heights—eight feet, nine feet. It is time to dunk.

For NBA guys this is a key element of the program, and on any given day they might dunk more than 150 times (on a 10-foot rim, of course). Thorpe wants his players to attack with force, be quick leapers and always finish with authority. This draws fouls and, for prospects who are on the cusp of making an NBA team, can be the best way to make an impression. When one of Thorpe's borderline players recently went to training camp with the Phoenix Suns, Thorpe's advice was simple: Go find Amar'e Stoudemire and try to dunk on him. It's your best shot at making the team.

So, like the pros, we practice. I pair with a big guy who's a beast down low, and we proceed to do unspeakable things to a nine-foot rim. At least that's how it feels to us. There are few things more primal, more gratifying, than throwing down monster dunks. By the end, we're trading roars with each jam. To be honest, it's the closest I feel to being a "pro" all week. Who cares that it's nine feet?

Like everything, the work is structured to mimic game conditions. So we toss the ball off the backboard, catch the "rebound" and try to take one step and dunk. First righthanded, then lefthanded, then off one foot, then off two. We hook dunk from the baseline (to put our off shoulder between us and the defender). We take one step, head fake, then dunk to draw contact. And we stand under the rim and jump straight up and dunk, then try to catch the ball and go straight back up by quick-jumping off our toes, and then do it 20 times in a row. By the end, we are sopping with sweat, our calves on fire—and it's not over.

Next comes Thorpe's pièce de résistance, the Superman drill. Here's how it works: Stand on one side of the lane, throw the ball off the backboard at an angle and then sprint and leap to catch it in the air and land on the *other* side of the lane. Now do it 20 times in a row. It is ridiculously tiring. Dunking was a lot more fun. But then—salvation!—we are told to incorporate the two. So now we throw, rebound and dunk, again and again.

Alas, it's one of our final drills. By noon we're headed back to the lodge to pack up, grab one final meal and disperse, lugging quads stuffed with concrete. Thorpe asks me if I want to stick around and practice with the postgrad kids that afternoon. My mind says yes; my hamstrings say no. I wisely decline. Within two hours I'm as sore as I've been in years. It feels fantastic.

In the weeks and months that followed, I found myself clinging to the glow of the experience, fighting to make it part of my daily life, which again revolved around typing and diaper changes and unfreezing food that looked like perhaps it should stay frozen. I exchanged e-mails with my fellow trainee Henry at ESPN, who wrote, "I really, really, really need some time to perfect the things I kind of learned." And I couldn't have agreed more.

At my local YMCA in Berkeley, Calif., I continued practicing elements of the warmup routine and focused on the little details when I played—keeping that foot forward on the drive, curling tight off screens. Once, I even found myself inadvertently blurting out, "Pinch post! Pinch post!" to a teammate. Since it's Berkeley, he wasn't fazed in the least. (After all, people shout crazy stuff all the time around here.) But expecting someone in a pickup game to run the pinch post was completely lunacy. It's like going to McDonald's and asking for your burger medium rare. I couldn't help myself. The impulse was like a vestigial tail from my week at IMG.

A few months later I saw Courtney Lee, the Orlando guard, at a game. We spoke about Thorpe—Lee deemed him "a good man who's made a big difference in my game"—and then I told him about our experience. He looked skeptical.

"You guys make it through?"

I told him we did.

"Two-a-days?"

Yup.

He nodded, mildly impressed. "How long?"

Four days.

He nodded again, then smiled. "Try doing it all summer."

Fine Tuning: Secrets of the Hoops Whisperer

It takes one kind of trainer to take a raw recruit like me and hone some basic skills. It takes quite another to tell LeBron James he can't dribble.

In the summer of 2008, on the recommendation of Chris Paul, James worked out for the first time with trainer Idan Ravin, whose clients include Paul, Carmelo Anthony, Gilbert Arenas and Elton Brand, among others.

When the two men met at a gym in New Orleans to work out with Paul and a few other players, Ravin (pronounced rah-VEEN; first name pronounced ee-DON) knew he had to make an immediate impression on James, as he always must with new players. A 38-year-old former lawyer, Ravin boasts none of the credentials that carry weight in the NBA world. He didn't play the game (at least not past high school), never coached (unless you count junior high kids), hasn't worked for an NBA team and isn't even certified as a trainer. Neither does he look the part. The son of an Israeli mother and a Russian father, Ravin is neither tall nor particularly athletic looking and in conversation comes off more as a sociologist than a club promoter.

Thus Ravin's first goal is to humble any new player, and do so quickly. In the case of James, Ravin believed his weakness was his dribbling, so he immediately ran him through a series of intricate ball-handling exercises. When James would look down to locate the ball, Ravin would occasionally gently tap him under his chin, a reminder to keep his head up. Now, granted, this exercise could go horribly awry—

you want to try telling LeBron he can't dribble? But provided Ravin is correct in his critique (and in this case he was), his method establishes him as an authority figure. "The only way to tame a 10,000-pound tiger is to immediately show a level of control," says Ravin, drawing an analogy to the book *Life of Pi*. "When LeBron's head goes down and I tap his chin up, nobody does that to him. He's not used to it."

Next, Ravin ran James through grueling conditioning drills, all within the context of game situations because, again, he'd noticed James was a bit out of shape at the time (at least by LeBron's high standards). By the end of the hourlong workout, the Cavaliers star was lying on the floor, gassed. Only then, once James was humbled, did Ravin address him.

"You are far and away the most talented player in the league, way more talented than Kobe," Ravin told LeBron. "But you don't even have a go-to move in isolation, you can't handle the ball that well and you can't shoot really. Think about that."

James sat silent, biting his fingernails and looking "sort of pissed," as Ravin remembers it.

"Look, I'm not here to hurt your feelings," Ravin continued. "But I'm not on your payroll either. I'm not trying to be mean, I'm trying to help you get better. You're a 30, eight and eight guy, and there's so much yet to do. That's *exciting*."

James came away impressed. "It was tough, but it was good," James said when I asked about the workout a few months later. He said he liked Ravin's methods. "He's good. I see why a lot of NBA guys work out with him."

They come because Ravin isn't afraid to tell them what they need to hear. "I try to convey it's not about anyone else, it's about you," explains Ravin. "Guys like LeBron can cut all the corners and still get an A on the exam. Eighty percent of Chris Paul or LeBron is better than 99 percent of anyone else. But I ask them: What if you maximized it? What if you were 99 percent? Isn't that interesting? I try to intrigue them. I say, 'What if?'"

In NBA circles Ravin inspires a wide range of reactions. Some coaches, like Eddie Jordan, see him as a resource. When Jordan was coach of the Wizards, he was having a hard time talking with Brendan Haywood, the Washington center who was then sharing minutes with Etan Thomas and was none too happy about it. Remembers Jordan, "Brendan loved working out with [Ravin], so I went to Idan and asked, 'How do you keep a positive relationship with Brendan?'" Ravin explained that Haywood merely wanted to be involved, to be part of the process. "You think he's challenging you, but all you have to do is ask his opinion," Ravin told Jordan. "Brendan's a cerebral guy. Empower him." Jordan took the advice to heart and, as he says, "I carried it over to my daily regimen, the idea that this is what I have to do with Brendan. And by the end we had a great relationship."

Other coaches, however, are not as welcoming, dismissing Ravin because he is not part of the basketball fraternity. (Ravin says Larry Brown in particular challenged him about his credentials.) And this is true: he has not apprenticed under a legendary coach or played for one or paid his dues as an assistant.

But the players don't care. They see him as a welcome alternative to the hierarchical infrastructure of the NBA. Carmelo Anthony flies him in for workouts during the season (and calls him Crouton because "his name rhymes with crouton, but he's a lot cooler than a regular cracker"). Suns guard Jason Richardson swears by him. And Wizards guard Gilbert Arenas used Ravin for almost all of his knee rehab during the 2008–09 season. If high school and college coaches provide fundamentals, Ravin is a final step in the development process. His is a business of refinement. "He knows the game so well and in turn knows his clients so well that he knows exactly how to get into their head," says Anthony. "Especially mine. Not only does he push me physically, but he also pushes me psychologically. He's a gym rat. He could go all day without stopping."

Ravin's training methods can be exotic, but what sets him apart is the way he relates to players, especially those like Anthony who have a history, at least with more traditional basketball types, of being difficult to reach. That's how Ravin got the half-joking nickname "the Hoops Whisperer," and it's why many of the world's best players now seek him out. "People say, 'What you do is not rocket science,' and it's not," says Ravin. "But you get Carmelo on the plane, get him to fly to L.A., get him to show up at 8 a.m., get him to run through a wall, get him to pay you. Now *that's* rocket science."

How Ravin accomplishes this, how he motivates his clients, provides a window into the inner life of elite NBA players.

———————

I first met Ravin in the summer of 2008, over coffee in Washington, D.C. We spoke for a few hours and then, over the course of the next nine months, kept in touch. (That was him in Chapter 1, breaking down Kobe's killer instinct.) I wanted to see more of his work, so in April 2009 I headed back to Washington. The goal was twofold: to witness his methods as he worked out players before the NBA draft; and to examine the results with him by watching two of his clients, Paul and Anthony, square off in the first round of the NBA playoffs.

We meet up on a warm spring morning in Potomac, Md., at the house of Andy Gold, a friend of Ravin's who works in finance. Though "house" doesn't do the place justice. Deep in the woods of D.C. suburbia, Gold's estate has, among other amenities, a spacious indoor gym. Built in 2000, the basketball floor is roughly three quarters of regulation length and the gym features breakaway rims, glass backboards, a scoreboard and a booming sound system. Ravin uses the court to work out his clients because a) it's private; b) it's motivational (as Ravin explains: "the players can relate to Andy because they're trying to make the kind of money he has"); and c) it's free.

In earlier years Gold would play in the games, living out every fortysomething guy's fantasy. (This is a dude who's been to five of the Michael Jordan fantasy camps, at $15,000 a pop, so he's obviously committed.) He was impressed with Alonzo Mourning, remembers Elton Brand as "soft and jiggly" when he first entered the league and talks about Anthony's striking ability to "turn it on."

On this morning Gold stays upstairs in his office ("trying to pay for this house," he jokes), while Ravin skips down a spiral staircase to the gym, followed by the day's clients, Sam Young (of Pittsburgh) and Jack McClinton (of Miami), both of whom have been sent to Ravin by Lance Young at Octagon Sports. Both players are early in their draft prep—neither has begun working out for NBA teams—and eager and optimistic. Young is hoping to be a lottery pick—he is pegged as a late first-rounder in mock drafts—and McClinton, who is projected as a second-rounder, is trying to move up to the first round.

As Young and McClinton put on their gear in silence, Ravin walks the court arranging a couple dozen small orange cones. He has a shaved head, prominent nose and large, hangdog blue eyes and is wearing a Washington Wizards sweat suit and a Dallas Mavericks workout shirt, none-too-subtle reminders of both his credentials and the goal at hand.

Ravin was raised in the Washington, D.C., area in a traditional Jewish household. After graduating from the University of Maryland and California Western School of Law, he joined a New York City law firm but soon soured on the field. During his 20s he began coaching kids two nights a week at a YMCA in San Diego, using unconventional drills of his own creation. Soon enough, as he recalls, all the kids wanted to be on Mr. Ravin's team. A few years later, back in the D.C. area, he casually ran some workouts for some college-level players, using those same drills. His big break came when Steve Francis, then a star at Maryland, showed up to one of the workouts and got hooked. He in turn brought another NBA-bound friend, Elton Brand. One referral led to another, and Ravin's client base grew. Before arriving, both Young and McClinton had already heard about Ravin's techniques, through Grizzlies forward Rudy Gay, so they knew what to expect. Sort of.

The workout begins without a warmup. Going one at a time, Young and McClinton dribble the length of the court through staggered sets of cones and finish with layups. With each time up and back, they perform a different move: crossover, then behind the back, then hesitation. As they work out, Ravin runs in front of them, commanding them to call out the number of fingers he is holding up (to ensure that the players keep their heads up), then behind them doing the same thing (to make sure they're aware of defenders), then has them finish with jump shots.

It's a relatively elementary drill, but Ravin's process can seem counterintuitive. For starters, his workouts rarely last longer than an hour, but with good reason. Rather than hours of running or repetitive drills, Ravin focuses on applying the lessons to game situations—remember, his players are already accomplished—using exercises he devises himself, and each is designed to provide conditioning along with skill development. When Richardson first hooked up with Ravin, he was a bit bewildered. "It was only 45 minutes, but it felt like two hours," Richardson told me. "It was weird. It was basketball, but at the same time it was conditioning. It was a whole bunch of things mixed up into one. I was like, 'I don't really know what all this is, but it helps out.'"

Many of Ravin's drills are intended to create a state of confusion. In one he throws tennis balls at the player who must catch them while maintaining his dribble. (Ravin can be seen doing this in a Nike ad with Anthony from a few years back.) The goal is not to improve hand-eye coordination, as one might assume, but rather to create sensory overload. "You make the player focus on everything else except the game so that the game skills become automatic," explains Ravin. "You try to make the unreasonable feel reasonable."

With Young and McClinton, for example, he sets up 13 cones within the key extending to the top of the circle and has the two players dribble between the cones without hitting them. With two balls. Moving forward and backward, left and right. Then bouncing one high and one low. This is Young and McClinton's fifth day with this drill, and upon seeing Ravin setting up, McClinton turns to me and says, "This is some hard-ass shit right here."

Indeed, it looks to me like a nearly impossible drill, like being asked to ride a bike through the pieces of a chess board. Still, both players fare pretty well, occasionally backing into a cone. "You should have seen us when we started," McClinton tells me.

With his two trainees Ravin dispenses subtle draft tips and motivation as he goes. While Young runs sprints, he shouts, "Lengthen your strides. Show them you're an athlete." As McClinton runs: "Avoid your heels when you run. It makes you look heavy and slow."

He throws in references to draft position—"Let's say you're picked 10th by the Hornets," he says at one point to Young—trying to keep them aspirational but realistic. As Ravin explains to me later, "You never want to lower expectations. You're stepping on dreams here."

And because this is all about the draft, Ravin sometimes focuses not necessarily on a player's greatest weakness but on his *perceived* weakness—in this case the perception of the NBA G.M.'s who will be doing the drafting. For Young, then, the focus is on ball handling. "He has to make sure he's spotless in the workouts because there's already the idea that he has trouble," Ravin explains. "The way the NBA guys look at it, when Sam loses the ball, they say, 'There he goes again, losing the ball.' Whereas with McClinton, when he loses the ball, they say, 'Oh, it just slipped.'"

If the flaw is elemental, however, Ravin doesn't even address it. In Young's case, that means living with his jump shot. At 6' 6" and 220 pounds of lean muscle, Young is a true specimen. When he first arrived at the University of Pittsburgh, as the story goes, he impressed coach Ben Howland by doing backflips down the court. His collegiate jams filled up many a highlight reel. But his jumper is something out of a basketball house of horrors. He uses two hands and spins up a flat shot. Rather than trying to fix it, though, Ravin knows it's better to reinforce it. "If I had five months, then I could try to change it," Ravin says. "In four weeks, though, all you're going to do is hurt his confidence. So instead I want him to shoot a million jump shots that way so he can make them when he needs to rather than breaking it down and stripping the guy of his confidence—because then he won't be effective."

As the players train, Ravin maintains a calm patter. Even when criticizing, he doesn't raise his voice. When he says, "Terrible shot, Jack," it is in just the same tone and volume as when he says, "Finish strong, Sam." Jordan, the former Wizards coach, believes this is an undervalued aspect not only of Ravin's approach but of modern coaching in general. "The voice is important these days whether you're a head coach or an assistant coach," Jordan says. "It's crucial that players know that you respect them. They've been yelled at so much during AAU and on up. You need a confident, direct voice, and [Ravin] has that."

Ravin also keeps the workout moving at an efficient pace, with no frills. He doesn't use a chalkboard, doesn't lecture and does most of his talking during the action. When he introduces a new drill, he doesn't explain it but rather runs it himself to demonstrate. Once the players understand what to do, he provides verbal reinforcement, for example saying, "Sit! Sit!" to remind someone to stay low when dribbling, or "Feet parallel!" during crossover drills. "You have to give them bits," says Ravin. "They all have ADD. They can't sit through two hours of coaching theory. Not one kid wants coaching theory." Instead, Ravin makes everything interactive. "I have ADD too. As a player, I'd rather do it and fail, do it and fail than have a coach move my hand to see what to do. These guys learn by movement."

The higher the skill level of his client, the more evolved the drills. When working with NBA players on finishing at the rim, for example, Ravin addresses a common shortcoming. On a drive to the basket, most players bring the ball down to help drive their leg up, thereby exposing the ball to the defense. So Ravin reprograms how his players jump, keeping the ball high and using their knees to drive upward.

To drill the move, Ravin stands to the side of a player—let's say it's Carmelo Anthony; as Anthony runs, Ravin keeps his hand waist-high, where the ball is. "I tell him to visualize Earl Boykins," Ravin says, referring to the superquick, 5' 5" former Nuggets guard. "You have to give them someone in the league they recognize to visualize. They all know Boykins or Brevin Knight, guys who have quick hands. So if I say, 'Brevin Knight is here,' they think, Fucking Brevin Knight, and if the ball gets too low, I strip it."

Often Ravin concentrates on a very small detail, the kind that can make a difference at the NBA level. Many players, for instance, catch a pass and bring it in to the chest, giving a defender an extra split second to close on the player. "If I'm Tayshaun Prince, and I'm closing out, I want to see that," says Ravin. So he has his players practice catching the ball and "pushing" it—that is, catching and sweeping in one direction, in one motion. He'll have them run, touch the baseline, run to the wing, catch the ball and "push" one direction for one dribble and shoot it. Then he'll do the same thing on the other wing, and so on, with myriad variations. "Then, when they get good at those, I show them a counter for that move," says Ravin. "Everything is a real-life situation."

After an hour Ravin tells Young and McClinton they're done. Both are drenched in sweat. McClinton stays on the court to work on a dribble move, while Young shows off his post pivot fake, then the three men fall into an easy conversation. There is no formal evaluation, just five or 10 minutes of small talk, with Ravin mostly listening. They talk about teammates, mutual friends, eating habits. To Ravin, this postworkout banter is essential time, especially with his longtime clients. He has found that it is after the workout, rather than before or during, that he learns the most about his players. "That's when you can understand a guy: What do they want, how did they get here. And they're pretty candid. You see where they struggle and excel." From that he knows which buttons to push. "You try to emphasize the struggle, because that creates the humility and the rawness, which allows people to see where they're not so good. From there, you learn by how he responds. Does he talk, does he complain, does he curse? Does he show up the next day earlier?"

Ravin rarely asks questions of his NBA athletes. "It's about understanding where they're coming from and how they learn, and those answers don't come from direct questions," he tells me. "Even something so small as a guy telling me that he's going to make sure he takes his mom out for Mother's Day—now maybe I come at him in a more sensitive way."

To be successful, Ravin realized, he has to see the world through the players' eyes. "The biggest mistake you can make is thinking these guys are stupid and inarticulate. Whatever language they speak, they speak it well. And it's not incumbent on them to understand me; it's up to me to understand them." His approach was evident in the different ways he communicated with McClinton and Young during their workouts. McClinton was eager and unafraid to fail; Young was more guarded. "It's just how each guy learns," says Ravin. With Jack [McClinton], I can give him the whole platter right away, and he'll dig in. With Sam, I just need to cut up the steak bite by bite. And it's up to me to figure that out."

Failure to understand a player's psyche is a flaw Ravin sees in the disciplinarian style of some coaches. Rather than empowering a player, they strip him of his authority. "At the end of the workout, I'll give players the option to run," explains Ravin. "I'll say, 'I think you've got more in you, but it's your choice.' They'll always run if you present the option in a fair way. And then when they're done, I'll say, 'I'm impressed with you. I think you have half a tank of gas left. I think it'd be great if you did another one.' And they'll say, 'Really?' And they'll do it. Players want to be part of the process."

Ravin's rapport comes in part from spending time with his clients' friends and family. Sometimes he has to win them over. When he first met Anthony's fiancée, the deejay LaLa Vasquez, at Anthony's house in Denver, she was skeptical. She looked Ravin up and down, then demanded, "What do you know about basketball?"

"Let me show you," Ravin said, and the two headed to the gym in the basement of the house. (A gym comes in handy in these situations.) For half an hour Ravin worked on Vasquez's shot—she'd played in high school. When they emerged again at the top of the stairs, she said to Anthony, "O.K., he's all right." As Vasquez remembers it, "In minutes he improved my shot, and I knew he was the one."

———

Workouts provided one perspective on Ravin's work, but I was also curious how he observed his clients from afar. During my visit the Nuggets are facing the Hornets in Game 2 of the first round of the Western Conference playoffs, so we meet up at a hotel bar in Bethesda to watch the game—and two of his prized pupils.

Right off the bat, Ravin notices an edge to Chris Paul as he walks onto the court. The Hornets are down 1–0 in the series. Ravin notes the way Paul is chewing his gum, as if trying to crush walnuts.

Paul is perhaps Ravin's most intense client. The two began working together after Paul left Wake Forest before the draft, and Paul is now so familiar with Ravin's drills that he does his workouts by himself when he travels, even for extended periods of time. "For six weeks," says Ravin, astonished. "It's a Navy Seal type of attitude. He has an inexhaustible spirit." Paul, in turn, appreciates that Ravin pushes him. "When I get tired, he'll motivate me to push through," Paul says. "He'll say, 'Gilbert Arenas ain't resting right now.' 'Steve Nash isn't resting.'"

Early on with each client Ravin begins to compile a mental dossier of sorts. He quickly learned that Arenas, for example, is very inquisitive and needs validation. So Ravin will say, "You're great doing this, but you could be greater or the greatest." Anthony is emotional and needs to be convinced of why he's doing things; says Ravin, "There has to be more dialogue."

Paul, on the other hand, doesn't need validating or convincing. "He has a natural chip on his shoulder, so all you have to do is remind Chris that just as he has evolved, so will other people," Ravin says, looking up at him on the TV screen. "There's always another kid out there that's just as hungry. He may be in high school, but he's coming."

Paul is also exceptionally competitive. As we watch the game, Ravin tells the story of when Paul was still preparing for the draft and got the chance to work out with Arenas, who was then an All-Star and an accomplished NBA scorer. For weeks Paul had worked out alone, and finally Ravin let him take on Arenas. As Ravin remembers, "Chris was like a dog let off the leash." Ravin had them play a series of one-on-one games designed to prepare players for the pace of the NBA. The rules force creativity. One game is two dribbles from the top of the key, no rebound, and a deflection results in change of possession. Another is one dribble from the wing, or three from half-court. (You'd be amazed how far an NBA player can get from half-court on three dribbles.) So Arenas and Paul play six of these games, each one a contest to seven points. "If I remember correctly," says Ravin, "Chris won the first four or five in a row. Gilbert looked at me like, This kid's going to be pretty good."

On the TV at the hotel bar, Anthony hits a pull-up jumper on his first touch. After the first game of the Nuggets-Hornets series, in which Anthony shot 4 of 12 and played poorly, Ravin sees the first shot as a good omen. "Gonna be a long night for the Hornets," he says. "He didn't rely on the catch-and-shoot. He put the ball on the floor. And believe me, that's an important first bucket for Melo. When you're the star player and you play poorly and the team still wins, part of you says, 'I want to be a part of this.'"

It is a pivotal time for Anthony, in Ravin's eyes. After five years as an NBA wild child, he is trying to be taken seriously. He's never taken the Nuggets past the first round of the playoffs, but this looks like the year. He even recently cut off his cornrows. "That's the evolution of Melo," says Ravin. "We're seeing him mature in front of the world."

It's a side of these players that Ravin says fans rarely see: Despite the stereotype, money is not the driving force for the great ones. "All these guys have a certain ambition to them," explains Ravin. "They've made generations worth of money. Motivation is no longer money. You can only have so many bedrooms in your house. Instead, these guys are consumed with being the absolute best at what they can do." In some respects, Ravin sees money as a demarcation line. "The average player may talk about girls, or cars. You give me the great players, and money's never part of the discussion. The great ones want to win a ring, want to make an All-Star team. They're motivated by each other. CP is wondering what Kobe is doing right now. Gilbert is thinking about LeBron."

Now it is the middle of the first quarter, and Anthony passes for the second consecutive time out of an isolation. "That's the evolution on the court," says Ravin. "He's making the pass there. Count his touches per shot—that's how you know how well he's playing." A minute and a half later Anthony hits a catch-and-shoot from the right side after one pump fake. "He's the most efficient wing scorer in the NBA," says Ravin. "Watch, and you'll see that he takes limited dribbles on everything. No more than three dribbles."

As the game goes on and Anthony continues to score, Ravin watches Anthony's body language. "Here he goes again. He's on fire. This is where if I'm George Karl, I let him play until he misses, because if not, Melo will get pissed. If I were Karl, I wouldn't pull him until early in the second. You have to remember, Melo's had five years of not getting past the first round. He's very excited. He's very motivated. Especially after a bad first game. You want him to feel like he's a big part of this."

Paul, on the other hand, is having a harder time as his Hornets fall behind early. Still, watching his client play, Ravin points out a couple of moves the two have worked on together. At one point Paul shoots a running two-hand floater. ("We work on doing that off either foot, so the defense can't time it.") Later, it's a "dribble-skip" move on the perimeter, where Paul dribbles sideways, almost literally "skipping" before punching through the defense. ("Watch how he never crosses his feet on the perimeter, so he's always in shooting position.") Then Paul gets a mismatch and dribbles back first, before attacking, to create more of a speed advantage against the bigger player. ("Derek Rose does that a lot too.")

By the end of the third quarter it's clear Denver is the better team this night. "This one's over," Ravin declares, and indeed it is. The Nuggets go on to win 108–93. As Paul walks off the floor, he is scowling, face scrunched up like a man whose wallet has just been stolen. Ravin shakes his head, then looks at me. "Tell you what," he says. "I don't think you need me to interpret that expression."

10

The Superbigs: Shaq, Yao and the Rise of Size

Late one evening, driving back to my hotel after covering a Suns game in Phoenix, I encountered a most unusual sight. This was in February 2009, and the Suns, struggling at the time, had cruised to a rare blowout win earlier in the night. Center Shaquille O'Neal had inflicted much of the damage, scoring 45 points and playing like a man a decade younger than his 36 years. Repeatedly he caught entry passes, dribbled once or twice—burrowing into the soft Toronto interior defense—then pump-faked before cramming the ball in the basket so hard the stanchion nearly collapsed.

I was 20 minutes into my postgame drive, tooling along in my rental car, a Volkswagen Jetta, when I pulled up to a red light on a two-lane suburban road in Scottsdale. I heard a strange gurgling to my left. Glancing over, I saw the longest, shiniest motorcycle fork imaginable, above which ran a similarly extensive set of silver handlebars, all of it attached to a tricked-out three-wheeler boasting a resplendent, sparkling spoiler. The machine was so big and otherworldly, like some vision from an apocalyptic future in which all earthly things had grown exponentially, that at first I didn't recognize the man astride it, for he looked comparatively normal-sized. Helmetless, eyes covered by sunglasses, he wore a tan T-shirt, tan sweatpants rolled up to his knees and tan hightops. The same clothes, it occurred to me, that O'Neal had been wearing in the locker room after the game.

The light turned green, and the three-wheeler tore off the line and into the distance, an SUV following a ways behind (which I figured to be Shaq's trail car). It was a surreal experience seeing the big man out and about like this, and that would have been the end of it except that, down the road, O'Neal came to a stop at another red light. My hotel turnoff was at hand, but I couldn't resist; when would I have another opportunity to drag-race Shaq? So I ignored my turn and kept going, pulling up next to O'Neal at the light. Glancing in his direction, I revved the rental Jetta's engine, producing a noise akin to a garbage disposal choking on a fork. O'Neal looked over, mildly surprised.

Now, at this point, let's stop to consider what this encounter tells us about O'Neal. First of all, here is an NBA Hall of Famer and global icon who, on a Friday night after a game, does not hide behind tinted windows or the bulk of a giant SUV but rather rides home on some crazy look-at-me contraption, instantly recognizable to every other motorist. Can you picture Kobe or Jordan doing this? Second, O'Neal must anticipate the reaction when he does this, because who knows how many other civilians get it into their heads, as I did, that they should try to race the Big Fella off the line, hoping to goad him into doing something spontaneous and human and, yes, probably a little dumb. Surely he was inured to such provocations by now, right? I figured it was worth a shot anyway.

The light turned green, and I let him have it, slamming the gas pedal down and pushing the Jetta for all it was worth, which, to be honest, was about a metaphorical buck-fifty.

After 50 yards or so, I was alone on the road.

Then, just as I was considering laying off the gas, disappointed that Shaq hadn't taken the bait, I glanced in my rearview mirror to see, approaching at approximately the speed of a cruise missile, the single, frosted headlight of O'Neal's bike. He passed me doing 100 or so and disappeared, taillights twinkling, like some crescent-bearded demon let loose into the Scottsdale night.

Only he hit another red light, so we did it again, and again Shaq torched my Jetta before continuing on to wherever it is All-Stars go after they score 45 points. Me, I U-turned and headed back to my hotel, where I immediately recounted this story to the bartender, who I'm pretty sure didn't believe a word of it. (Two nights later, when I saw Shaq at the arena and told him my tale, he smiled and said, "All right, so that was *you* in the Jetta.")

And here's the thing about Shaq: This was not some isolated instance. No NBA player in history has embraced his bigness quite as

O'Neal has. Figuratively and literally, he has lived an outsized life, the biggest, baddest, goofiest dude in every room. After all, this is a guy who once came out at an All-Star Game and performed an 80-second routine with the Jabbawockeez dance troupe; who became one of the first NBA athletes to employ Twitter and then, naturally, used it to invite fans to initiate conversations when he was out for lunch; who continued to make movies and rap albums even though it was clear early on that he wasn't especially good at either.

Likewise, he is totally content in his own skin when on the court. When coaches told him to lose weight, he ignored them. When they counseled that, in deference to increasing age, he should develop finesse moves to complement his bull-to-the-basket approach, he instead opted to bull harder. Sure, he claims to have a diverse game. As he once told Bob Young of *The Arizona Republic,* detailing his post repertoire, "My game is different. It's a mixture of everybody's game. When I was coming up, I was like, 'O.K., spin lob—David Robinson. Get the knees up—Rony Seikaly. Bow people in the face and look mean—Patrick Ewing.' Then I just added a little of my own." Really, though, for the entirety of his two-decade NBA career O'Neal's offensive strategy could be summed up as Just Try to Stop My Big Ass.

Now, this may seem like an obvious basketball strategy for any NBA giant, but it is not. Not all big men think of themselves as big, or even know *how* to be big for that matter. After all, scores of 7-footers have come into the league, but the great majority have been role players. Stand there and clog the lane. Stand there and grab offensive rebounds. Stand there on the sideline and wave a towel.

Obviously, talent plays a role. Some 7-footers are in the league primarily because they are 7 feet, not because they're especially good at basketball. Take Chuck Nevitt. During the '80s and early '90s the 7'5" Nevitt played for five teams in nine years but logged a total of 826 minutes, or the equivalent of about 17 games. His nickname was the Human Victory Cigar—because if he made it into a game, you knew it was a blowout. For a while the Houston Rockets kept him around primarily because he was good company for the coaches. Good-natured and quick-witted, he lists his career highlights as "blocking Kareem's sky hook in practice," "dunking on Bill Cartwright" and "talking to Jack Nicholson during timeouts." (He's not kidding. As Nevitt explained it to me, "When I was with the Lakers, Jack Nicholson had season tickets for the Clippers just so he could watch the Lakers play the Clippers. His seats were at the end of the bench, so a lot of the time I got to sit next to Jack. After a timeout, he'd ask what we were planning to do—if it was a special out-of-bounds play, what were we looking for. He really was interested in the game, and not just as a spectator. Those are some of my fondest memories.")

Like other big men of his era, Nevitt was expected to always do certain things and to never do others. "When I was coming along, the tall center's role was to stand in the middle, play defense, pass it out, then jog down the court," he says. "You were always considered the slowest guy on the team. In some ways it was a self-fulfilling prophecy."

With time, however, the position evolved; it became clear that there is an art to being big. Not just in the way personified by Shaq—the embracing of one's size—but in the deployment of that size. To understand how this came to be, let's examine three key steps in the evolution, beginning with a springy Navy grad and ending with the great, ongoing Yao Ming experiment, which is expanding the very boundaries of bigness.

———————

When David Robinson entered the NBA in 1989, opposing players had no idea what to make of him. Here was a man who, at 7'1" and 235 pounds, looked like a post player but preferred to play facing the basket. In many ways Robinson played like a very, very large small forward.

In evolutionary terms, Robinson was a mutation. It wasn't that some brilliant coach said, "Let's take this big kid and have him play like a small forward," but rather that Robinson *was* a small forward in his early basketball life. When he arrived at the Naval Academy, he was 6'6" and weighed 175 pounds. It was only when he proceeded to grow seven inches during college that he began to resemble an NBA center. But Robinson had already developed all the athletic traits of a smaller man. Better yet, he retained his coordination through his growth spurt. "To be honest, the main thing I couldn't do as well was gymnastics," says Robinson when I reach him on the phone. "I could still walk on my hands, but pull-ups became more difficult. Swimming became more difficult too, because my legs would drag." (Later in his career Robinson got back into swimming and, naturally, decided to challenge teammate Tim Duncan, who'd been an elite swimmer in the Virgin Islands when young. "I'd been taking swimming lessons with my boys," says Robinson, "and I thought maybe it was time to test it out." The two men swam a 50-meter freestyle. "It was ugly," he says laughing. "I was lucky to even finish.")

After entering the NBA, Robinson became a nightmare for opposing big men because of his speed and quickness. Here was a man the same height as they were, but he had a 34-inch waist and blazed around the floor. When other behemoths would take him aside to ask how he could move that way, Robinson would shrug. "I'd tell them it was because I grew late in childhood," he says. "I was a guy who ran high hurdles and track, so the running and jumping was easy. I just told them, 'All I am is a 5'9" guy in a 7-footer's body.'"

But just as the lumbering giants envied Robinson, he in turn envied them. When I asked Robinson to name one thing he wished he could have done but couldn't, he didn't choose playing point guard or bombing threes, as most bigs do. Rather he replied, "I always wish I had bigger hips, just more mass on me. It would have been fun to be a guy like Shaq who could just move guys out of the way, because I could never do that. I had to jump over them." Which, it should be noted, he did with remarkable success, winning an MVP award among all manner of other honors while averaging 21.1 points and 10.6 rebounds for his career. He became, in many respects, a prototype for the mobile 7-footers to come—lithe, agile big men like Kevin Garnett.

––––––––––––

If Robinson was the catalyst for one phase in the evolution of big men, Dirk Nowitzki represents the next. Nowitzki grew up in Würzburg, Germany, the son of athletes. His mother, Helga, was a basketball star, and his father, Jörg-Werner, played handball for the German national team. Like Robinson, the young Dirk played a variety of sports, including tennis and handball, before turning to basketball at 13. But here is where their stories diverge: Though already significantly taller than his peers, Nowitzki was not forced into the post and ordered to grab rebounds—like virtually every tall American kid. Rather, Pit Stahl, his first pro coach with DJK Würzburg in 1994, played him on the perimeter to take advantage of his shooting touch.

By the time Nowitzki entered the NBA draft in 1998, Dallas coach Don Nelson saw in him the potential for a genre-busting perimeter player. Inspired, Nelson helped engineer what has to be the greatest set of draft-day trades in NBA history—dealing first-round draft choice Robert (Tractor) Traylor, the sixth pick, to the Milwaukee Bucks for Nowitzki (the No. 9 choice) and Pat Garrity (No. 19). Dallas then shipped Garrity, two other players and a first-round pick in '99 to Phoenix for a backup point guard named Steve Nash. That's two MVPs for two bench players. (It is in moments like these that Nelson comes off as a crazy genius, making up for those times when he seems just plain crazy.)

Immediately, Nelson set about turning Nowitzki into a point-forward, a longtime obsession for Nelson; the experiment had limited initial success. In his first year Nowitzki was pushed around endlessly and was such a defensive liability that his nickname became Irk as in "No D." Under another coach, Nowitzki might have been sent into the paint, or down the bench, but Nelson didn't waver in his faith, insisting Nowitzki would "revolutionize the game." And, with Nash holding the reins of the racehorse Mavs offense, Nowitzki soon flourished as the first true perimeter big man. He became the first 7-footer to finish in the league's top 10 in three-pointers made and attempted (in 2000–01), the first 7-footer to win the All-Star three-point shootout (or even to be invited to compete, for that matter) and the first 7-foot, non–post player to be named league MVP. In retrospect, it seems the most natural concept in the world. "You don't normally see people of that size with such good touch," says Carroll Dawson, who was the Rockets' G.M. when Nowitzki entered the league. "If you can shoot off the dribble and you're 7 feet tall with long arms and you can also fall back, you can't be guarded."

That Nowitzki was such a good shooter was no doubt due in part to genetics, but there are two other factors not to be overlooked. First, despite his size, he was encouraged to shoot from the outside, both as a boy growing up and then as a Maverick. Second, he practiced his ass off. When Avery Johnson was coach of the Mavs, he became so concerned by Nowitzki's obsessive practice habits that he started fining his star if he found him in the gym on an off day. Nowitzki's solution? "He would sneak off to a high school gym," says Del Harris, an assistant with Dallas from 2000 to '07. "He and Jason Terry and whoever else they could drag with them. They'd find ways to get into a gym, or a high school or a health club and go shoot at night." I asked Nowitzki about this, and he smiled. "Yeah, whatever it takes, man." he said. "I remember in Philly we went to some health club that was like 100 years old and had wooden backboards."

Like Robinson before him, Nowitzki inspired a wave of imitators, multiskilled 7-footers, most of them European and most proving irresistible to NBA G.M.'s hoping for the next Dirk. Darko Milicic, the 7-footer from Serbia, was taken second in the 2003 draft but has never lived up to his promise. Three years later Toronto spent the first overall pick on Andrea Bargnani from Italy, another three-hoisting giant; and he has shown promise. And in 2008 New York used the sixth pick on Danilo Gallinari, a 6'11" Italian big man with a soft outside touch. Interestingly, there have yet to be any American-born 7-footers of a similar ilk who've had success, with the possible exception of Brad Miller, a 7-foot center adept at both passing out of the high post and dropping in 20-footers. And Miller takes exception to the stereotype of being a "European-style" big man. "European?" he says with a smile. "Before there was European there was Indiana." Indeed, Miller's skills can be traced to small-town Hoosier-ball. His marksmanship from the foul line is rooted in the free throw shooting contests he won at the Elks club in his hometown of Fort Wayne; and he developed his court vision in the share-and-share-alike flex offense at East Noble High, where as a 5'11" freshman he sometimes ran the attack.

(This gives me an excuse to pull out one of my favorite NBA anecdotes. While doing a story on Miller in 2003, I spent some time with him at his off-season home in Kendallville, Ind. On the morning we met, Miller looked pretty wiped out, and when I asked him why, he told me about the Drunk Olympics, a daylong contest of wills and livers that Miller considered nearly as important as any playoff game. Held every summer at the house of his best friend Steve's parents, outside Kendallville, the games began with a shotgun blast at 7 a.m., at which point everybody furiously chugged a beer. Eight teams of two, drawn from a hat the night before, then competed in a taxing day of competition, starting with nine-hole golf and continuing through half-court hoops (in which Miller was not allowed in the paint), grass volleyball, a three-legged sack race and, finally, the tricky around-the-lake canoe sprint. Any disputes were settled by chug-offs. "In seven years of the Drunk Olympics," Brad said very seriously and with obvious pride, "I have never finished worse than second.")

Unlike the versatile Miller, though, most American big men remain stuck in the paint. Orlando Magic center Dwight Howard is a perfect example. Growing up, he played point guard and idolized Magic Johnson, watching a VHS tape of *Magic Fundamentals* so many times he can recite some of the stilted dialogue by heart. Even after Howard enjoyed a freak five-inch growth spurt during his sophomore year at Southwest Atlanta Christian Academy, he harbored dreams of becoming the first 6' 11" point guard in the world. He practiced threes, made no-look passes and was his team's second option to bring the ball up against pressure. When playing *NBA Live,* Howard even created his own character every time he played: a big man who runs the offense.

Yet when Howard got to the Magic, drafted with the No. 1 pick out of high school in 2004, he was promptly sent down to the blocks. "What we do to most 6' 11" guys, unless they're named Dirk Nowitzki, is to take the ball out of their hands and put them on the block and take two dribbles," says Magic G.M. Otis Smith. "Which, don't get me wrong, is what you want to do, but it doesn't allow them to show off those skills."

———————

Chances are, the mobile big man and the sweet-shooting 7-footer could have emerged at an earlier time in the game's history if players had been given the opportunity. Surely Bill Walton, with his soft touch and feel for the game, could have stepped out further from the basket, and just imagine Wilt Chamberlain, who could dunk from the free throw line, running the wing in a Mike D'Antoni–style fast break. In the last 20 years, though, we've seen two players who exemplify a different breed of big man, a breed defined not by skill (though both players certainly possess it) but by extraordinary size. Shaq came into the game as the first successful 7-footer with the body of an offensive lineman. Now comes Yao Ming, the 7' 6" Rockets center who entered the league in 2002 as a curiosity, the giant from a faraway land, but has since become a player unique in the history of the NBA. Unique not because of his nationality but because he has evolved into the first truly dominating "supersized" player, that breed of NBA colossus taller than 7' 4".

Consider: Never before has there been a supersized player who wasn't a specialist or limited by physical shortcomings. Mark Eaton (7' 4") and Manute Bol (7' 6") were one-dimensional, useful only as shot blockers. Seven-foot-six Shawn Bradley of the Mavericks couldn't adapt to the pace or contact of the league and averaged only 8.1 points and 6.3 rebounds for his career. Gheorghe Muresan, the Bullets' 7' 7" center, had skills but played only three full seasons. The 7' 4" Ralph Sampson never played more than 50 games in a season after his third year in the league. None of them were ever asked to play 35 minutes a night and carry a team. Even Rik Smits (7' 4"), the Pacers center who made one All-Star team and had a successful 12-year career, never averaged more than 31 minutes, 19 points or eight rebounds in a season. In only seven seasons Yao is already more accomplished than any of his supersized predecessors, having made seven All-Star teams and averaging 20-plus points for three consecutive seasons to go with career averages of 9.3 rebounds, 1.9 blocks, 52.5% from the field and 83.2% from the line. Despite a series of injuries, Yao has also managed to log 77 or more games in four of his seven seasons while averaging 32.7 minutes a game for his career. (In 2007–08, he averaged a whopping 37.2 minutes.)

Yet, according to conventional medical wisdom, he has no business even being on the court. And so, for the last seven years, the Rockets have embarked upon a grand experiment in a quest to create and maintain the first supersized superstar. It has involved equal parts basketball training, physical conditioning and cultural education and has been remarkably successful, all things considered. To examine the process is to get a glimpse at what may be the outer limits of big-man play, for Yao is as close to a finished product as there is in the NBA, a player who, according to one NBA scout, "has maxed out his potential as much as any player in the league."

To understand how this has happened, it's helpful to know first just how unusual Yao is, from both a cultural and a genetic standpoint. As detailed in Brook Larmer's book *Operation Yao Ming,* Yao was the product of a government's obsession with athletic success. Hoping to create a basketball player of extraordinary height and skill, the Chinese government encouraged the coupling of Yao Zhiyuan, a 6' 7" star basketball player, and 6' 3" Fang Fengdi, one of the best female players of the era. Yao, the couple's only child, was 11.2 pounds and 23 inches at birth—nearly double the size of the average newborn in China—and was 5' 5" by the time he turned 10. He joined the Shanghai Sharks junior team at 13, practiced 10 hours a day and was playing against grown men on the senior circuit by 17. By the time he left for the NBA, at 21, he was not only a national icon but the country's primary hope for global sports relevancy. In his final season with the Sharks, he averaged a preposterous 38.5 points and 20.2 rebounds while shooting 76.6% from the field and, in one game of the playoffs, finishing 21 of 21 from the field.

The Rockets, from the beginning, treated him like a science experiment, albeit one with a potentially enormous payoff. Upon arriving in Houston, Yao weighed 300 pounds; five years later he weighed 302. (He has since gone up only slightly, to 310.) This was by design. The Rockets have wanted him to stay around 300 pounds to reduce the stress on his joints, in hopes that he will not be hobbled like so many of his outsized predecessors. "Most guys gain three or four pounds a year, which doesn't sound like much, but after 10 years it adds up," says Jeff Van Gundy, Yao's coach in Houston from 2003 to '07. "Not Yao. No player I've been around works harder. None. Ever."

Only once did Yao stray, after his first season. He'd gone home to Shanghai, then returned to Dallas to practice with the Chinese national team (coached by Del Harris). The Rockets sent their strength coach, Anthony Falsone, to check up on Yao. The two met in the lobby of Yao's hotel. "He looked good," recalls Falsone, "and he said he felt good. So I say, 'Let's go up to your room and check your body fat.' Well, I get up there and there are about 30 beer cans in the room."

Yao protests, smiling. "But only about 20 percent of them were mine! I had an old friend in town."

The beers were not lonesome; Yao had been enjoying his summer and had thickened to 330 pounds. It would be the last time. "At that time, I don't know how much more work I need to put into my career," he says. "I don't know how to keep myself in shape. Then, I stay here and train with [Rockets assistant] Tom Thibodeau, and that was the first year that Anthony totally worked for me. I feel good after that summer. I feel really, *really* good. I feel the next year is totally different."

Under the direction of Falsone, who became his personal trainer, Yao steadily gained strength without adding bulk. By the spring of 2007 he had transformed his body. Unfortunately he was also recovering from his third major injury in as many years. In December 2005 he had undergone surgery to clean out an infection in his left big toe that required doctors to shear off part of the bone. Four months later he broke a bone in his left foot, requiring surgery. Then, just before Christmas 2006, he suffered a bone fracture under his knee when teammate Chuck Hayes toppled onto his leg.

Yao began his rehab five days after the injury. By this time, he had ceased brooding, deeming it unproductive. (This is how Yao thinks.) He started by lifting weights, working with Falsone, then moved on to working with Thibodeau on his touch, shooting baskets from a chair. By early February, Yao was running again, weeks ahead of schedule. Curious to see the recovery in action, I flew down to Houston for a couple of days.

On a cool morning Yao arrives at the Toyota Center in downtown Houston at 9 a.m. for his workout. The Rockets are on the road, playing in Dallas, so it is eerily quiet in the arena. Yao is greeted enthusiastically by Falsone, a short, energetic man with a shaved head who is the kind of guy who shows off his biceps by declaring, "Welcome to the gun show!" He puts Yao to work right away in the weight room. The only sounds come from the clanking of iron and Falsone's constant patter.

"Quality. Always quality."

"Pause. You're not pausing."

Though he doesn't look bulky, Yao is far and away the strongest player on the Rockets. (He can bench 310 pounds.) When he first arrived as a rookie, never having done much weight training, he struggled to perform incline presses with 45-pound dumbbells and then watched teammate Jason Collier hefting 100-pounders. Yao turned to Falsone and asked if he'd ever be able to do that. "This year," Falsone tells me, "we bought 120-pound dumbbells just for Yao."

At first the opponent who drove Yao to become stronger was Shaquille O'Neal. Now it is Dwight Howard. When Howard's name comes up during the workout, Yao peppers me with questions. "Does Howard have a trainer?" "How much is he lifting—Steve Francis said Howard was *always* lifting." With Shaq on the downside of his career, Howard is the one NBA center athletic enough and strong enough to pose a threat to Yao over the next five years. "A lot of NBA centers are not that strong," Yao says. "They are big but a little soft. But he is strong, *very* strong." (Howard sees their dynamic in much the same way. "Every time we play each other it seems he plays extra hard," Howard said when asked about Yao. "It's sort of like a rivalry." Told Yao is benching 310, Howard smiled. "Oh, that's pretty good." He waited a beat. "My highest is 345.")

After an hour of lifting, Yao and Falsone head to the practice field at Reliant Stadium, home of the NFL's Texans, so Yao can run on its forgiving rubberized surface. It is a 20-minute drive, and on account of Yao's knee, Falsone drives Yao's Infiniti QX56 SUV. Though it's not on display this morning, Yao's erratic driving is a source of great delight to many of the Rockets. When he first came to the U.S., Yao had never driven a car—"He was riding a bike the day I first met him [in Beijing]," says G.M. Carroll Dawson. He learned to drive in parking lots, then passed his driving test (a source of great pride). But he remains less than expert. He once backed into a teammate's car in the Rockets parking lot and has been known to poke along on the highway at 40 mph.

As Falsone drives, Yao sits in the front passenger seat, one enormous leg crossed over the other. Falsone puts on a U2 CD and cranks it up. Yao asks him to skip forward one track, then one more.

"This one?" says Falsone.

"Yes," says Yao.

The opening chords of "Desire" rumble through the car, Bono's opening exhalation followed by that staccato guitar riff.

"I can't listen to this song and drive," proclaims Yao, moving his head. "I begin to drive too fast."

They arrive at Reliant. Once inside the practice bubble, Yao begins running, starting at one goal line and loping toward the other. Each day, Falsone will ratchet up the pace. The following week, responding to pressure from his team and representatives, Yao will fly to Las Vegas for All-Star weekend on one condition: that he can continue his rehab work. Though he is booked for a half-dozen events each day, Yao is up at 6 a.m. working out. "I guarantee you he was the only NBA player who didn't attend a party that weekend," says Bill Sanders, the vice president of marketing for BDA Sports Agency, which handles Yao's affairs. "When you talk about the Americanization of Yao, that's the one part I'm glad he hasn't taken on."

It is now late March of the same year, and after missing 32 games, Yao is back in the lineup. The Rockets have won 6 of 8 since Yao's return, and the team feels good about its chances of passing the Utah Jazz for home court advantage in the first round of the playoffs. On this night the opponent is the Indiana Pacers.

As he does on the day of every game, Yao arrives at the arena at 9 a.m., an hour and a half before the team shootaround. And here we see another aspect of the great experiment: the relentless honing of skills—for even the simplest of basketball tasks do not always come easy to a man of Yao's size.

As always, Thibodeau is there to meet him. A former assistant at Harvard, Thibodeau is a thick-chested man with short, thinning hair and an unvarying baritone that makes him sound as if he should be doing voice-over work. (Rockets guard Rafer Alston calls it "his commando voice.")

Thibodeau begins by going over tape, showing Yao how he will be defended by Jeff Foster, Indiana's center, and Jermaine O'Neal, the Pacers' power forward. (Regularly, Thibodeau will make tapes for Yao to take home with him—of Kevin McHale's jump hook, of all of Yao's fouls. Other times, Yao requests tapes, as he did over the winter when he asked to watch teammate Dikembe Mutombo's rebounding.) After 45 minutes of video, Yao and Thibodeau head to the practice court, where Yao runs through shooting drills for 45 minutes. Then, sweaty and breathing hard, he joins his teammates, who have now arrived, some still sleepy-eyed, for the morning shootaround. The old trope comes to mind about the guy who does more before 9 a.m. than most men do all day.

Yao is also the first on the floor at the Toyota Center that evening, arriving at 6 p.m. for an 8:30 game. He begins with spot shooting, circling through nine locations, seven on the perimeter and the two "short corners," which are 15-foot baseline shots. The goal is to hit 8 of 10 at each spot; if he fails, Thibodeau gives him a second chance. Most of the time, he doesn't need it. As he shoots, Thibodeau calls out his make percentage. "One-two, two-three, three-four."

Yao makes 9 of 10 from the left elbow, then only 7 of 10 from the wing.

Yao curses under his breath. On other misses, he grimaces, or shakes his large head. Alston calls Yao's approach "almost perfectionist"; Rockets forward Juwan Howard calls it "extreme, in a good way." To watch him shoot is to see the motion at its most refined. He keeps the ball high and releases it with his right hand in a short flicking motion, as if playing Pop-a-Shot. He does not jump and barely even moves his legs. His form is entirely replicable, almost robotic. By contrast, when Alston begins shooting jumpers 15 minutes later, his form is an intricate series of bodily tics and jerks. He takes the ball from near the floor and whips it to his shoulder, then splays his elbow forward, leaping and catapulting the ball. It does not look as if Alston is even engaged in the same activity (and, considering Alston's 38.6% field goal percentage, in some respects he is not).

Next Yao steps to the line, where he hits 10-of-10 free throws. He is, at the time, shooting 86.0% from the line for the season, second only to Kobe Bryant among players who average eight attempts or more per game. Yao's percentage not only leads all Rockets—he regularly shoots the team's technical free throws—but is nearly 10 percentage points better than any other NBA center's. In fact, there has never been a back-to-the-basket center as accurate from the line. (Former Bucks center Jack Sikma shot 84.9% for his career, but he was a 6'11" jump shooter.) Yao's free throw accuracy provides the Rockets with a unique weapon. In late-game situations, they can go to their best post player and simultaneously put the ball in the hands of their best free throw shooter.

"O.K., post moves next," commands Thibodeau.

Yao sets up on the right block, practicing jump hooks, then turnarounds. It is part of his continuing education as a low post player; developing counters, taking angles, rooting for position. "What people forget is that he was an elbow player when we got him," says Dawson, referring to the area at the edge of the free throw line. "He had a lot of finesse things in his system, and we felt like power moves were what he needed."

As Yao works, Thibodeau reminds him to "crab" in the lane—to keep his legs bent and the ball low to prevent it from being stripped—because Yao's primary weakness remains turnovers. (He averages 2.7 for his career.) Because of his height, the moment Yao puts the ball on the floor, he is prey to double-teaming guards or shorter, quicker defenders. The same is true when a cutter runs off his hip. "He struggles when a point guard throws it in and cuts baseline," says McGrady, whom Thibodeau credits with helping Yao with double teams. "Yao tends to forget that some of those defenders come back right on the baseline on his blind side." For his part, Van Gundy would prefer that Yao never even dribble the ball. "You got a bunch of fucking midgets on you," says Van Gundy. "Just turn around and shoot the ball."

When Yao secures good position and faces up, he is virtually unguardable, as is clear two hours later against the Pacers. When he squares up in the first quarter, Foster, the Pacers center, doesn't even try to alter his shot. Later, against Jermaine O'Neal, one of the leading shot blockers in the league, Yao has only to turn his shoulder to shoot uncontested jump hooks. Though his knee is still balky—it is the first night he has worn a sleeve rather than a brace—he makes 10 of 17 shots from the field (and 12 of 13 from the line) and finishes with 32 points and 14 rebounds in an 86–76 Rockets win.

He is also more confident on the floor, another element of his evolution. At one point he even breaks off a play—"he never used to do that!" says Van Gundy, almost giddily—to go at his man on the block. For a player versed in strict obedience, as all Chinese athletes are, it is an encouraging sign. Van Gundy says Yao has added the proper amount of stubbornness, and Thibodeau says, "His self-assurance now is as high as it's ever been." Yao agrees that he feels more confident, but despite his numbers, he still sees himself as an outsider among the NBA elite. "I still have a long way to go," he says. "I feel that every year I am getting better, better, then—boom—next level. And then a new, stronger player is coming. And I feel, Where is the end?" He pauses. "If you relax or take it easy for yourself, they will beat you, someday. Maybe tomorrow, maybe day after tomorrow."

Told this is a rather fatalistic viewpoint for a five-time All-Star, he smiles: "That is what 1.3 billion people watching you will do."

––––––––––––

Flash forward two years. It is spring 2009, and the experiment continues. But some things have changed. On Feb. 26, 2008, Yao was injured again, this time suffering a stress fracture in his left foot and missing the remainder of the season.

He returned to the court in time for the Beijing Olympics, serving the role of global ambassador for which he was literally conceived, and arrived healthy for Rockets training camp. Three quarters of the way through the 2008–09 season, when I see him next, he is once again an All-Star and the dominant offensive big man in the league—though increasingly challenged by Dwight Howard. The difference between the two men is, still, Yao's skills. "You can throw the ball into Yao 20 times and play a game through him because he's a phenomenal passer out of double teams," one scout tells me. "You can't do that through Dwight. He can finish at the rim, but you can't just run turnouts and post-ups for him 20 times."

The Rockets' primary concern remains Yao's health, and with good reason. Per 100 possessions, when Yao is on the court, Houston scores 5.6 more points on offense and allows 5.4 fewer points on defense than when he is not on the floor. He will finish the season with his typical numbers: 19.7 points and 9.9 rebounds, to go with 1.9 blocks while shooting 54.8% from the field and 86.6% from the line. He doesn't get included in the MVP debate, obscured by the extraordinary seasons of LeBron James, Dwyane Wade and Kobe Bryant, but he really ought to be.

Over breakfast at a restaurant near the Toyota Center, Hinkie discusses the ongoing challenge that is Yao's health. Especially for someone like Hinkie, a big proponent of quantitative analysis, it is a flummoxing proposition. "We are swimming in a sea of data," he says, exasperated. "You can find whatever you want to find. You can find guys who had foot problems, guys who kept playing. Everyone's got theories [about the superbigs]."

One involves Yao's circulation. When he suffered from an ingrown toenail, Yao required surgery. Afterward, according to Hinkie, the doctors posited that it wasn't a problem with the toe itself so much as poor circulation: Because of Yao's size, perhaps his heart just had too far to pump the blood to reliably get it to his toe. "Maybe it's true," says Hinkie, "but call me a skeptic. I don't trust any of the theories."

What *is* certain is not to trust the diagnoses from Yao himself. Ask him about an injury, and his response tends to be either a) it doesn't hurt; or b) it hurts a little, but I can play through it. "That's part of the medical process, you know?" says Hinkie, laughing. "If the patient feels pain, then A, and if not, then B. But he never says he feels pain. So we always get X-rays with Yao."

There are also concessions. When I arrive three hours early before a Rockets-Cavaliers game, intent on watching Yao go through his grueling workout again, I find it has changed a bit. For one, Thibodeau is gone, hired away by Boston. So Yao goes through his routine with the help of whoever is around—an assistant coach, or, in this case, a ball boy. "It's all up here anyway," he explains, pointing to his head.

The workout is also truncated. Yao jokes to me that "I'm getting old and lazy," but this is, of course, not the case—he continues to display one of the best work ethics in the league. Maybe, Rockets coaches believe, if they can curtail that ethic a bit, they can lessen the chance of injury. Similarly, Yao is asked to take it easy during some practices. "It's all part of the compromise," explains Jonathan Feigen, the *Houston Chronicle* writer who covers the team. "They just want to see him in the playoffs for once."

At the time, with a month to go in the regular season, the Rockets hold the second seed in the Western Conference, well-positioned for the postseason (and as it happens, they will finish with the fifth seed, and Yao will make the playoffs. He will finally win in the first round and then, sadly, go down with yet another injury three games into the second-round series against the Lakers, this time with a broken left foot. The hairline fracture will require surgery and, in July, the Rockets will announce that they don't expect Yao back until the start of the 2010 season, setting back the grand experiment once more).

Across the brackets Howard is leading the Orlando Magic, now the second seed in the East. As for Shaq, he put up impressive numbers for the remainder of the season in Phoenix, but the Suns missed the playoffs. Of course, this doesn't stop him from continuing to enjoy the ride, or preaching the gospel of bigness.

An example: On the same weekend of our one-sided street race, I watched as O'Neal lumbered into the Suns' locker room before a game and, midway through his stroll to the training room, fixed his eyes on Robin Lopez, the Suns' 7-foot, 255-pound rookie reserve center with the haystack hairdo.

"Why you always bending over?" Shaq asked, though it was really more of a declaration.

"Huh?" said Lopez.

"You're always bending over. You're a 7-footer. Be a 7-footer!"

Lopez blushed.

"Seriously, you're down here, and it's like you're six-three"—and here Shaq mimicked Lopez, bent at the waist playing defense—"You do that, and I can just turn and shoot over you."

Lopez nodded, unsure of what to say.

Shaq continued. "There's only a few guys in this league who can hurt you down there. Gasol, Jefferson, Howard, Yao. The rest ain't gonna do shit."

O'Neal started walking, continuing toward the treatment room on the far side of the locker room, then swiveled. "You know what it is? You don't like being tall. You don't like being tall at all."

"Huh?" said Lopez

Now O'Neal turned to Grant Hill, the Suns' forward, who was sitting at his locker nearby, checking his cellphone.

"Am I right, Grant? He don't like being tall."

Hill looked up. "I'm not getting in the middle of this one."

"Tell you, man, you don't like being tall."

Shaq paused, then summed up what may be the real secret to being big. "The thing about being a seven-footer," he said. "You gotta like it. You gotta *like* it."

Shot Blockers: A Rare Affection for Rejection

The dunk is electrifying, it is emphatic, it is a coronation. But it is also something else: common.

During the typical NBA season, there are more than 8,000 dunks. That works out to an average of more than three per game. In other words, a fan can attend any given NBA matchup and reasonably expect to see at least a few jams, knowing that almost any player on the floor is capable of the feat. *Blocking* a dunk, however, is a different matter.

The snuffed jam is one of the most exotic of NBA sights, the hoops equivalent of a birder seeing an endangered spoon-billed sandpiper. Most seasons, there are fewer than 300 blocked dunks, a scarcity that is attributable in part to the difficulty of the act: The odds are always stacked against the defender. He is stationary; the man with the ball has a running start. He must go straight up and down and worry about a foul call; the dunker can roar in at any angle—and when have you ever seen a player get called for an offensive foul on a dunk? Then of course there's the pride factor; only certain players are willing to risk the potential embarrassment of trying to block a dunk and failing.

One such risk-taker is Emeka Okafor, the center for the New Orleans Hornets (recently traded from the Charlotte Bobcats). Okafor is a regal-looking man, with a high forehead, sharp cheekbones and deep-set eyes you could almost describe as pretty. He could be a senator or an African king, albeit it one built like an oversized NFL tight end. Okafor carries most of his weight in his thickly muscled torso, which appears disproportionately large compared to his legs. Though 6' 10" tall, his wingspan is 88 inches, which makes him quite handy if you need a lightbulb changed or a basket protected.

Watch him in action. It is a January evening a few years back, and the Bobcats are hosting the New Jersey Nets. On one side of the lane Okafor is standing and staring intently away from the basket. He looks like a man lost in thought, and this is on purpose: He is baiting a hook, hoping one of the Nets will bite.

On the other side of the key, New Jersey center Mikki Moore obliges. Receiving a scoop pass on the right baseline, Moore takes one dribble and aims his 7-foot frame at the rim for what appears to be an easy dunk. Okafor, who has been waiting for just this moment, swivels and, with shocking quickness, takes one long step and launches himself toward the far side of the rim. Now, when Okafor leaps to block any other kind of shot, he prefers to turns sideways, like a waiter navigating a crowded room, so that he can extend his right arm as far as possible. But when he leaps to block a dunk, he likes to go straight up, the better to absorb some of his opponent's body weight. In this situation, however, he must cover so much ground that he has to jump at an angle, making his odds of success even worse than usual.

The two men meet above the rim, and there is a thudding sound. It's a violent moment and can be a dangerous one; meet the dunker too close to the basket, and the shot blocker risks having his hand slammed back into the iron, an easy way to break a finger. This time, however, Okafor prevails, stuffing the shot and sending the ball spinning back to the floor. The crowd at Bobcats Arena is momentarily roused, and they cheer politely; but it's unlikely that many understand the difficulty of what Okafor has just done. Nearly halfway through the season—in this case 2006–07—it is only his 11th blocked dunk. Still, that is enough to lead the league; no other player has even reached double digits.

For Okafor, that play against Moore is the product of years of practice. Growing up in Houston, his favorite sport was football; he only began playing basketball because his father enrolled him at the local Y when he was eight years old. Even so, as he remembers, "blocking shots was basically my first basketball skill." As a high school senior he averaged six stuffs per game. At the University of Connecticut he averaged 4.3 a game. During his first five years in the NBA he averaged 1.9, and on one memorable night in January 2007, Okafor blocked 10 shots against the Knicks. When I later asked which of the 10 he remembered most fondly, he smiled. "They were all good," he said. "I love all my children."

Okafor's barrage of blocks against the Knicks is especially notable because, increasingly, such performances are anomalies. The dominant shot blocker, once a common sight on the NBA landscape, is a disappearing breed. Gone are the days of lumbering giants like Mark Eaton—of whom *Los Angeles Times* columnist Jim Murray wrote, "The Empire State Building has grown arms." Today's practitioners are a more disparate group, consisting of undersized centers, lanky forwards and the occasional old-school specialist. And while there are still standouts—namely Dwight Howard and Marcus Camby—the group as a whole is blocking fewer shots. While the blocked dunk has always been the rarest, blocks of all kinds have become increasingly scarce. From 2002 to 2007 the league-wide average declined almost every year, hitting a nadir of 378 per team in 2006–07, the fewest blocks in a season since 1976. The following season the number was only marginally better, at 388, and in 2008–09 it was 394. "You need the mentality to do it," says Alonzo Mourning, who averaged 2.8 blocks per game over his career. "And I don't see a lot of guys having it today."

Also to blame: 7-footers who play 20 feet from the basket; the increasing popularity of the three-pointer; running teams that rarely post up; the defensive three-second rule; and a dearth of coaches willing to start a purely defensive center. "I think a lot of teams are caught up in points per possession," says Nets coach Lawrence Frank. "People will tell you the best shot is a layup, the second is a corner three, the third is another three not in the corner. There's such an emphasis on having offensive players on the floor that if a shot blocker isn't multidimensional, then it's harder for him to be out there. Plus, shot-blocking is a very hard skill to find."

It also suffers from something of an image problem, starting with the word itself. To block something is to halt its progress. Football linemen block defenders, e-mail filters block spam, toilets get blocked up. This is not a glamorous word, making it much more satisfying to employ euphemisms. So we call them swats and stuffs and snuffs. We talk about the ball being "rejected!" and "returned to sender!" And, ever-popular, "getting that shit out of here!"

Whatever you want to call it, the block seems to be on the wane, and elite swatters have become more valuable than ever. Consider the case of Dikembe Mutombo, the Houston center who retired ranked second alltime in blocks. In 2006–07, even at 40 years old, Mutombo had a significant impact on Houston's defense when he filled in for an injured Yao Ming. When Mutumbo was on the court, opponents scored four fewer points per 100 possessions and shot about 3% worse.

So why doesn't every team train one of its big men to patrol the paint? Well, because it's not that easy. First off, just being big does not a shot blocker make. There are plenty of 7-footers who, for one reason or another, seem incapable of swatting anything more than houseflies. Second, not all blocks are equal—send a ball out-of-bounds, for example, and you give it right back to the offense. Talk to those who've mastered the craft, and they'll tell you that it is a science, one that can be studied and refined but, as it turns out, rarely taught.

———————————

Until the 1973–74 season the NBA didn't keep statistics on blocked shots, but if it had, Bill Russell surely would have put up some gaudy numbers. The original defensive stopper, Russell was only 6' 10" but played as if he'd sworn an oath to protect the basket. Most players played defense; Russell *lived* it. Here he is, describing his shot-blocking philosophy to *Sports Illustrated* in a 1958 story. "Look," Russell said, "If I tried to block all the shots my man takes, I'd be dead. The thing I got to do is make my man *think* I'm gonna block every shot he takes. How can I do it? O.K., here. Say I block a shot on you. The next time you're gonna shoot, I *know* I can't block it, but I act exactly the same way as before, I make exactly the same moves. I'm confident. I'm not thinking anymore, but I got *you* thinking. You can't think and shoot— nobody can. You're thinking, Will he block this one or won't he? I don't even have to try to block it. You'll miss."

Russell saw each defensive possession as a psychological challenge—later stating that he figured he could only block "eight to 10 percent of the shots taken against me," but he endeavored to make his opponent think he was going to go after at least 90%. His tactics were often not only counterintuitive but also required some intelligent restraint. "The year before I came into the NBA, Neil Johnston was third in the league in scoring, and I was worried about him from the start," he said in a 1965 *SI* cover story he cowrote called "The Psych . . . and My Other Tricks." "I wasn't worried about his shooting; Neil had a low-trajectory, soft little hook, and I figured I could block nine out of 10 of them. But this created a new problem for me. If I did block them, Neil would surely change his style against me and come up with something I probably couldn't handle as easily. So I took the psychological route. I would let him alone just enough to keep him puzzled; block just enough so that he wouldn't get riled and try something new. I would keep a little mental box score and make sure the score came out in our favor. Or try, anyway."

More than any player before or since, Russell proved that defense alone can dominate a game, that intimidation could be not only cool but effective. As such he inspired countless big men to come. "I remember there were times when Russell wouldn't come past the top of the key on offense," says Kareem Abdul-Jabbar. "He'd let them run the fast break and stay back because that's where he thought he belonged." Naturally, Abdul-Jabbar says, he patterned his own shot-blocking after Russell's.

In Russell's wake, many of the next generation of centers focused on defense as much as offense. It wasn't until the 1980s, however, that the league saw the advent of the first true shot-blocking specialists, offensively inept giants like the 7' 4" Eaton and Manute Bol, the 7' 7" Sudanese tribesman turned NBA scarecrow who played for the Warriors and the Bullets. Because of their height, neither man had to jump to block a shot, so pump fakes were useless against them. While with the Warriors, Bol once blocked eight shots in a *quarter,* and he had more blocks than points in all but two of his 10 NBA seasons. Eaton still holds the NBA record for blocks in a game with 14, and during the 1984–85 season he blocked an astonishing 456 shots—or a good 50 more than most NBA *teams* do these days. That season he averaged 5.6 a game. Eaton never topped this mark, and with obvious reason, he says. "You know you're really changing the game as a shot blocker when your numbers go down," he told me. "That means teams aren't even attempting certain shots because you're in there."

Eaton and Bol gave way to a golden age of multitalented big men in the early '90s: Hakeem Olajuwon, who played with instincts he developed as a young soccer goalie in Nigeria; David Robinson and Patrick Ewing, who relied on length; and Shaquille O'Neal, whose girth alone shut down driving lanes. A few years later they were joined by Dikembe Mutombo, who was fond of wagging an enormous ET finger in the direction of the blockee. (This, I must note, was actually a point of contention for Dikembe. He started wagging in 1996, shaking his finger at the victims of his blocks. But in 1999 the NBA banned his gesture. Four years later a compromise was reached, and he was allowed to wag the finger, for the fun of the fans, as long as it wasn't a taunting gesture made at the opponent.) At the same time as Mutombo entered the scene, along came Alonzo Mourning, who boasted great timing and a willingness to challenge every shot. Blocked shots were now very much in vogue.

Ten years later, as late as 2008, Mourning remained, tellingly enough, the league's most-feared big man. Never graceful or even especially athletic, Mourning preferred to lurk near the rim and rely on timing and pursuit. "Even when I can probably get there a little earlier and prevent them from taking a shot, I'll wait for a guy and make him think he has an opportunity to get a shot off," he explained. "Then I'll go get it."

This ploy, the bait-and-block, is one of many tricks of the trade. A primer might include these tips: 1) know your pump fakes (Kobe Bryant and Tracy McGrady are especially dangerous); 2) swat with the hand opposite the shooter's for better extension (a favorite of Ben Wallace's); 3) watch your man's jersey, not his eyes ("the eyes lie," warns Eaton); 4) beware the nearly unblockable floater of guards like Tony Parker (it's the blocker's mirage, there one second, gone the next); and 5) know who loves to get to the line (Utah's Andrei Kirilenko rates Boston's Paul Pierce as the easiest "good" player to block because Pierce is forever trying to get a shot off near the basket in hopes of getting to the free throw line, sometimes offering up easy block opportunities).

Another tip would be this: Beware those players who jump into shot blockers. On this last count, Wizards guard Gilbert Arenas is the most notorious, barreling into the paint and creating contact, then waiting to release the ball. Okafor says he won't even try to block his shot, instead backing up to avoid the foul. (Then a suddenly worried Okafor adds, "Wait, no, don't use Gilbert's name because he'll read that this is what Mek does against me." Sorry, Omeka, but I'm pretty sure Gilbert already knows.)

If there is a blocker's mantra it is this: Know your adversary. Certain big men like Eddy Curry and Zach Randolph like to muscle inside with the ball, then go straight up, affording ample opportunity to pick off the ball from behind. Dirk Nowitzki likes to fade on his jumper; meaning the best way to pick off his shot, according to Kirilenko, is to sneak in from behind and time the release. And some are just easy targets, often rebounding specialists whose offensive game is more wishful than skillful. For example, almost one out of every five shots Reggie Evans took during the 2008–09 season (18%) was blocked, the highest rate in the league among players with at least 100 attempts. When Reggie shoots, big men thank him.

For sheer dramatic impact, no block is more impressive than a Karch Kiraly–style spike that whistles six rows deep in the crowd. Of course, no block is less valuable either, as the defense has no chance of gaining possession. Still, year after year young players enter the league airmailing balls (because it feels good) and driving their coaches crazy (which may feel good too). Even when a player knows better, the temptation is strong. "I've been trying to keep my blocks in-bounds," said Dwight Howard, who led the league in 2008–09 with 2.9 blocks per game (and also led the league in shots blocked out-of-bounds, with 55). "It's tough though, because I like to watch it go out-of-bounds, and then the crowd *oohs*. It's just *fun*." Then he added with a grin, "If I send it out-of-bounds, the other team gets the ball back, and there's probably like a 10 percent chance that I might block *another* shot in the same sequence."

Howard is kidding, sort of. Whether he practices it or not, he knows as a shot blocker you always try to keep the ball in play, preferably by tapping it to a teammate. Russell was a master at this, as was Kevin McHale; Eaton developed soft hands on his blocks by pretending he was tipping a jump ball. Mourning had to teach himself to hold back, and by the end of his career, he says, he sometimes tapped it *too* lightly, mistakenly sending the ball back to the player who shot it. Others have naturally soft hands: During the 2005–06 season Raptors forward Chris Bosh blocked 74 shots without sending a single one out-of-bounds.

There's also such a thing as an overzealous shot blocker. Chase too many jumpers, and you end up out of position for the rebound; gamble too much on the weak side, and your man is open for a layup. The worst result is, of course, the goaltend, which gives away free points. (Philly's Samuel Dalembert is one of the more egregious offenders, accumulating an average of 34 a season from 2005 to 2009. He is still no match for the ever-busy Howard, who has averaged 51.5 goaltends over the last two seasons.) Committing a foul is almost as bad. All of which makes players like Marcus Camby (consistently near the top in blocks per foul, at a career average of 0.893) and Mourning (0.838 for his career) more valuable than less-controlled leapers like Brendan Haywood (0.536).

Those who excel at foul-free shot-blocking achieve it in different ways. Mourning and Mutombo waited near the rim, like human gargoyles; Okafor uses lateral quickness and anticipation; Andrei Kirilenko, the spider-armed Utah sixth man, prefers to come from behind the shooter after hiding "in the shadow of my teammate," as he puts it. And Howard, well, he has the advantage of not being human, or so it seems when a man that large leaps so quickly and rises that high.

Most grew up with a gift for it. Okafor says he was "blocking shots before I knew what a block was." Kirilenko played point guard as a boy in Russia but still averaged "probably three blocks a game." Mourning remembers as a teen violently spiking anything that came near him.

The 7' 4" Eaton, however, is a different story. Eaton was an aspiring auto mechanic as a teenager when, by virtue of his inescapable stature, he was persuaded to play basketball at a junior college. From there, he transferred to UCLA, where he sat on the bench and was largely ineffective. Still, he *was* 7' 4", and there's not a lot of 7' 4" going around, so in 1982 he was drafted into the NBA by the Utah Jazz in the fourth round. He appeared, however, destined to be little more than Chuck Nevitt with better facial hair. But the previous summer, while playing a pickup game at UCLA, Eaton had had an epiphany, spurred by some unsolicited advice from a retired Wilt Chamberlain, who was then in his 40s but still running the floor against men half his age. "We had a guy on our team named Rocket Rod Foster, to this day the fastest guy I've ever seen," says Eaton. "He'd get to the basket about the same time that I got to the top of the key. So I was standing there, huffing and puffing, and I felt a large hand on my shoulder. It was Wilt. He said, 'You're never going to catch that man, first of all. Second, it's not your job to catch him. Your job is to guard the basket, then cruise up to half-court to see what's going on. Because if a quick shot goes up, you have to go back." Eaton pauses. "That day, a lightbulb went on. I figured out my niche in basketball. This is my house, the paint. This is where I live."

Eaton became the prototypical low-post shot blocker. The Jazz funneled opposing players to him, allowing their own guards to gamble for steals, and treated every Eaton block as essentially an outlet pass, looking to turn it into a transition basket. Today, with so many running teams, few shot blockers can afford to stay rooted near the basket. They have to show on the pick-and-roll, cover out to the three-point line and get up and down the floor. This explains in part why blocked shots are down. So does the trend of glorified power forwards playing the center position. But Mourning also sees fewer players with the requisite desire. "You have to want to go after it," he says. "I've seen many players that will be in the lane and guys will be coming full speed at them, and they'll just get out of the way. You're seven feet, and all you got to do is jump straight in the air and you can make him change the shot or contest it. But you got to *want* to do it. You got to *want* to feel contact. Because you're gonna run into bodies."

Actually, there *are* reasons why some players "just get out of the way," and in some cases it's hard to blame them. First, there's a physical toll to being a shot blocker. Check out a big man's fingers, and you can tell if he goes after shots. Mourning holds up his own, which are plumcolored, as proof. "Blood blisters on the tips from hitting the backboard," he says. "They'll turn purple."

If the backboard doesn't do the damage, the rim will. Adonal Foyle, the longtime Warriors center and shot blocker, has dislocated his pinkie after clanging it against the iron. Eaton once broke the little finger on his left hand when he jammed it against the bottom of the rim trying to swat a shot. And plenty of others, like Kirilenko, have suffered sprained ankles and tweaked backs from flying in for a block and landing awkwardly.

The most likely injury, though, is not to the body but to the ego. No matter how skilled a shot blocker, he *will* get dunked on. Hard. And, just as likely, that dunk will make it on *SportsCenter,* to be looped endlessly, in slow-motion. "To be a good shot blocker," says Foyle, "you have to stare getting dunked on in the eye almost every time. People are going to attack you at the basket, and you have to be confident enough to stay in there at the last second. Because one of these days you're going to miss, and eventually you're going to miss maybe two or three times in a row and you're going to get dunked on."

Mourning, for one, relishes the showdown. "The slowest shot in the world is a dunk," he says. "You got to gather yourself, you got to grab the ball and you got to jump. So I'll wait. You gather yourself, O.K. You jump, I know where you're going. I'll meet you there."

It is still a losing proposition. Kirilenko estimates that he blocks only 30% of attempted slams. Okafor guesses he gets eight out of every 10 (a dubious estimate) but admits that "sometimes you get got." All agree that it's easier to block a power dunker who exposes the ball (as

Okafor puts it, "You start advertising, someone's gonna buy") and a two-handed dunk (because it provides a bigger target).

The most dangerous players are those who, like Kobe Bryant, can lean, tuck the ball away and then expose it only at the last moment. "We don't like them much," says Foyle. Worse still are the leapers who can hang, foremost among them Vince Carter during his heyday. In one infamous dunk from 2005, Carter took off from the right side of the key and went at Mourning, who met him in front of the basket and, by all appearances, had the shot blocked with his right hand. Only, as Mourning began to inevitably descend, Carter continued to levitate, then hook-dunked the ball over Mourning with jarring ferocity. It is a move so astonishing it has gained something of a cult following. Go on YouTube right now, type in "Alonzo Mourning and Vince Carter and dunk" and you can watch the clip, again and again if you like. "Unfortunately, that particular dunk will be remembered for a very long time," says Mourning, who dispenses praise in such matters quite grudgingly. "But, hey, that's a part of the game. If I cared about that, I wouldn't have blocked half as many shots as I've blocked." But he does care, of course. At the end of our long conversation about the art of the block, he couldn't help himself. "That dunk Vince had on me?" he said. "By the way, we won that game."

Contrary to the easy assumption, blocking shots has little to do with leaping ability. In fact, with a few notable exceptions (like Howard), many of the NBA's best-jumping big men are surprisingly poor shot blockers (such as the 6'10", spring-legged Chris Wilcox, whose career average is only 0.4 of a block per game). "Jumping's not even important, actually," says Mourning. "It's timing. I don't care how high you [the dunker] jump, you got to come down with the ball. You can jump as high as you want over the rim, but you're coming down, and that's when I time it, and I meet you at the rim."

As easy as rejecting shots comes to men like Mourning—who once blocked 27 in a high school game—it remains a confounding skill to some NBA big men. To watch Raptors center Primoz Brezec in action is to see a physiological mystery. Brezec is 7'1" and 255 pounds, yet he rarely blocks a shot, though not for lack of effort. He hustles from one side of the lane to the other, but gives the appearance of waddling more than running. During his seven-year career, he has averaged 0.4

of a block per game. His coaches try to be diplomatic: Former Bobcats coach Bernie Bickerstaff once told me of Brezec, charitably, "He's more about providing a presence." Brezec himself has no illusions. "I'm a terrible shot blocker," he says. "I think it's just about timing. You just have that ability or you don't. I don't."

For others, it is a matter of tactics. Michael Doleac (6' 11", 0.4 of a block per game for his career) says his preference is to take a charge rather than try to block. The same goes for 7-foot Jason Collins of Minnesota (0.6 per game). Jason's twin brother, Jarron, the Utah center, is so unsuccessful at swatting shots—averaging 0.2 per game—that he says, "I've stopped jumping altogether."

The most glaring example of a placid giant may be Knicks center Eddy Curry. At 6' 11" and 285 pounds, Curry is one of the most impressive physical specimens in the league, endowed with both tremendous strength and leaping ability. Yet he has averaged less than a block per game for his career. "He just doesn't make the effort," says one Eastern Conference scout. "Look at his body language. He plays with his hands down, and he's not very active defensively."

So why not coach him? Why, in a league where there are conditioning coaches and lifestyle coaches, is there not a single shot-blocking guru? Says Eaton, "I don't know why more people don't spend more time thinking about it. It can have a profound impact on the game."

Perhaps it's because, as Abdul-Jabbar says, "it's mostly instinct." Foyle believes that you can teach strategy to those who already have the knack to block, but you can't teach timing. Maybe, though, it is the desire that can't be taught. Take that Bobcats-Nets game in which Okafor blocked Mikki Moore. Well, that wasn't the only dunk Okafor tried to block that game. In the second quarter Vince Carter drove the right baseline and took off toward the hoop. Okafor, who had earlier described to me exactly how he would stop a hypothetical Carter dunk—"I'd crowd him, get to him early"—came late and had no chance. Bam. Instant highlight. But at least Okafor had tried. The same couldn't be said for Bobcats backup center Melvin Ely—who is 6' 10", 261 pounds and a great leaper. In the third quarter of the same game, when Carter came down the lane again, Ely took one look at the Nets forward, then put his hand up and jogged under Carter's dunk, as if waving to some imaginary friend at the other end of the court. "Yeah," Okafor noted. "Mel got out of the way fast, didn't he?"

———————

Great swats stick in the memory. Think of Tayshaun Prince chasing down Reggie Miller in the 2004 Eastern Conference finals and wiping his layup off the glass to save the game. Think of Michael Jordan, late in his career with the Wizards, pinning the ball against the backboard with two hands on an attempted layup by the Bulls' Ron Mercer. Or Mutombo (then of the Denver Nuggets) smacking away eight shots against the Sonics in the climactic game of the 1994 first-round play-offs, then lying on his back blissfully, holding the ball aloft as if the two were being reunited after a long absence.

Asked to recall his favorites, Foyle gets a dreamy look in his eye, as if remembering a particularly good Cabernet. "Well, there was Latrell Sprewell. He came in with two hands and just wanted to take the basket home, just bring the house down, and I met him at the rim." He smiles and continues. "I got one on Shaq once, and that's huge because with that I have the maximum probability that he will break my fingers."

Eaton can recall his highlights but just as clearly remembers the ones that got away. He ranks Hakeem Olajuwon, Kevin McHale and Jack Sikma as the three players of his era most difficult to block—Olajuwon because he was so crafty and the other two because they shot the ball from so far behind their heads. He also recounts a run-in with Larry Bird. "I blocked one of his shots, and if I recall correctly, the next time we played them, he beat one of the players on our team, and as he drove into the middle, my teammate said, 'Mark, help!' And Larry in mid-stride said, 'Yeah, Mark, get this,' and launched one of those runners, down the middle off of one leg. He shot it straight up in the air and it hit nothing but net. Then he ran back down the court with a little smirk on his face."

For Kirilenko, his most memorable sequence came, as he recalls it, when he blocked three Kobe Bryant shots in a row on the same possession, a feat made even more impressive by the fact that he was guarding him one-on-one. A foul was called on the third block, but Kirilenko's pride was undiminished. "Three times in a row, same attack," Kirilenko says, "and the third was a pretty clear block!" That said, Kirilenko's most satisfying stuffs come against big men. He cites Tim Duncan as a frequent target—though he's quick to point out that Duncan will burn you with a pass if you commit too early. He also has a Shaq tale. "One time I blocked Shaq, and the next attack, I get elbowed in the face." He laughs. "It is part of the business."

A memory of a particular block can run deep and last a long time. Consider the case of Tom Wilkinson, as recounted by my colleague Alexander Wolff in *100 Years of Hoops*. In the late '70s Wilkinson played point guard for Penn State. One afternoon, a decade after his college career ended, he was in Manhattan shopping for clothes when he spotted a familiar figure across the store. It was Darrell Griffith, the Utah Jazz shooting guard who had starred at the University of Louisville as a member of the team's Doctors of Dunk. In a 1978 preseason tournament, the Nittany Lions had played against the Cardinals, and even though Penn State lost by 31, it was, for Wilkinson, a sort of brush with greatness, since Louisville had gone on to win the NCAA title the next season.

Wilkinson walked over, introduced himself, reminded Griffith about the game, and the two men chatted. There was one play in the game Wilkinson chose not to mention, however: Wilkinson had gotten free for a fast break and was all alone as he went to lay the ball in. But Griffith, charging from behind, somehow caught him and stuck the ball to the backboard.

After a few minutes of conversation, the two men parted ways, heading off to different parts of the store. Before he could get too far, however, Wilkinson heard a voice from across the way. It was Griffith.

"Yeah, I remember you," Griffith said, brightening up. "Didn't I pin your shit?"

Prototype: The Anatomy
of LeBron James

et's say that you could inhabit the body of any current NBA player
for one day. Who would it be?

No doubt some people would pick Kobe Bryant. Or, perhaps, Dwight
Howard—surely it would be immeasurably fun to view every basket as
if it were a 7-foot Nerf hoop. And maybe the love-starved among us
might go with Wally Szczerbiak, the high-cheekboned Cleveland forward whose impact upon young women is greater these days than his
impact upon the game.

But, more than any other, I'm guessing the answer would be LeBron
James. No NBA player—perhaps no human being—combines power,
skill, speed and grace as he does. Don't take it from me, though. When
Sports Illustrated asked 190 NBA players in the fall of 2008, "Who is
the best all-around athlete in the NBA?" an overwhelming 66% chose
LeBron. No one else got more than 7% of the vote (Josh Smith of the
Hawks), and Howard came in fourth at 4%, behind third-place finisher
Kobe Bryant (6%).

Curious how James uses his physical prowess to his advantage, I
decamped for Portland in January of 2009 to follow him for the better
part of a week on a Cavaliers West Coast road trip that took the team
through the Bay Area and on to Utah. As familiar as I was with him—
I'd written two stories on LeBron for *SI* in '06 and '07, and I'd seen him
play in person more than a dozen times—I wasn't prepared for what I
saw during that week.

In the game I watched against the Warriors, there was a moment where it looked as if Golden State center Andris Biedrins, no small man at 6'11" and 245 pounds, had been sucked out of an airplane hold, so quickly did he fly backward upon colliding with James. Biedrins was attempting to protect the rim when the 6'8" James came charging down the lane in that straight-line, parting-the-waters manner of his. Gamely, Biedrins took to the air to try to block the shot, and then—*whoomp!*—next thing you knew he was hurtling onto his backside. As for James, he remained both on balance and on course, as if he'd merely hit a patch of turbulence on his solo commuter flight—*nonstop from basket to basket, departing 15 times nightly*—and finished with a forceful layup. Later LeBron did it again, only this time he toppled *two* Warriors, then finished with a one-handed dunk of surpassing violence. Afterward, Warriors forward Stephen Jackson tried to describe to me the perils of such defensive encounters. "As big as he is," said Jackson, "you got to hope he don't just run over you and give you a concussion."

The fact that James was big and powerful wasn't itself shocking—after all, coming out of high school in 2003, he weighed 240 pounds and was already built like a construction worker. Rather it was just *how* big and powerful James had become. Despite spending vast chunks of each waking day burning calories at a prodigious rate, LeBron had somehow gained weight every season. By the time I caught up with him, he was far north of 240 and looked suspiciously larger than the 250 pounds listed in the Cleveland media guide. At the time there were whispers that it was more like 265 or, as one ESPN report had it, 274 pounds. When I talked to other NBA players about James, they were hungry for clarification. "How much *does* he weigh, anyway?" wondered Portland Trailblazers forward Travis Outlaw. Stephen Jackson guessed "at least 260, right?" and then described D-ing up James as akin to "guarding a brick wall." (If so, it is a brick wall much-envied by others; when I asked Portland All-Star guard Brandon Roy what one part of LeBron's game he would most want to steal, Roy responded, "Can I steal his body?")

In an attempt to settle the weight debate, I brought a scale when I met James for an interview at a ballroom of the St. Regis Hotel in San Francisco during the road trip. He laughed, commending my industriousness, but didn't bite. He joked that he'd "gotten fat"—this from a man with 5% body fat whose veins run like tiny interstates up his arms and calves—then hemmed and hawed before confiding that he'd gained eight pounds that summer, "even though I was trying to lose 10." Still, he wanted the exact figure to remain a mystery—more than any other NBA star save perhaps Shaq, James understands the value of mystique and theater, saying, "I can't let everybody know everything about LeBron." That said, a Cavs source told me James's weight was "between 265 and 270."

Considering his skill set and athleticism, that is a staggering number. After all, there are plenty of centers who don't weigh that much, including Cleveland's own 7'3", 260-pound Zydrunas Ilgauskas. Karl Malone, as massive as he was at 6'9" and popping with muscles, was listed at only 256 and had little of James's agility. That LeBron was an all-state wide receiver in high school is not really surprising; what's shocking is that anyone could tackle him. "He even makes reads like a football player," says Nate McMillan, the Portland Trailblazers' head coach, who worked with James for three years on the U.S. national team. "And he has enough speed he could probably play free safety." (In a 2009 TV ad, James was portrayed playing for the Cleveland Browns, and what was scary was that it didn't seem far-fetched in the least.)

It would be one thing if LeBron were merely a physical marvel, but over the course of his still-young career his game has improved steadily. Coming into the league in 2003, LeBron was an impressive athlete and already an exceptional playmaker, but he had little in the way of a jump shot and even less of an idea how to play defense (not uncommon with players who skip college, which can serve as a four-year course in D). "I didn't think LeBron was going to improve that much, especially defensively," one Eastern Conference scout told me. "It's not usual to see a guy his age come back better and stronger every year. He really is a freak."

If so, then let us examine this freak who, lest we forget, turns all of 25 in December 2009 having already scored 12,000 points (sooner than any other NBA player in terms of both games played and age). As impressive as this is, in another era James might be posting cartoon numbers. Consider: The last NBA player to average a triple double for a season was Oscar Robertson, who put up an ungodly season line of 30.8 points, 12.5 rebounds and 11.4 assists for the Cincinnati Royals during the 1961–62 season. LeBron isn't close to those numbers (28.4, 7.6 and 7.2 for the 2008–09 season), but that is a product, at least in part, of the era he plays in. In a fascinating comparison Basketball-Reference.com notes that the 1962 Royals averaged 124.7 possessions a game while James's Cavs averaged 89.2 in 2009 and estimates that if James's '09 Cavaliers played at the same pace as Robertson's '62 Royals, James's line would extrapolate to 40.1 points per game, 10.3 rebounds and 10.0 assists.

So if Kobe represents the game's pinnacle of mental prowess in basketball (Chapter 1), LeBron represents the apex of its physical skill. And it is skill that's married to an innate feel for the game. Here is a man who passes like a point guard, runs like a sprinter, leaps like a high jumper and, as Biedrins found out, hits like a linebacker. If you were to create the prototype for the NBA player of the future, it would look an awful lot like James. So let's take the measure of the man, at times literally. Consider it Lebronatomy 101.

Chest (XXL)

This is sure to exasperate scrawny teenagers toiling in weight rooms the world over, but despite his bodybuilder's physique, LeBron has never really lifted. At least not in the way a normal human would need to lift in order to develop such musculature (think heavy weight, low reps, loud grunting and Metallica).

Rather, James only really began working out seriously in 2008, five years into his career. "He just messed around in the weight room and got by on raw strength his first few years," said Cavs trainer Mike Mancias, who oversees all of James's conditioning work. Even now James eschews power lifts like the bench press—"I leave that to Body," he said, using the nickname of former Cavs center Ben Wallace—and instead opts for core exercises, dumbbells and, more recently, yoga. Not that he was an easy convert to the last. "I had to start with poses he wouldn't think were too goofy, if you catch my drift," said Mancias. Still there was LeBron by a hotel pool in L.A. while in town for a commercial shoot in the summer of 2008, busting out some downward dog.

That James has gained weight each year is as much a mystery to him as to anyone else. He doesn't gulp protein shakes, instead eating three low-fat meals daily, prepared by his chef (oatmeal, chicken, salmon), with the occasional candy snack in between. "Honestly, this past off-season, I wanted to lose some pounds, and I ended up gaining some," he told me. "I worked out as hard as I ever did. It's kind of crazy. My body's like reversed. So I was like, 'O.K., well, let me stop working out for a little bit before I gain 20 pounds.'" He laughed. "You could put me in one of those magazines, *How to Gain Weight,* huh?"

(Considering that last comment from James, this is perhaps as good a place as any to address an issue that, in this day and age, must be addressed. When I asked Danny Ferry, the Cavs' G.M., the "steroid question," he seemed shocked. "Honestly, you are the first person who has ever asked me that," he said. Ferry's logic: First, LeBron has never needed performance enhancers, as he's always been physically imposing, dating back to high school. Second, it's not necessarily to his advantage to add muscle mass: Usually when a basketball player puts on too much muscle, he loses some quickness, and quickness is the coin of the realm for a wing player like James. [A few years back, Kobe spent the summer bulking up only to quickly shed the muscle, feeling it slowed him.] Finally, until recently, LeBron showed neither the interest nor the dedication to the lifting required to take advantage of steroids.)

Starting in 2008, James began a light lifting regimen every game day for 20 to 30 minutes, focusing on flexibility and core muscles. Ferry credits James's experience on the U.S. national team, especially during the run-up to the 2008 Olympics, for his new dedication. "He always worked out, but now he works out with a purpose," says Ferry. "He got to see how hard Jason Kidd works, and Kobe works. From a corporate sense, it's like those guys spent their summers sharing best practices. If they have a meeting in the morning and Kobe comes in already sweaty, LeBron's going to say, 'Holy shit, this guy's already working. That's what it takes.'"

The result of the workouts is that LeBron feels he's better able to control his power. For example, Wallace, the former Cavs center, who was one of the strongest players in the league, says he didn't stand a chance against James in practice. "I learned early that I can't run alongside him and then hope to body him or get in front of him," says the 6'9", 240-pound Wallace. "If you are even with him, you've already lost."

James, of course, is not the first NBA player to leverage his strength; he is just the most agile. During his heyday Karl Malone was as finely conditioned an athlete as ever played the game. (The Denver Nuggets' team doctor once told me the only player he's ever seen even close to Malone is retired forward Kevin Willis.) Malone maintained 4% body fat, lifted for an hour on the mornings of games and spent his "off days" in the Wasatch Mountains snowshoeing or taking grueling straight-line hikes (no trails allowed). As Utah assistant coach Mark McKown, Malone's good friend and hiking partner, once told me, "He needs a strength coach like Einstein needed a math tutor."

Likewise, Corey Maggette is built like the NBA version of the Ultimate Soldier, all bulbous muscles and shoulders, and David Robinson combined strength and athleticism with a tapered 34-inch waist and superhero biceps. But not one of these three was able to combine both bulk and quickness as James does. The closest comparisons anyone can come up with are a young Charles Barkley and, as Ferry suggests, a young Shawn Kemp.

What's flummoxing for opponents is that, at least outwardly, LeBron doesn't appear to absorb any punishment when he bangs through the lane. Privately, though, it's a different matter. After the Portland game, in which James at one point crashed into Greg Oden as if in a human monster-truck rally, I lingered in the locker room until James eventually exited the shower. He walked stiffly, then leaned against the wall, propped up by his arms, while Cavs head trainer Max Benton began kneading his back. As Benton focused on "trigger points," attempting to work out a spasm that spanned the width of James's lats-encompassing CHOSEN1 tattoo, James commenced swearing.

"Shit. Aww, shiiiiiiiiiiiit."

Watching him, bent over and grimacing, was somehow comforting. Not because it's fun to watch another man's pain; but it was reassuring to know that LeBron could, in fact, hurt like the rest of us.

The illusion was short-lived though. When I talked to Benton afterward, he told me that James's recovery time from such ailments is remarkable. "Oh, it's much shorter than for most players," Benton told me. "He's different. Real different."

Feet (Size 16)

James's feet aren't especially big, at least not for an NBA player; it's his ability to move them quickly and efficiently that is impressive. The trainer Idan Ravin (Chapter 9) was struck by how quickly James covered ground when the two worked together. "Most players can go full speed from baseline to baseline in somewhere between 11 and 14 strides," Ravin told me. "LeBron covers that in nine or 10 strides."

This is especially valuable on defense. Draw a circle of, say, six feet around most players, and that is how much space they can patrol—call it their defensive radius. For James, make your circle almost twice as big. "He can be all the way in the lane on that skip pass and still close out [on the wing on the shooter]," said Cavs assistant Mike Malone, the team's defensive coordinator. "And it's not a guy like me closing out; it's, 'Holy shit, this is a *big guy* coming at you.'"

Not long ago LeBron's close-outs were inconsistent. "Early in my career I just did a lot of on-ball defense, and once the ball was swung, I kind of lost my man and got unfocused," James admitted. By 2009, however, Brandon Roy called James "arguably the best one-on-one defender in the game," while scouts pointed to his continued improvement. "He's leaps and bounds better on defense this year," an Eastern Conference scout told me, citing James's footwork, balance and understanding of defensive schemes. "You always hear coaches talk about, 'He helps the helper, he digs back on the dig-back man.' Those are priceless things coaches love, and he is doing that now. I think before, that's what separated Kobe from him, but LeBron has stepped it up to his level. I don't think there's a big difference anymore."

In essence, James has become the coolest toy any defense-inclined coach could imagine—long, powerful, fast *and* smart. (He was one of only two players to average more than one block and 1.7 steals in 2008–09, the other being Dwyane Wade. As a result LeBron finished second to Dwight Howard in the voting for Defensive Player of the Year.) When the Cavs play the Hornets, for example, Cleveland coach Mike Brown puts James on point guard Chris Paul. Now, when New Orleans runs a pick-and-roll with forward David West, there is no longer a mismatch. "Instead of a little guy like Mo [Williams] or Daniel Gibson, now it's LeBron switched on to West, and he can bang him," said Mike Malone. "You know how tough that is for a team?" McMillan even went so far as to tag LeBron as the rare player who can guard "one through five."

But James says he can't guard everyone. "There are some players you just can't guard in this league one-on-one," he said. "Guys like Kobe, Chris Paul, Dwyane Wade, you can't hand-check as much and can't be physical because it's an automatic foul. Sometimes you have to get help." He also said that, when it comes to pure size and strength, there are a few bigs he can't slow down, primarily Shaq and Yao Ming. (The two guys who deliver the toughest beating while he's guarding them, James said, are Ron Artest and Matt Harpring. "You just hope you don't have a back-to-back after covering either of those guys.")

As consistent as LeBron has become on defense, there are, of course, still lapses. Occasional ball-watching. Losing his man on the weak side. Not crowding a shooter. "But then," said Mike Malone, "he goes and does something ridiculous you could never teach a player." For example, according to the Cavs, James finished the 2008–09 season with 22 "chase-downs"—that is, 22 times he caught an opponent on a break-away in time to erase the shot. Often, it should be noted, with great gusto.

Eyes (New and Improved)

In the aforementioned game against the Warriors, the most impressive play I saw LeBron make was not the finish against Biedrins or even his hellacious block on Kelenna Azubuike, when he sprang from under the basket like some monster of the deep to spike the ball back toward the three-point line. Rather, it was a more mundane sequence. While running the baseline in the third quarter, James received a poorly timed pass. Falling out-of-bounds under the basket, he looked as if he had no options. Yet, in one motion he caught the ball and redirected it at a nearly 90-degree angle along the baseline about 15 feet to his right, through a two-foot gap in defenders, to a surprised Anderson Varejao, the Cavs forward.

That James would see Varejao on such a play is extraordinary. (That Varejao would blow the layup is not; one wonders how many assists LeBron would average if he weren't surrounded by big men with hands of concrete.) This impressive court vision is made more interesting by the fact that, for the first four or so years of his NBA career, James had a hard time seeing things. Like, say, road signs.

Growing up, James told me, he had poor eyesight. "I was in the classroom, and I couldn't see the chalkboard, so I had to move to the front," he said. "I couldn't see a sign three blocks down. I couldn't see a lot of shit."

So, obviously, he got glasses, right?

"Nah," he said with a sheepish smile. "My pride wouldn't let me."

Which means James was operating in something of a haze, which must surely make all his peers feel even better about getting torched by him. He claims, though, that it never affected his game. "I could see everything on the court. I never had a problem with here"—he holds his hands to the side of his head, indicating his peripheral vision—"it was right here in front that I had the problem."

Impressive, but I was skeptical, so I contacted Dr. Kevin Gee, director of the Sports Vision Performance Center at the University Eye Institute in Houston. Gee has worked as a consultant to the Houston Astros, the Houston Comets of the WNBA and teams at the University of Houston. When I told Gee about LeBron's experience, he said it was possible his court vision was fine, considering "his surroundings on the court are pretty confined, and you've got big gross objects around him, if you will, but the fine details would be blurry." He paused. "But are you saying he was running around with his eyes uncorrected?" When I told him this was the case, Gee murmured, "Wow, that's a testament to him that he can shoot a free throw and not be clear. I don't have a hard time believing he could see fine in his peripheral vision, but his central vision he must have learned to compensate. The younger they are, they learn to compensate for their shortcomings." (Interestingly, Gee told me that the eyes can be trained for basketball by increasing the range of peripheral vision. Gee works with players to train their "up vision." "These are gazes that aren't customarily performed by you and me," Gee explained. "We sit in front of a computer for the most part, and sometimes we turn our head, but that's still straight ahead. But the majority of basketball players and volleyball players are used to looking up, and we'll have them looking at 45-degree angles, 60-degree angles, to train their ability to use their eyes efficiently in that area.")

When LeBron had Lasik surgery in September 2007, it had a profound effect. "It's kind of cool," he told me afterward, "because I can see stuff in the distance. I'm like, 'So that's what that is!'" Pressed, he admitted it probably helped his game, too, saying, "Well, I *have* gotten better."

Whether or not he can actually *see* the floor more clearly, *seeing* the floor has always been his most impressive pure basketball skill. In 2006, his third year in the league, I sat and watched game footage with James in a luxury suite at Quicken Arena in Cleveland. I was struck immediately by his recall. The footage we were reviewing was from a game played more than a month earlier, but as the DVD ran, he'd say things like, "I'm about to get my second foul here; it was a good call," and, "Watch this: Z's going to tip this ball."

He was also surprisingly enthusiastic for a man who is generally so measured. Usually in public interactions James maintains an even keel. He is smooth, self-assured and has the long-practiced smile of a child actor—a thin, cheeky grin that makes him look innocent and slightly self-conscious, as if he's hiding a mouthful of braces. He is charming and polite, if rarely forthcoming. "He doesn't necessarily like the attention," Cavaliers owner Dan Gilbert told me. "But you watch him talking to the media after games, and it's almost like you couldn't script the answers better than what he says." Indeed, James's voice and cadence sound eerily like Jordan's—clipped, definitive, rising at the end to signal a finality of discussion—and his comments are efficient and declarative, more often than not two sentences delivered in the following structure: statement of fact followed by brief elaboration. (For example, on a stellar performance in a Cavs win against Chicago, James said, "I used the whole court tonight. My teammates did a great job of putting me in different spots where [the Bulls] couldn't double-team or they didn't know where I was going to be.")

Yet, away from the cameras, where he could just watch and dissect the game, he seemed almost childlike in his passion. When I asked him about learning to jump stop, for example, LeBron's answer was extensive (10 sentences), specific (he cited a coach he'd had as a kid), emotional (it was "frustrating at first") and accompanied by enthusiastic gestures. Here is how it ended: "It was hard for me to go, *Whoooosh!*" he said, pantomiming hurtling through the air, "and then—*choo!*—come to a stop. Once I got it, it really helped, because then I knew I could alter the pace of a defender. It put some control into my game."

In analyzing plays from that '06 game, he often sounded more like a coach than a player. At one point in the game tape he had the ball and was isolated on Paul Pierce on the left wing. Dissecting the sequence, however, James did not focus on whether he thought he could have scored on Pierce's defense but instead homed in on the team dynamics. "My main focus isn't on the guy that's guarding me; it's on the second level of defense, because I feel like I can get past the first guy who's guarding me," James said as we watched. "But there comes a time where the weak side can come and double you, they can load the box on you and right here"—he pointed to the screen, paused at the point where he sized up Pierce—"I'm not really looking at Paul. I know he's in front of me, but I'm looking at Raef LaFrentz and [Ryan] Gomes and seeing if they see me or if they predetermine my move. Right now, they don't really know what they're doing backside, so that gave me a good chance to try to drive baseline before they got there."

It was an exceptionally nuanced perspective for a third-year player, especially one who hadn't played college ball. His coaches on the Cavs told me he has a rare ability to remember plays, that he can see a play drawn out once and then envision all five players' roles. To listen to LeBron talk, it's as if he sees the game as a series of interlocking pieces. At one point he described having teammate Drew Gooden's man "in attendance," explaining that he knew he could dribble all the way back to half-court and the defender would follow. At another, he explained how the movement of Delonte West, who was the farthest Celtic from the ball, would affect what type of pass he threw on a pick-and-roll to teammate Eric Snow (depending on whether he wanted to get Snow the ball in position to shoot or to dribble).

This level of awareness makes James a unique defensive challenge. When I talked about James with Tyson Chandler, the Hornets center who is an excellent help-side defender, he said that, with James, he has to hide his intentions. "A lot of scorers get tunnel vision, and you can help, and they're kind of just looking at you and waiting for the opportunity to go," Chandler explained. "But with him, you help and he burns you. He hits your man or he makes you think he doesn't know, then he drives at you and makes you come and kicks it to your man. It's kind of like when you watch Magic back in the day. Thinking of plays before they happen."

This is why Pat Riley compares James to Nash, not Jordan, and why one Eastern Conference scout told me that LeBron is behind only Kidd and Nash as a playmaker. It's also why one of the problems Cavs coaches had for years was that James was too good for practice. "We can't create a matchup that challenges him," Hank Egan, the longtime assistant, told me. "We can double him, but we can only do that for so long because we have to run our own stuff." At a loss, coach Mike Brown eventually turned to Johnny Bach, a former Bulls assistant during the Jordan years. Bach recommended putting James on the reserve team during practice. "At first I don't think LeBron understood what we were doing," said Brown. "Then, since he's so competitive, he'd get into it." And who won those practice scrimmages? Brown nodded. "Usually LeBron's team."

Midsection (No Ab Roller Needed)

To explain James's uncanny body control, which emanates from his core, let us turn to teammate and LeBron aficionado Mo Williams. Asked the most amazing thing he'd seen James do, Williams chose not a soaring jam or twisting finish but a loose ball early in the 2008–09 season. "Most guys have to bend down, pick it up and take their time to get up," said Williams. "In one motion he dove down to the floor, scooped it up"—and here Williams mimicked a low pirouette—"and without touching the floor he's back on his feet for one dribble and a dunk. In *one motion.*"

Here, then, is the evidence of James's newfound interest in yoga and working on his core, the slab of muscles in the stomach and lower back that controls much of an athlete's balance. Especially in a sport like basketball, a player's core is often the most important area of his body, guarding him against injury and providing balance and stability. Steve Nash, for example, does little or no traditional weight training—unlike James and Dwight Howard, you won't find him wearing any tight shirts—but he is renowned for his core workouts. When he lifts weights, he often does so while balancing on a stability ball (often on one leg), and when he does off-season conditioning, it sometimes involves skateboarding, which is powered almost entirely by the middle of the torso. In James's case, he began doing serious stretching a few years ago, after suffering from lower-back spasms, and moved on to yoga in the belief that it would extend his career. Now, like some oversized suburban mom, he can cycle through any number of poses, from the thunderbolt to the hero pose, and he believes it has given him the flexibility, balance and core strength to play heavy minutes through a long season. "Guys forget it, but being on balance is something you should always keep in your game," he said. "That's a large part of the game for me."

Legs (Full of Fast-Twitch Fibers)

A vertical leap test is just what it sounds like: You jump straight up from a standing position. For someone like Dwight Howard, a two-footed leaper whose post game is predicated on such explosion, this is a meaningful measure. (For the record, Howard's vertical leap is 30 inches.) But for someone like James, who does most of his damage on the move, usually launching off one leg and at high speed, it is less illuminating.

A truer test would be to measure LeBron's lift off one leg after a running start, something he told me he's never tested.

At the NBA predraft camp six years ago, LeBron's vertical leap was measured at 38 inches or 44 inches, depending on whom you believe. (I believe the former measure, as 44 is essentially unheard of.) But even at 38, it's an impressive number. Given that he estimates he gets about half a foot higher jumping off one leg, that means that with a running start James could probably leap over your dresser without even turning horizontal. This, it goes without saying, is a useful basketball skill. When asked what one part of James's game *he* would steal, teammate Wally Szczerbiak said, "That Go-Go Gadget calf muscle on his left leg."

This is not to imply that James's two-footed jumping is subpar. "Not at all," said Szczerbiak. "I didn't realize how good he was off two feet until I got here [in a trade in 2008]. Then you see him at shootaround, with no warmups and no stretching, going up and doing 360s at 9:30 in the morning. I'm over here trying to stretch just to get through a drill."

At times during his career, usually when Cleveland was depleted by injury, LeBron has even jumped center. (He won a tip against 7' 1" Marc Gasol of the Grizzlies, for one.) And during the 2008–09 season, he *played* center for nearly 12 minutes against the Hornets and held his own, which should come as no surprise, considering he did the same at times during the 2008 Olympics. "He would switch off on opposing centers and say, 'Don't worry about him; he ain't going anywhere,'" said McMillan. "Because he understands leverage, he would get underneath bigger guys so they couldn't move."

Arms (In Progress)

Shooting has very little to do with upper-body strength; just ask Reggie Miller. In some cases muscular bulk can be an impediment—can you think of any pure shooters who were really jacked up? Not surprisingly then, this is one area where James does not come naturally by his skills. Rather, it has been an ongoing struggle for him.

In his first five years in the league LeBron had an inconsistent jump shot, to put it kindly. Annually, his shooting percentage on shots around the basket would be in the 60s—64.1% in 2005, 66.1% in 2006, 67.1% in 2007 and 68.5% in 2008–09—and drastically lower from elsewhere on the floor. Some years, as in 2006–07, he shot below 30% from entire sides of the floor on mid-range jumpers (in that case, the left side). This despite the fact that they were often wide open: Fearful of his penetration, opponents played off James, allowing him his choice of pull-up jumpers. But too often it looked like he was chucking pumpkins at the backboard, hurling the ball from behind his ear.

Then, just as Tiger Woods remade his swing at the height of his career, James spent the summer of 2008 quietly reconstructing his jumper, working with Cavs assistant and former NBA sharpshooter Chris Jent five days a week, for an hour and a half per session. Over that summer LeBron worked to develop what Jent described as a "calmer" shot. This meant better balance—when shooting on the move, James had to contend with the considerable momentum created by his weight—and keeping his shooting elbow locked at his side so that, as James put it, "the ball will go straight instead of veering off sometimes."

So, like a peewee player, James began by tossing up one-handed shots (unlike a peewee player, he did so while wearing an iPod blasting Jay-Z). Next came one-dribble jumpers and free throws, then mid-range. Incredibly, never once during the sessions did he shoot a three-pointer. (Go ahead, let's see you spend an hour at the gym and resist the temptation to let one go from long distance.) "He's so strong that he can shoot a jumper from half-court," explained Jent, whose motto was, "Form first and the range will come."

The results were encouraging, if still indicative of a work in progress. During the 2008–09 season James shot 39.4% from the mid-range spots on the court, those outside the paint but inside the three-point line. And on good nights, as in the Portland game I saw on the West Coast road trip (an 88–80 Cavs win), he could become unstoppable. Using his quickness to create space, he hit a succession of deep one-dribble pull-ups, many from 22 feet or so. "That's the shot he didn't have before," said one Eastern Conference executive at the game. "A couple of those I was like, 'No way,' but he hit them." And indeed, the shots, daggerlike, were reminiscent of—what's his name again?—oh, yes, Mr. Bryant.

On other nights, though, James could threaten to shoot the Cavs out of games. He spent much of the second half against the Warriors missing the same deep one-dribble pull-ups he'd hit against Portland just two nights before. Only a last-second buzzer-beating jumper from the left wing got him off the hook. Remarkably, it was the first buzzer-beater of his career.

(It's worth clarifying that a buzzer beater is different from a potential game-winning shot. James has hit plenty of those. For a shot to be classified as a potential game-winning shot, according to the game-tracking website 82games.com, it must fill two criteria: 1) It comes with 24 seconds or less on the clock, and 2) the team is either tied, down one, or down two. It's not a perfect measure, admittedly, but it serves its purpose. During the time he's been in the NBA through the end of the 2008–09 regular season, LeBron has hit 17-of-51 shots in such situations, second only to Vince Carter [18 of 55 in that same period of time] but leading Kobe [15–58]. In just the playoffs, James and Bryant are co-leaders over the same time period, both having hit 4 of 8.)

LeBron's shot against the Warriors, his first true buzzer-beater, was a relief not only to him but to everyone in the Cavs' organization. For years James has been criticized for passing in big moments, even when doing so was obviously the sound basketball play. Most notoriously, he found Donyell Marshall in the corner against the Pistons during Game 1 of the Eastern Conference finals in 2007, and Marshall missed the jumper. Afterward, James said, "I go for the winning play. The winning play when two guys come at you and a teammate is open is to give it up. It's as simple as that."

Except it's not as simple as that when it comes to public perception. It's almost as if James has skipped a step in his evolution as a dominant NBA player, and the critics will not allow it. It took Michael Jordan the better part of his career before he trusted his teammates in those final critical moments, memorably finding both John Paxson and Steve Kerr for game-winners. And one can argue that Kobe Bryant still hasn't reached that point. James, on the other hand, came into the league already willing to trust his teammates, feeding them as the clock ticks down. Yet this will continue to be viewed by some as a negative until he wins a championship, whereupon those same people will instantly start lauding LeBron for being an "unselfish superstar."

Hands (Matching Pair)

They measure 9¼ inches from the bottom of his palm to the top of his middle finger, and he's been able to palm a basketball since the 10th grade. This allows him not only to wave the ball around on drives if he so pleases but also to grab a disproportionate number of one-handed rebounds. It also enables him to throw passes with astonishing velocity. "At first I had to get used to it because he'd surprise me," said Szczerbiak. "He'll be on the other side of the court and—*bam!*—the ball's right in your shooting pocket."

This is the element of James's game most likely to surprise new teammates. While he has led the league in scoring, James is at heart a passer. Elton Brand, the Sixers forward, found out as much when he played with James on the U.S. national team in Japan. "What you realize when you play with him is that he's very selfless," said Brand. "Because of the commercials and the fame, all the fans over there [in Japan] wanted to see him score and dunk, but he seemed like he didn't care if he was sacrificing points. He wanted to be the distributor."

It is the burden of any playmaker to try to make four other men happy when, by necessity, three of them (or all four), may not shoot on any given possession. James's strategy is to be supportive of his teammates when warranted but never to tolerate poor shot selection. "There ain't no leeway for a bad shot," he explained. "A bad shot is a bad shot, and you got to tell them right away. You can't have a guy just jackin' up shots."

Brain (Like a CEO's)

As physically gifted as James is, Ravin thinks his greatest assets are what he calls James's "soft skills." "He's so engaging and able to command so much attention and respect that people will mimic him," Ravin told me. "That's very powerful, especially in a league of guys trying to fit in."

Part of LeBron's appeal derives from the fact that despite his global celebrity, he is capable of acting like the 15-year-old he never really was. When I interviewed him in 2006, for example, he had more handlers than a teen starlet, and his time was doled out in five-minute increments. Our *SI* photographer was told he'd have but five minutes to shoot a portrait, and it had to be during the interview. This put the photographer, Michael LeBrecht, in the awkward position of trying to take a closeup shot while James sat in a chair, talking to me. So, trying to be unobtrusive but finding it impossible, LeBrecht ended up just straddling James's legs and firing away from point-blank range.

Now, as I relate what happened next, it's worth noting that LeBrecht and James had known each other for six years and were friendly. So when LeBron lifted one cheek off his chair and let rip a long, stuttering fart, the duration and power of which was surprising even for a man of his physical capabilities, it was meant as a sign of affection. Or at least I think it was. To his credit, LeBrecht kept straddling and snapping, eventually pulling his shirt over his nose while LeBron giggled like a teenager and let fire again.

James deploys this type of humor—if indeed hotboxing a photographer with flatulence qualifies as humor—to put his teammates at ease. Act like a goofball off the court, he figures, and he can lessen the divide between himself and others. But don't be fooled: He is in control and he is confident. "You never need to reinforce LeBron," said Rachel Johnston, his personal stylist, who outfits James for all his appearances. "He always thinks he looks good."

The challenge during his first six years in the league was to inspire similar confidence in his teammates. Considering the motley assortment of players the Cavs brought in to play alongside James—only Williams and Ilgauskas have played in the All-Star Game during that span—this has not always been easy. I can remember him, in '06, trying to inspire teammate Donyell Marshall. In the first half of a game against the Bulls, Cleveland ran a pick-and-roll that called for Marshall to throw the ball to Ilgauskas, but in the process Marshall found himself wide open at the top of the key.

"Shoot the ball!" demanded James.

"But I'm running the play," Marshall countered.

James, adamant, yelled back, "Shoot the fucking ball!"

After the game Marshall sat at his locker. "It's funny because you feel guilty, but he'll say, 'The next time I pass it to you, shoot it again. If you miss, you miss it. If it's a good shot, then that's your shot, just shoot it again.'" The 32-year-old Marshall chuckled and looked over at James at his locker. "It's funny because you're here to teach him and be the leader, but then there are times when he picks you up. When I was 21, I was the second-youngest player in the NBA and just learning the game. He's 21, and he's the third-leading scorer in the NBA."

By the 2008–09 season James had become even more vocal. With coach Mike Brown's blessing, James cajoled, ribbed and commanded. During huddles he suggested plays and had the freedom to change defensive matchups when he pleased. So when viewers saw LeBron switch onto an elite scorer like Kobe Bryant or Brandon Roy, it was his decision, not Brown's. Explains the coach, "When I first got here, I took the approach Pop had with Tim Duncan in San Antonio"—that is, saving your best player on defense by having him guard a secondary option. "We're at the point now where, as the game goes along, LeBron knows when it's time to switch onto a scorer. It's part of the growth of his leadership skills."

Such is James's feel for all the moving parts of a team that McMillan thinks he could coach one day. ("I think I'd be pretty good," agreed LeBron, who nonetheless says that just being asked that question "makes me feel old.") Says McMillan, "He understands the game so well, he could play all five positions if he wanted to. You're talking about a game IQ like Magic's, Michael's, Kobe's. When you have that type of mind and then the talent that he has, he could do pretty much whatever he wants."

And that's the really scary part. At 24 James is already one of the best players the game has ever seen, yet he is far from a finished masterpiece. After all, Jent calls James's jumper "unfinished business." And Ravin considers James a work in progress. Ferry, the G.M., puts it in perspective. "We saw him grow up from 18 to 24. And we're going to see him change again from now until 30. We just don't know how."

Even James can't help but marvel at his potential sometimes. "If I'm just getting my man-strength now," he said, "I don't want to see me at 32."

Epilogue

In researching this book, I spent most of my time talking to NBA players, men who have mastered elements of the game and get paid sizable amounts for this mastery. Their passion is evident, but so is their prodigious skill.

In closing, however, I thought it was worth sharing a different kind of story, one that concerns not an All-Star—at least not as its protagonist—but rather someone whose passion for hoops perhaps surpasses his talent. Someone who is probably more like me and you: just a man in love with a game. Only in his case, he can lay claim to perhaps the greatest bar boast ever: "I beat Michael Jordan one-on-one."

I first heard rumor of the feat many years ago from a friend in Chicago. The details were hazy: It (probably) occurred at MJ's basketball camp (about) five years ago, when Jordan lost to a camper for the first time—an old(-ish) guy who threw up a (musta-been) crazy lefty hook to which Mike (undoubtedly) yelled, Nooooo!

What's more, my friend said, the whole thing was (purportedly) videotaped.

Curious, I decided to look into it. A call led to a call led to a name, John Rogers Jr. Now 52, Rogers is a Princeton grad and Chicago rainmaker. The founder and CEO of Ariel Mutual Finds, the nation's largest minority-run mutual fund, he is friendly with Oprah and even friendlier with Barack Obama (who used Rogers's conference room for mock debates while running for president). Most important, Rogers could afford Jordan's Senior Flight School, a three-day summer camp in Las Vegas for the 35-and-over-and-loaded crowd that ran 15 grand, or more than twice what it would cost to go to, you know, actual flight school.

Simply put, Rogers was (and is) a hoops addict. Despite knee surgery five years ago, he not only plays often but also practices regularly. How many pickup players do you know who actually *practice*
in their free time? And while Rogers was captain of the 1979–80
Princeton team, he's not one of those naturally gifted types. He's six
feet tall, a tad nerdy-looking, and not too athletic. As Rogers puts it,
"Coach [Pete] Carril always said I wasn't a good dribbler and I was
a terrible passer, but I could finish." To watch him now, rec-specs
on nose and brace on knee, moves equally herky and jerky, is to see
bits of every middle-aged guy at every YMCA, juiced on pregame
Advil and hoping that this time his ball fake will work on a younger,
springier defender.

Before we get to the one-on-one video, which Rogers was kind
enough to share with me and which was shot by camp staffers, some
caveats. For starters, the game is short: first to three, make-it-take-it,
no rebounds. And this is not vintage MJ but rather the Floor Jordan
model after his final final season, 2002–03 with the Washington Wizards. Even so, bear in mind that (1) MJ had never lost to a camper in
the seven years of Flight School, and (2) this is Michael Jordan we're
talking about, for many years the most competitive athlete alive. As
Steve Kerr told me, "I played with Michael for [five] years, and I never
beat him one-on-one."

The game begins, fittingly, with Jordan still ribbing a previous vic-
tim. "Don't be mad at me, I'm just too good," he booms. "What, you
think I had this camp just so you all could beat me?" Taking the ball
first, Rogers drives right and lofts in a runner. Then he goes left to hit
a leaner. The crowd of 150 or so—campers, but also coaches like John
Thompson and Mike Krzyzewski—begins to murmur. Predictably, Jordan evens it with a pair of jumpers, and the end appears imminent
until . . . Michael misses a jumpshot. Then he clangs another!

Here is Rogers's big chance. He again hurtles left and, nearing the
hoop, jumps off both feet. Jordan, clearly into it now, times his leap
to swallow up the shot. Only Rogers, in a move he's practiced a thousand times but that still appears impossibly awkward, leans away from
MJ as if eluding the curl of a crashing wave. He spins the ball up, up,
up and over Jordan's fingertips, off the glass and in. On the video the
first thing you hear is Jordan ("Oh, no!"), followed by comedian and
camper Damon Wayans, who jumps at the chance to mock MJ, shouting, "How you feel about that, that's what I want to know . . . losing at

your own camp!" (Lest you think Jordan had lost his edge, he immediately brought Wayans onto the court and humiliated him 3–0.)

Naturally, Jordan demanded a rematch with Rogers, right? Actually, he didn't. Instead he hugged Rogers—the two go back a ways from Jordan's days in Chicago—and said, not so huggably, "Next time we're on the court together, I'll show you what it's like to play in the NBA." But that has yet to happen. Six years have passed since that day and Rogers hasn't been back to Flight School, and MJ stopped playing campers a few years ago. As for Rogers, he had DVDs made from the tape, complete with a soundtrack and post-game interviews, and dispensed them to friends and employees, because, well, wouldn't you?

It's tempting to want to take away an inspirational morsel: On the right day Everyman can take down Superman. But I prefer to see it from a different light. When it comes to basketball, Jordan may be Jordan. But when it comes to crazy-ass, spinning, over the shoulder, no-look lefty layups—which require a specific talent just as much as a fadeaway jumper—well, I daresay that John Rogers Jr. may be the Michael Jordan of such shots. In which case it was not luck that won that game but passion, guile and obsessive practice. In other words, it was artistry.

Acknowledgments

This book wouldn't have been possible without the contributions of a great many people.

At *Sports Illustrated,* Terry McDonell believed in the idea from the start and provided unwavering support throughout the process; anyone who's worked with him knows he's a rare advocate of the writer's voice in this day and age. Chris Stone provided invaluable early structural advice and oversaw a couple of *SI* stories that provided inspiration for the book, while David Bauer applied his sharp editorial vision to the manuscript, provided frequent counsel and helped shape the book's feel and tone over many months. I feel fortunate to work with both men. Jill Jaroff did her usual peerless copyediting. Stefanie Kaufman did a masterly job of coordinating all the moving parts and keeping everything running smoothly. Joe Lemire contributed not only assiduous fact-checking but editorial counsel (being a fundamentally sound big man himself). And Hank Hersch, a longtime friend and mentor, was instrumental in the development of my writing style and approach to NBA coverage.

I'm indebted to David Rosenthal at Simon & Schuster for taking a chance on this unusual joint venture. Colin Fox inspired confidence from the beginning and not only provided a steady editorial hand but was an unflagging advocate of the book. I also want to thank the Simon & Schuster p.r. team.

This is my third book, and once again I am grateful to be teamed with John Ware, the consummate old-school literary agent (and I mean that in the best way possible). John is the rare agent with an editor's eye, and he remains tireless and meticulous in his work. You're still the Charles Oakley of the biz, John.

Of course, the book wouldn't have been possible without the cooperation of the many athletes who provided their time and expertise. In all, I interviewed more than 150 NBA players, current and retired, and while I won't list everyone here, special thanks go out to Steve Kerr, Shane Battier, Steve Nash, Craig Ehlo, Nick Anderson and Kobe Bryant. I'd be remiss if I didn't also mention media-relations guru Julie Fie of the Suns, who went above and beyond to assist me in the research for two chapters, as well as Nelson Luis of the Rockets and George Galante and Joel Glass of the Magic.

A hearty shout-out to David Thorpe of IMG for not only kicking my ass at his camp in Florida but also providing ongoing basketball advice. I wouldn't be surprised if we're all working for you soon enough, David. Similarly, I'm indebted to Idan Ravin for his cooperation and keen insight into the NBA psyche, and to Sam Hinkie of the Rockets, who patiently answered all my dumb questions—may the odds always be in your favor, Sam.

A number of people read portions of the manuscript, and I owe a round of beers (or more) to Nick Grener (Pliny the Elder), Duffy Ballard (Lagunitas IPA), Phil Ballard (Anderson Valley Boont Amber), Roberta Ballard (um, Zinfandel) and especially Pete McEntegart (Harp), who provided crucial editing support late in the process.

A number of books and published stories proved helpful, both for background and as the source of anecdotes. While I won't mention them all, a partial list would include: *100 Years of Hoops* (Alexander Wolff), *Operation Yao Ming* (Brook Larmer), *Seven Seconds or Less* (Jack McCallum), *Basketball on Paper* (Dean Oliver), *Men at Work* (George Will), *Bird Watching* (Larry Bird) and *The Physics of Basketball* (John Fontanella). Print pieces include Jonathan Last's piece on Michael Jordan in *The Weekly Standard,* a David Halberstam *Vanity Fair* story (the source for the anecdote about Jordan playing pool), Curry Kirkpatrick's 1987 *SI* story on Michael Jordan, a wonderful 2008 story by Jackie Mac-Mullen in *The Boston Globe* about Ray Allen's superstitions, and Phil Taylor's 1996 *SI* story on Dennis Rodman (where I found a number of great Rodman anecdotes and strategies—thanks, Phil). Thanks also to Wolff for the Stacey Augmon anecdote.

For research and perspective I employed a number of valuable resources, including Basketball-Reference.com, Synergy, Hoopshype and TrueHoop.com, where Henry Abbott runs the best basketball blog in the country. (Most people don't know that Henry is also a world-class lobster hunter.) Roland Beech not only operates a remarkable website at 82games.com but was gracious enough to dig deep into his database to provide the arcane numbers you find in many of these chapters, for which I'm indebted to him. Others who assisted in the project include Brian Windhorst, Chris Mannix, Mike Moreau, Jason Levien, the Berkeley noon hoops crew, Jack McCallum, Ian Thomsen, Chris Heine, Max Cann, Riley Ballard, Bob Roe, David Matinho, John Rogers Jr., Dan Greenstone, Tom Amberry, Malik Rose, Mike Malone, Alexander Wolff, Walter Iooss Jr. and Pat Cottrell, the best "research assistant" imaginable.

Finally, I am in awe of my wife, Alexandra, who not only provided support and editorial guidance throughout the process but also did so while managing a newborn and a two-year-old, which surely qualifies her for some sort of Hall of Fame. And to those girls, Eliza and Callie, thanks for making each day more exciting than the last. May you find beauty in whatever games, whatever pursuits, you end up being passionate about.

Index

About the Author

Chris Ballard is a senior writer at *Sports Illustrated,* where he covers the NBA and writes features and back-page "Point After" columns. He has written for *The New York Times Magazine,* his work has been reprinted in the *Best American Sports Writing* anthology and his first book, *Hoops Nation,* for which he traveled to 48 states researching pick-up basketball, was named one of Booklist's Top 10 Sports Books of 1998. He lives with his wife and two daughters in Berkeley, California. Though not proud of it, he's starting to seriously consider joining a 35-and-over league.